ELECTORAL INTEGRITY IN TURKEY

Edinburgh Studies on Modern Turkey

Series Editors: **Alpaslan Özerdem** and **Ahmet Erdi Öztürk**

International Advisory Board

- Sinem Akgül Açıkmeşe
- Samim Akgönül
- Rebecca Bryant
- Mehmet Gurses

- Gareth Jenkins
- Ayşe Kadıoğlu
- Stephen Karam
- Paul Kubicek

- Peter Mandaville
- Nukhet Ahu Sandal
- M. Hakan Yavuz

Books in the series (published and forthcoming)

Turkish–Greek Relations: Foreign Policy in a Securitisation Framework Cihan Dizdaroğlu

Policing Slums in Turkey: Crime, Resistance and the Republic on the Margin Çağlar Dölek

Spatial Politics in Istanbul: Turning Points in Contemporary Turkey Courtney Dorroll and Philip Dorroll

Islamic Theology in the Turkish Republic Philip Dorroll

The Kurds in Erdoğan's Turkey: Balancing Identity, Resistance and Citizenship William Gourlay

The Politics of Culture in Contemporary Turkey Edited by Pierre Hecker, Ivo Furman and Kaya Akyıldız

Peace Processes in Northern Ireland and Turkey: Rethinking Conflict Resolution İ. Aytaç Kadioğlu

The British and the Turks: A History of Animosity, 1893–1923 Justin McCarthy

A Companion to Modern Turkey Edited by Alpaslan Özerdem and Ahmet Erdi Öztürk

The Alevis in Modern Turkey and the Diaspora: Recognition, Mobilisation and Transformation Edited by Derya Ozkul and Hege Markussen

The Decline of the Ottoman Empire and the Rise of the Turkish Republic: Observations of an American Diplomat, 1919–1927 Hakan Özoğlu

Religion, Identity and Power: Turkey and the Balkans in the Twenty-first Century Ahmet Erdi Öztürk

Turkish-German Belonging: Ethnonational and Transnational Homelands, 2000–2020 Özgür Özvatan

Contesting Gender and Sexuality through Performance: Sacrifice, Modernity and Islam in Contemporary Turkey Eser Selen

Turkish Politics and 'The People': Mass Mobilisation and Populism Spyros A. Sofos

Industrial Policy in Turkey: Rise, Retreat and Return Mina Toksoz, Mustafa Kutlay and William Hale

Electoral Integrity in Turkey Emre Toros

Memory, Patriarchy and Economy in Turkey: Narratives of Political Power Meral Uğur-Çınar

Erdoğan: The Making of an Autocrat M. Hakan Yavuz

edinburghuniversitypress.com/series/esmt

ELECTORAL INTEGRITY IN TURKEY

Emre Toros

EDINBURGH
University Press

To Seçil and Emek

Edinburgh University Press is one of the leading university presses in the UK. We publish academic books and journals in our selected subject areas across the humanities and social sciences, combining cutting-edge scholarship with high editorial and production values to produce academic works of lasting importance. For more information visit our website: edinburghuniversitypress.com

Edinburgh University Press Ltd
13 Infirmary Street
Edinburgh EH1 1LT

First published in hardback by Edinburgh University Press 2024

Typeset in 11/15 EB Garamond by
IDSUK (DataConnection) Ltd

A CIP record for this book is available from the British Library

ISBN 978 1 4744 9234 8 (hardback)
ISBN 978 1 4744 9235 5 (paperback)
ISBN 978 1 4744 9236 2 (webready PDF)
ISBN 978 1 4744 9237 9 (epub)

CONTENTS

Part 4 Conclusion

FIGURES

TABLES

ABBREVIATIONS

AKP	Adalet ve Kalkınma Partisi (Justice and Development Party)
ANAP	Anavatan Partisi (Motherland Party)
AP	Adalet Partisi (Justice Party)
BP	Birlik Partisi (Unity Party)
CHP	Cumhuriyet Halk Partisi (Republican People's Party)
Cİ	Cumhur İttifakı (People's Alliance)
CKMP	Cumhuriyetçi Köylü Millet Partisi (Republican Peasant Nation Party)
DEHAP	Demokratik Halk Partisi (Democratic People's Party)
DeP	Demokrasi Partisi (Democratic Party)
DeTP	Demokrat Türkiye Partisi (Democratic Turkey Party)
DIEV-T	Database of Incidents of Electoral Violence in Turkey
DP	Demokrat Parti (Democratic Party)
DSP	Demokratik Sol Parti (Democratic Left Party)
DTP	Demokratik Toplum Partisi (Democratic Society Party)
DYP	Doğru Yol Partisi (True Path Party)
EI-T	Electoral Integrity in Turkey (database)
EMB	electoral management bodies
HADEP	Halkın Demokrasi Partisi (People's Democracy Party)
HDP	Halkların Demokratik Partisi (People's Democratic Party)
HEP	Halkın Emek Partisi (People's Labor Party)

HP	Halkçı Parti (People's Party)
İBDA-C	İslamî Büyük Doğu Akıncıları Cephesi (Muslim Great East Raiders)
İP	İşçi Partisi (Labour Party); also İyi Parti (Good Party)
MBK	Milli Birlik Komitesi (the National Unity Committee)
MC	Milliyetçi Cephe (the Nationalist Front)
MDP	Milliyetçi Demokrasi Partisi (Nationalist Democracy Party)
MGK	Milli Güvenlik Komitesi (National Security Council)
MHP	Milliyetçi Hareket Partisi (Nationalist Action Party)
MKP	Milli Kalkınma Partisi (National Development Party)
MP	Millet Partisi (Nation Party)
MSP	Milli Selamet Partisi (National Salvation Party)
OSCE	Organization for Security and Co-operation in Europe
PACE	Parliamentary Assembly of the Council of Europe
PEI	Perceptions of Electoral Integrity (database)
PKK	Partiya Karkeran Kurdistan (Workers' Party of Kurdistan)
RP	Refah Partisi (Welfare Party)
RTÜK	Radyo ve Televizyon Üst Kurulu (Radio and Television Authority of Turkey)
SEÇSİS	Seçim Bilgi Sistemi ([Turkish] Electoral Information System)
SHP	Sosyal Demokrat Halkçı Parti (Social Democratic Populist Party)
SODEP	Sosyal Demokrasi Partisi (Social Democracy Party)
SP	Saadet Partisi (Felicity Party)
TBMM	Turkiye Büyük Millet Meclisi (Turkish Grand National Assembly)
TRT	Türkiye Radyo Televizyon Kurumu (Turkish National Radio and Broadcast Agency; now Turkish Radio and Television Corporation)
UN	United Nations
UNDP	United Nations Development Programme
V-Dem	Varieties of Democracy (database)
VP	Fazilet Partisi (Virtue Party); also Vatan Partisi (Patriotic Party)
WVS	World Values Survey
YSK	Yüksek Seçim Kurulu (the Supreme Election Council)
YSP	Yeşil Sol Parti (the Green Left Party)
YTP	Yeni Türkiye Partisi (New Turkey Party)

PREFACE AND ACKNOWLEDGMENTS

As a student of Turkish politics, my interest in electoral integrity dates back to 2014, when Turkey passed through a series of turbulent elections. However, this academic curiosity entered another phase when I met Professor Sarah Birch in 2015. I was thinking about building a comprehensive project on the subject, and she was kind enough to support my application for a British Academy Newton Advanced Scholarship, which was eventually funded. Hence my primary intellectual obligation is to her since it would not have been possible for me to carry out this research without her initial motivation and academic support throughout the whole process.

I am also grateful to KA Analytica, Mert Moral, Emre Erdoğan, Efe Tokdemir, Burcu Harmankaya and Lenore Martin for their support, which took place at different phases of the project. Similarly, I would like to thank Erdi Öztürk and Edinburgh University Press staff for their patience and understanding, especially during the COVID-19 pandemic. I am also indebted to Atılım University, Hacettepe University, King's College London, The Turkish Fulbright Commission, Harvard University and especially to the British Academy Newton Advanced Fellowship programme, which funded most of this research with the grant number AF160050.

Last but not least, I want to thank my family, Seçil and Emek, who have always supported me wholeheartedly. This book is dedicated to them . . .

Part 1

INTRODUCTION

1

CONTEXT, ARGUMENTS AND STRUCTURE

I am not joking, a cat entered the power distribution unit.

Taner Yıldız, Minister of Energy, 2014

The above epigraph is an excerpt from energy minister Taner Yıldız's official statement on the widespread power blackouts during the March 2014 Turkish local elections. Admitted by Yıldız himself, it sounded like a joke. Indeed, when BBC viewers heard Yıldız's statement on their evening news, they thought it was an April Fool's Day joke set by the channel and made it the number one hashtag on Twitter the following day. However, the reality was way beyond a joke: the March 2014 local election in Turkey was the most controversial in the country's recent political history owing to numerous accusations related to electoral integrity. Allegations included various types of rigging, including lost ballot papers, ballot-box tallies missing legally required stamps and signatures, high numbers of invalid votes in constituencies that were likely to have close races, power blackouts and electoral violence. Actually, what happened in 2014 and the subsequent elections in Turkey has followed patterns similar to what students of electoral integrity have observed throughout the globe in recent years. Several countries have experienced problems related to electoral integrity that range over a wide field, including vote-rigging, ballot-box stuffing, abuse of state resources by partisan officers, exclusion of opposition candidates, courts failing to show impartiality and violence, among others too many to mention. Although the research focusing on these issues is towering, a comprehensive and contextual outlook that tests the theoretical and empirical understanding of global and context-based driving forces and consequences of electoral integrity utilising a case study is still missing. This book is an attempt to fulfil that gap.

As Pastor puts it, 'democracy should be more than free and fair elections, but it cannot be less' (1998, 154). The existence of elections and electoral governance provides the opportunity for citizens to contribute on an equal basis to collective decision-making, thereby making democracy work. Democratic functioning necessitates far more than having legitimate elections, 'yet if credible elections are not a sufficient condition for democracy, they nevertheless remain a necessary condition for any polity to be considered democratic' (Birch 2011, 2). In other words, although elections are the *sine qua non* of democracies, many factors shape the quality of elections in a democratic state. However, what is problematic is the increased number and diverse content of problems related to electoral integrity. More interestingly, such issues are on the rise in the so-called grey-zone democracies of the world and in well-established systems with centuries of electoral tradition. Although these failures raise eyebrows in academic and policymaking circles, we still do not have adequate theoretical and conceptual apparatus for making complete sense of what is going wrong with elections worldwide.

Electoral integrity is an umbrella term for defining the *ideal* practical and normative context within which elections occur (Norris 2018, 220, italics added). Consequently, the existing research has analysed the phenomenon by controlling the proximity to this ideal context by utilising several diverse subject areas. The heading 'electoral fraud' seems to be the most dominant line of research among these subject areas. The early works on electoral fraud, which the existing literature defined as clandestine and illegal efforts to shape election results, argued that a) electoral fraud can take diverse forms, such as unjust legal arrangements and violence, b) it is indecisive, i.e. when there is a fraud, it may or may not have an impact on election results and c) fraud tactics change with the level of competitiveness of the electoral race (Lehoucq 2003). For example, following the above logic, in their early study Elklit and Reynolds (2005) proposed a framework to assess elections' quality, freeness, fairness and administrative efficacy. These pioneering works on electoral fraud attracted considerable attention in the field, and the subsequent studies developed accompanying concepts like 'electoral malpractice' and 'electoral manipulation', which considerably deepened the available literature. For example, Birch (2011) produced one of the earliest theoretical and conceptual approaches to the subject, focusing on electoral malpractice. In this seminal work, she first set the normative ideals that underpin democratic elections and then showed that, owing to manipulations of electoral law, vote choice and electoral administration, many elections fall short of these ideals. Birch also revealed that a) political actors get involved in electoral malpractice only after calculating the costs and benefits and b) the existence of a robust civil society and free media hinder electoral malpractice.

Similarly, writing on electoral manipulation, Simpser (2013) showed that electoral activity is a way of transmitting or distorting information that may produce more benefits than merely winning an election. From this insight, the author developed a theory demonstrating electoral manipulation's informational role coupled with its direct effect (i.e. winning the election) and indirect effects (e.g. consolidation of a manipulator's power, impact on future vote choice and formation of opposition). Speaking in Andreas Schedler's (2002) terms, these theoretical discussions displayed the fact that there are constant meta-games at play. These puzzles increased attention on studies of electoral fraud and manipulation, leading several researchers to test these theories in various settings such as Russia (Skovoroda and Lankina 2017), Scotland (Birch and ElSafoury 2017), Brazil (Hidalgo and Nichter 2016), Turkey (Aygül 2016; Akkoyunlu 2017; Toros and Birch 2019a), Nigeria (Isma'ila 2016; Steve, Nwocha and Igwe 2019), Britain (Hill et al. 2017; Finn 2019), Malaysia (Ostwald 2017), the USA (Norris, Garnett and Grömping 2019; Norris, Cameron and Wynter 2018; Curini 2019), Australia (Karp, Nai and Norris 2018) as well as comparatively (Kuo and Teorell 2017; Collier and Vicente 2012; Van Ham and Lindberg 2015; Bader 2012; Beaulieu and Hyde 2009; Norris 2016; 2015).

The concepts of 'electoral malpractice' and 'electoral manipulation' were accompanied by the concept of 'electoral violence'. This particular area of study linked the phenomenon of electoral integrity with political violence and unfolded the causes of electoral violence and its impact on democratic functioning. As one of the earliest studies in the area, Höglund (2009) linked the enabling conditions and initiating factors of electoral violence to a) the nature of politics in societies, b) the nature of competitive elections, and c) the incentives created by the electoral institutions. In a more recent study, Norris, Frank and Martínez i Coma (2015, 9–10) underlined the increased number of contentious elections worldwide. They argued that outbreaks of electoral violence are positively related to the lack of conventional channels for mobilising dissent and to weak institutional mechanisms for resolving legal disputes. Like electoral manipulation and malpractice, electoral violence has also received considerable academic attention. While several studies have analysed the factors that lead to outbreaks of electoral violence (Beaulieu 2014; Basedau, Gero and Mehler 2007; Gillies 2011; Birch 2020), some others utilised electoral violence as an independent variable and questioned its link to civil wars in the multi-ethnic and economically underdeveloped societies (Mochtak 2019; Collier and Vicente 2012; 2014). Electoral violence has also received interest from other disciplines, for example international relations – where scholars have tried to link the phenomenon with international peacemaking and terrorism (Birch and Muchlinski 2017b; 2017a; Cho et al. 2015; Alihodžić 2013) – and gender and family studies – where studies have tried to understand the domestic dimension related to the phenomenon (Bardall 2011; 2015; Leveque 2018; Toros and Birch 2019b). The literature summarised above has usually underlined the importance of sustained, strong, electoral traditions, well-established institutional capacities and high international interconnectedness as mitigating factors for electoral violence. Even so, we have scant knowledge about electoral violence's political consequences at individual and institutional levels and how the concepts link with other components of electoral integrity.

More recently, another of these components has received increased academic interest: the role of electoral institutions and their capacity to manage elections. Fuelled by the increasing number of electoral problems worldwide, electoral integrity scholars have gradually tried to understand the tools and strategies employed during processes for administering elections and link these strategies with the phenomenon of electoral integrity. Furthermore, several recent studies have also attempted to unfold the consequences of flawed electoral management. Like other components of electoral integrity, electoral management literature has also utilised case studies (Kerr 2014; James and Jervier 2017; Clark and James 2017) coupled with international comparisons (Garnett 2019; James 2019; Norris 2019; Kerr 2018; Otaola 2018). This literature demonstrated that if elections are poorly run, the risks of protests, violence and even system breakdowns are increased (Birch and Muchlinski 2017b; Hafner-Burton, Hyde and Jablonski 2014; Norris 2015). This literature also focused on how electoral management bodies (EMBs) react to allegations (and practices) of fraud, improve polling day activities and regulate finance issues (Norris and Nai 2017; Alvarez and Grofman 2014). Elevating the existing literature to an advanced level, a more current vein in the scholarly work attempts to understand the consequences of EMB performance (Birch 2011; Birch and Van Ham 2017; Van Ham and Lindberg 2015; Magar 2012; Norris, Frank and Martínez i Coma 2014). Although these works are valuable, there is still considerable room for deepening the discussion on the link between EMBs and electoral integrity. As Norris aptly argues (2019), the analysis in hand, which heavily relies on cross-national datasets, 'typically treat[s] the structure, capacity, and ethos of the EMBs as largely fixed and stable'. In that sense, more research is needed on different EMBs, primarily focusing on contextual particularities.

Lastly, motivated by the opportunities created by this rich literature, researchers have started more recently to investigate the consequences of problems related to electoral integrity in many sub-fields of political science, including political attitudes and voting behaviour. What does damaged electoral integrity cost a political system? Does it have any impact on individual political behaviour? Do problems of electoral integrity shape the existing institutional structures of polities? One common vein for such analyses is to check the variation of voters' perceptions of democratic legitimacy attributable to problems of electoral integrity (Birch 2010; Norris 2014; Norris, Cameron and Wynter 2018). The findings link issues of electoral integrity to decreasing levels of political trust (Grönlund and Setälä 2012; Rose and Mishler 2009), turnout (Alvarez and Grofman 2014; Simpser 2012), political legitimacy (Robbins and Tessler 2012; Bratton 2008).

Following what I have summarised above, this book explores the causes and consequences of damaged electoral integrity not only through the lenses of explained theoretical explanations but also with a novel and comprehensive approach. The fundamental motivation behind this investigation is the substantial increase in the attention given to the causes and consequences of damage to electoral integrity in various countries in recent years. Taking these developments into serious consideration, practitioners in the related areas of electoral administration, electoral assistance and electoral observation operating at national and international levels have attempted to develop best practice standards. As a contribution to this developing literature, this volume aims to make additional contributions to the fields of electoral studies, electoral misconduct and democratisation, first by combining the existing literature that examines the same subject with different focus points and second by analysing a neglected but important case. Compared to the analysis of established democracies, few investigations have paused to integrate electoral integrity into the theoretical frameworks employed to examine electoral institutions in the grey-zone democracies. The studies on electoral integrity in such democracies have primarily identified the phenomenon as one of the fundamental mechanisms through which authoritarian regimes maintain power (Gandhi and Przeworski 2009; Geddes 1999; Hermet, Rose and Rouquié 1978; Magaloni 2008; Cox 2015; Schedler 2002; 2006). Nevertheless, most of this literature focuses on the broad strategies authoritarian leaders use in maintaining their regimes; the consequences of electoral malpractice and integrity have received far less attention (Bjornlund 2004; Beaulieu and Hyde 2009; Kelley 2009). Furthermore, although the literature on democratisation has developed considerably in incorporating consideration of electoral integrity into our understanding of democracy (Callahan 2000; Geddes 1999; Herron 2009; Howard and Roessler 2006; Lindberg 2006), the main focus of these studies has been on the improvement of democratic functioning, rather than on causes and consequences of damaged electoral integrity *per se* (Carothers 1997; Ottoway 2003; Elklit 1999; Elklit and Reynolds 2005).

Similarly, as explained above, although the research on electoral integrity is also on the rise, it still needs further development, especially in explaining the phenomenon in alternative contexts. The primary deficit in the current literature is its preference for checking whether the elections in specific contexts correspond with global liberal democratic procedures, and meet global norms and international conventions, covering the complete election cycle – that is, from the pre-election period, through the campaign, to polling day and the immediate aftermath (Norris 2013a; 2013b; Norris, Frank and Martínez i Coma 2013; Norris 2014; Norris, Frank and Martínez i Coma 2014; Norris 2015; Norris, Frank and Martínez i Coma 2015). Although this approach has produced revolutionary knowledge on the phenomenon, there is still room for explaining the particularities of electoral integrity in different contexts. Although the need to identify other democratic systems that go beyond the democratic/non-democratic dichotomy has resulted in a conceptual flood – including 'electoral democracies', 'semi-democracies' and 'semi-free' regimes (Freedom House 2019), 'hybrid states' (Diamond 2002), and 'electoral' or 'competitive' autocracies (Schedler 2006; Levitsky and Way 2010) – these efforts have only been linked minimally to the electoral integrity literature. Accordingly, by choosing Turkey as the empirical context to analyse, I aim to fill this gap.

Turkey, a second-wave democracy with a history of competitive elections since 1950, has undergone considerable political change in recent years. Since the 1970s, Turkey has been a hybrid state on the fuzzy border between democracy and authoritarianism. It has regularly held competitive, multi-party elections, yet concerns have periodically been raised about electoral integrity. Since the early 1990s, Turkey has been labelled 'partly free' by Freedom House, and though elections in the country are competitive, these elections were not conducted on an entirely level playing field. However, electoral integrity is moderately high by global standards, though the country has witnessed a decline in recent years, and Turkey can now be considered an electoral authoritarian state.

Against this background, allegations of electoral malpractice and falling integrity started to rise to the top of the country's political agenda by the early 1990s. The following two decades, from the 2002 parliamentary elections onwards, were marked by the successive victories of Adalet ve Kalkınma Partisi (the Justice and Development Party, AKP). During this period, the opposition parties launched many accusations of electoral fraud against the governing AKP, especially after 2010. These allegations included illegal use of overprinted ballot papers, misuse of state funds, media censorship, manipulation of the computer-aided voter index system and electricity cuts during the vote count. Thus, though Turkey has a history of polls that have elected legitimate governments based on the popular will, recent developments have raised eyebrows about the integrity of electoral processes. By the end of 2019, Turkey had held a total of nine elections in six years, including three parliamentary elections (two in 2015 and one in 2018), two presidential elections (2014 and 2018), a constitutional referendum (2017) and three local elections

(2014, 2019 and Istanbul repeat elections). Over the course of these elections, issues related to electoral integrity came under the spotlight, and concerns about the quality of elections have increased. The frequent allegations of fraud, undue influence and violence cast doubt on Turkey's claim to be an established democracy (Akkoyunlu 2017; Toros and Birch 2019a). These concerns reached a climax during the 2018 combined presidential and parliamentary election, which the *Economist* described as 'the most unfair election in Turkey in decades' (*Economist* 2018). The 2018 elections took place after an attempted coup in July 2016, coupled with a short but tense campaigning period, but more importantly, under a state of emergency. This situation raised severe concerns about the integrity of these elections since the state of emergency measures affected the judiciary, the police, the military, the civil service, local authorities, academia, the media and the business community, shutting down more than 1,000 institutions and private companies and seizing their assets (PACE Monitoring Committee 2017). The United Nations (UN) raised similar concerns, noting that 'protracted restrictions on the human rights to freedom of expression, assembly and association are incompatible with the conduct of a credible electoral process' (Zeid Ra'ad Al Hussein 2018). While the government maintained that the election was transparent, the atmosphere was hardly conducive to a level playing field, considering the opposition's limited access to the media and state resources (Kirişçi 2018). Confirming these concerns, the mission sent by the Organization for Security and Co-operation in Europe (OSCE) to observe the 2018 election recorded evidence of violations of electoral procedure, limitations on media freedom, intimidation and numerous violent attacks on candidates and partisans (OSCE 2018). These developments make the Turkish context ideal for probing the research questions related to the phenomenon in a grey-zone democracy.

Turkey is a country where problems with electoral integrity also take on a particular regional dimension. As part of the debate about electoral integrity, the regional dimension of electoral violence has recently attracted attention. Literature on this specific topic suggests that electoral violence tends to cluster in regions for two reasons. The first is the uneven capacity of different polities. This imbalance can leave certain parts of a country effectively ungoverned by the central state and ruled instead by organised criminal groups or local warlords. Examples of this phenomenon are Afghanistan, Indonesia, Italy, Nigeria and Paraguay (Alesina, Piccolo and Pinotti 2019; Harish and Toha 2017; Reno

2011). The second reason is that electoral violence tends to cluster in contexts where ethnic conflicts take place. Some examples include India, Kenya and Sri Lanka (Dercon and Gutiérrez-Romero 2012; Gutiérrez-Romero 2014; Höglund and Piyarathne 2009; Wilkinson 2004). In Turkey, the multi-ethnic eastern and south-eastern Anatolian region has historically been prone to violence of various types, including electoral violence. When considering the regional aspects of Turkish politics, one invariably must come to terms with what is often referred to in Turkish political discourse as the 'Kurdish question' (Toros 2012). Eastern and south-eastern Anatolia is an economically underdeveloped region with a dense Kurdish population and historically has advanced separatist claims. These claims have recently focused on securing ethnic rights within Turkish state institutions via utilising the primary political party for the ethnic Turkish population, the Halkların Demokratik Partisi (People's Democratic Party, HDP). Most research on the 'Kurdish question' has focused on the economic aspects of the topic and, in particular, the relative deprivation that affects many Kurdish-populated regions. However, uneven development also manifests itself in political terms, which has consequences for electoral politics. In this region, historical conflicts amplify ethnic tensions, which are highly relevant to aspects of electoral integrity in the country.

Based on the evidence discussed above, it is not hard to guess that Turkey's score on any card of comparative electoral integrity is declining. According to the Perceptions of Electoral Integrity Index published in Norris and Grömping (2019), Turkey ranked 21st, with the lowest score among the northern and western European countries. The evidence from the World Values Survey's (WVS) seventh wave (Haerpfer et al. 2022) also ratifies this argument. It displays Turkey as a country with characteristics similar to South American countries among which electoral integrity is also questioned.

This book attempts to re-use the literature on electoral integrity described in this chapter and propose a new framework for research and analysis. This framework offers a theory that identifies the causes and consequences of electoral integrity and malpractice at individual and institutional levels. This novel approach contributes to the literature by utilising the valuable research strategies of the existing studies, proposing alternative data sources that will describe the phenomena better and, most importantly, presenting a theoretical framework that will suit both singular and comparative cases. Figure 1.1 displays this two-dimensional theoretical approach combined with data sources and methods.

Individual

Individual Level Causes

Individual Level Consequences

Informational Sources

Polarization

Partisanship

Democratic maturation

Trust in EMBs

Damaged Electoral Integrity

Causes

Consequences

Manipulation

Low trust

Violence

Authoritarian backsliding

Malpractice

Institutional Level Causes

Institutional Level Consequences

Institutional

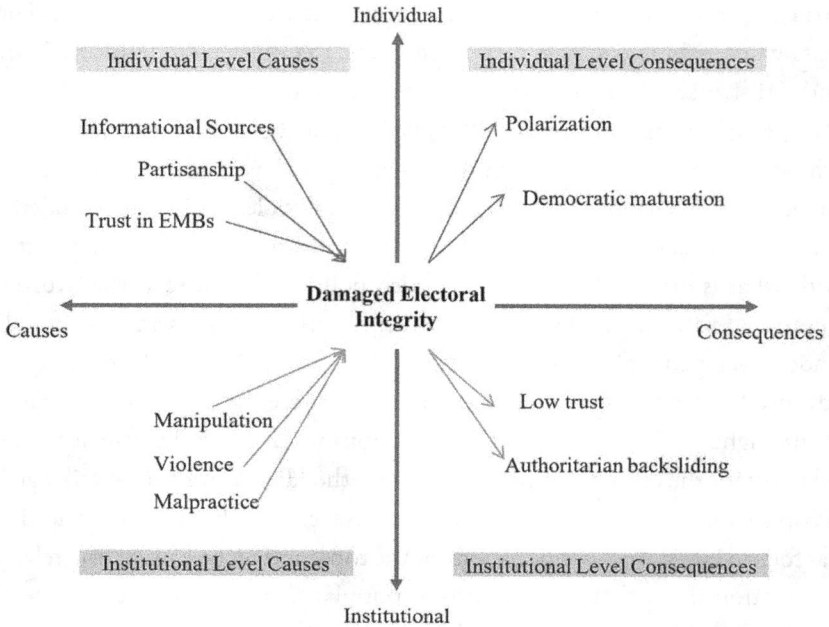

Figure 1.1 Two-dimensional approach to electoral integrity

The complex literature described above also comes with operationalisation and measurement problems. While early research heavily relied on elite-level studies such as the Electoral Integrity Project (EIP), Freedom House and Polity IV indices, more recently WVS included an electoral integrity battery which investigates the perceptions of electoral integrity and malpractices in multiple countries of the world (Norris 2014). While utilising datasets as such, this piece also employs alternative, qualitative and quantitative, methods because the subject matter is inherently complex. Accordingly, the following chapters include case studies exploring the mechanisms that underpin the statistical regularities uncovered through quantitative analysis. The original data utilised in the empirical analysis for this study consists of two sections, the print media-based DIEV-T database and the Electoral Integrity in Turkey EI-T survey research database. The DIEV-T is an incident-level database. It covers news in twenty-five newspapers related to electoral integrity, and covers every election that has taken place since 1950 in Turkey, including the 2019 Istanbul repeat elections. Conversely, the EI-T is survey-based research on electoral integrity in Turkey that includes field experiments and cross-sectional data, measures perceptions of electoral integrity and relates the phenomena to other factors, including party identification, region, media consumption and trust. The EI-T data was collected via a nationwide, representative, face-to-face sample survey in July 2018, immediately following the June 2018 presidential and parliamentary elections. Lastly, for analysing the Turkish case from a comparative perspective, this study has referred to other available datasets such as Varieties of Democracy (V-Dem), Index of Electoral Malpractice (IEM) and PEI.

In line with the framework described above, the second chapter focuses on Turkey and analyses the elections that the country has experienced since the 1940s through the lens of electoral integrity. By utilising the DIEV-T data, this chapter aims to display the nature and intensity of the issues related to electoral integrity and portray the evolution of the problems relating to electoral integrity in Turkey. The information provided in this chapter sheds further insights into recent electoral problems that the country has experienced.

The third chapter elaborates further on electoral integrity in Turkey from a comparative perspective. To that end, the chapter utilises several databases – WVS, PEI and V-Dem – to make global comparisons, accompanied by the DIEV-T data to portray a picture of the last two decades. This chapter also provides introductory information on EMB and the media in Turkey, which are the subject matter of the following chapters, where detailed descriptive and explanatory work is carried out.

In compliance with the approach proposed for the study, in the second part, Chapters Four and Five analyse the causes of problems related to electoral integrity in Turkey at individual and institutional levels. Accordingly, the fourth chapter focuses on the individual causes of damaged electoral integrity. It develops an informational model of perceptions of electoral integrity, building on literature on perceptions of electoral justice, electoral violence and information processing. The basic argument is that informational sources play a crucial role in individual perceptions of electoral integrity, influencing common expectations of elections' integrity. In a similar vein, the fifth chapter focuses on institutional drivers of damage to electoral integrity in Turkey. It provides a historical outlook on Yüksek Seçim Kurulu (the Supreme Election Council, YSK), the EMB of Turkey, combined with models presenting trust in the YSK.

Chapters Six, Seven and Eight provide evidence of the consequences of damage to electoral integrity at the individual and institutional levels. The sixth chapter uses the EI-T data on the Istanbul re-elections. The analysis demonstrates that voters having different party identifications stated that the re-election decision of the Turkish EMB damaged the credibility of elections in Turkey. Following this, Chapter Seven sheds light on the relationship between public perceptions of electoral integrity and trust in government. Lastly, Chapter Eight focuses on the link between electoral integrity matters and expectations of electoral outcomes.

During the course of writing this book, the COVID-19 pandemic broke out and triggered an unprecedented global crisis posing massive challenges to democratic institutions, including elections. The ninth chapter focuses on this issue and analyses the effect of the COVID-19 pandemic on a possible election in Turkey via a conjoint experiment planted in a country-representative face-to-face survey.

The conclusion chapter summarises the study's implications for the scholarly and policy communities. It also maps the further research agenda that this study seeks to lead. It also provides an inventory of the practical lessons drawn from this research and the study's recommendations for those involved in electoral integrity research. Finally, an epilogue looks at the elections of 2023.

References

Akkoyunlu, Karabekir. 2017. 'Electoral Integrity in Turkey: From Tutelary Democracy to Competitive Authoritarianism'. In *Authoritarian Politics in Turkey: Elections, Resistance, and the AKP*, edited by B. Başer and A. E. Öztürk, 47–63. London: I. B. Tauris.

Alesina, A., Salvatore Piccolo and Paolo Pinotti. 2019. 'Organized Crime, Violence, and Politics'. *The Review of Economic Studies*, 86 (2): 457–99. https://doi.org/10.1093/restud/rdy036

Alihodžić, Sead. 2013. *The Guide on Factors of Election-Related Violence Internal to Electoral Processes*. Stockholm: IDEA.

Alvarez, R. Michael and Bernard Grofman. 2014. *Election Administration in the United States*. New York: Cambridge University Press.

Aygül, Cenk. 2016. 'Electoral Manipulation in March 30, 2014 Turkish Local Elections'. *Turkish Studies*. https://doi.org/10.1080/14683849.2015.1135061.

Bader, Max. 2012. 'Trends and Patterns in Electoral Malpractice in Post-Soviet Eurasia'. *Journal of Eurasian Studies*. https://doi.org/10.1016/j.euras.2011.10.006.

Bardall, Gabrielle. 2011. 'Breaking the Mold: Understanding Gender and Electoral Violence'. IFES White Paper.

———. 2015. 'Towards a More Complete Understanding of Election Violence: Introducing a Gender Lens to Electoral Conflict Research'. https://ecpr.eu/Filestore/PaperProposal/ce51102c-24cb-4161-a3d8-ac125011be4a.pdf.

Basedau, Matthias, Erdmann Gero and Andreas Mehler, eds. 2007. *Votes, Money and Violence: Political Parties and Elections in Sub-Saharan Africa*. Uppsala: Nordiska Afrikainstitutet. https://doi.org/10.1353/arw.2008.0024.

Beaulieu, Emily. 2014. *Electoral Protest and Democracy in the Developing World*. Cambridge: Cambridge University Press.

Beaulieu, Emily and Susan D. Hyde. 2009. 'In the Shadow of Democracy Promotion: Strategic Manipulation, International Observers, and Election Boycotts'. *Comparative Political Studies*. https://doi.org/10.1177/0010414008325571.

Birch, Sarah. 2010. 'Perceptions of Electoral Fairness and Voter Turnout'. *Comparative Political Studies*. https://doi.org/10.1177/0010414010374021.

———. 2011. *Electoral Malpractice*. Oxford: Oxford University Press. https://doi.org/10.1093/acprof:oso/9780199606160.001.0001.

———. 2020. *Electoral Violence, Corruption and Political Order*. Princeton, NJ: Princeton University Press.

Birch, Sarah and Fatma ElSafoury. 2017. 'Fraud, Plot, or Collective Delusion? Social Media and Perceptions of Electoral Misconduct in the 2014 Scottish Independence Referendum'. *Election Law Journal: Rules, Politics, and Policy*. https://doi.org/10.1089/elj.2016.0393.

Birch, Sarah, and Carolien Van Ham. 2017. 'Getting Away with Foul Play? The Importance of Formal and Informal Oversight Institutions for Electoral Integrity'. *European Journal of Political Research*. https://doi.org/10.1111/1475-6765.12189.

Birch, Sarah, and David Muchlinski. 2017a. 'Electoral Violence: Patterns and Trends'. In *Electoral Integrity and Political Regimes: Actors, Strategies and Consequences*, edited by Holly Ann Garnett and Margarita Zavadskaya, 100–113. Abingdon: Routledge. https://doi.org/10.4324/9781315315126.

———. 2017b. 'The Dataset of Countries at Risk of Electoral Violence'. *Terrorism and Political Violence*, 1–20. https://doi.org/10.1080/09546553.2017.1364636.

Bjornlund, E. C. 2004. *Beyond Free and Fair: Monitoring Elections and Building Democracy*. Baltimore, MD and London: Johns Hopkins University Press.

Bratton, Michael. 2008. 'Vote Buying and Violence in Nigerian Election Campaigns'. *Electoral Studies*. https://doi.org/10.1016/j.electstud.2008.04.013.

Callahan, W. A. 2000. *Pollwatching, Election and Civil Society in Southeast Asia*. Aldershot: Ashgate.

Carothers, Thomas. 1997. 'Democracy Assistance: The Question of Strategy'. *Democratisation*. https://doi.org/10.1080/13510349708403527.

Cho, Seung Yeon, Erin Connors, Faizaa Fatima and Utku Yalim. 2015. 'Preventing Post-Election Violence Based on the Kenyan Experience'. Stanford Law School: Law and Policy Lab (13 March).

Clark, Alistair and Toby S. James. 2017. 'Poll Workers'. In *Watchdog Elections: Transparency, Accountability, Compliance and Integrity*, edited by Pippa Norris and Alessandro Nai. Oxford: Oxford University Press.

Collier, Paul and Pedro C. Vicente. 2012. 'Violence, Bribery, and Fraud: The Political Economy of Elections in Sub-Saharan Africa'. *Public Choice*. https://doi.org/10.1007/s11127-011-9777-z.

———. 2014. 'Votes and Violence: Evidence from a Field Experiment in Nigeria'. *Economic Journal*. https://doi.org/10.1111/ecoj.12109.

Cox, Gary W. 2015. 'Electoral Rules, Mobilisation, and Turnout'. *Annual Review of Political Science* 18 (1): 49–68. https://doi.org/10.1146/annurev-polisci-060414-035915.

Curini, Luigi. 2019. 'The Integrity of the 2016 US Presidential Election: Exploring the Possible Impact of Ideology on Experts' Judgments'. *Party Politics*. https://doi.org/10.1177/1354068818809524.

Dercon, Stefan and Roxana Gutiérrez-Romero. 2012. 'Triggers and Characteristics of the 2007 Kenyan Electoral Violence'. *World Development*. https://doi.org/10.1016/j.worlddev.2011.09.015.

Diamond, Larry. 2002. 'Elections Without Democracy: Thinking About Hybrid Regimes'. *Journal of Democracy* 13 (2): 21–35.

Economist, The. 2018. 'Recep Tayyip the First', 28 June.

Elklit, Jørgen. 1999. 'Electoral Institutional Change and Democratisation: You Can Lead a Horse to Water, but You Can't Make It Drink'. *Democratisation* 6 (4): 28–51. https://doi.org/10.1080/13510349908403631.

Elklit, Jørgen and Andrew Reynolds. 2005. 'Judging Elections and Election Management Quality by Process'. *Representation* 41 (3): 189–207. https://doi.org/10.1080/00344890508523311.

Finn, P. D. 2019. 'Electoral Corruption and Malpractice'. *Federal Law Review*. https://doi.org/10.1177/0067205x7700800204.

Freedom House. 2019. 'Freedom in the World 2019: Democracy in Retreat'. *Freedom House*, . https://freedomhouse.org/report/freedom-world/2019/democracy-retreat.

Gandhi, Jennifer and Adam Przeworski. 2009. 'Authoritarian Institutions and the Survival of Autocrats'. *Comparative Political Studies* 40 (11): 1279–1301.

Garnett, Holly Ann. 2019. 'Evaluating Electoral Management Body Capacity'. *International Political Science Review* 40 (3): 335–53. https://doi.org/10.1177/0192512119832924.

Geddes, Barbara. 1999. 'What Do We Know about Democratization after Twenty Years?' *Annual Review of Political Science* 2: 115–44.

Gillies, David, ed. 2011. *Elections in Dangerous Places: Democracy and the Paradoxes of Peacebuilding*. Montreal: McGill Queens University Press.

Grönlund, Kimmo and Maija Setälä. 2012. 'In Honest Officials We Trust: Institutional Confidence in Europe'. *The American Review of Public Administration* 42 (5): 523–42. https://doi.org/10.1177/0275074011412946.

Gutiérrez-Romero, Roxana. 2014. 'An Inquiry into the Use of Illegal Electoral Practices and Effects of Political Violence and Vote-Buying'. *Journal of Conflict Resolution*. https://doi.org/10.1177/0022002714547902.

Haerpfer, C., R. Inglehart, A. Moreno, C. Welzel, K. Kizilova, J. Diez-Medrano, M. Lagos, P. Norris, E. Ponarin and B. Puranen (eds). 2022. *World Values Survey: Round Seven – Country-Pooled Datafile Version 5.0*. Madrid and Vienna: JD Systems Institute and WVSA Secretariat. doi:10.14281/18241.20

Hafner-Burton, Emilie M., Susan D. Hyde and Ryan S. Jablonski. 2014. 'When Do Governments Resort to Election Violence?' *British Journal of Political Science* 44. https://doi.org/10.1017/S0007123412000671.

Harish, S. P. and Risa Toha. 2017. 'A New Typology of Electoral Violence: Insights from Indonesia'. *Terrorism and Political Violence* 31 (4): 687–711. https://doi.org/10.1080/09546553.2016.1277208.

Hermet, Guy, Richard Rose and Alain Rouquié. 1978. *Elections Without Choice*. London: Palgrave Macmillan.

Herron, Erik S. 2009. *Elections and Democracy after Communism?* Basingstoke: Palgrave-Macmillan.

Hidalgo, Daniel and Simeon Nichter. 2016. 'Voter Buying: Shaping the Electorate through Clientelism'. *American Journal of Political Science*. https://doi.org/10.1111/ajps.12214.

Hill, Eleanor, Maria Sobolewska, Stuart Wilks-Heeg and Magda Borkowska. 2017. 'Explaining Electoral Fraud in an Advanced Democracy: Fraud Vulnerabilities, Opportunities and Facilitating Mechanisms in British Elections'. *British Journal of Politics and International Relations*. https://doi.org/10.1177/1369148117715222.

Höglund, Kristine. 2009. 'Electoral Violence in Conflict-Ridden Societies: Concepts, Causes, and Consequences'. *Terrorism and Political Violence* 21 (3): 412–27. https://doi.org/10.1080/09546550902950290.

Höglund, Kristine and Anton Piyarathne. 2009. 'Paying the Price for Patronage: Electoral Violence in Sri Lanka'. *Commonwealth and Comparative Politics*. https://doi.org/10.1080/14662040903090807.

Howard, Marc Morjé and Philip G. Roessler. 2006. 'Liberalizing Electoral Outcomes in Competitive Authoritarian Regimes'. *American Journal of Political Science*. https://doi.org/10.1111/j.1540-5907.2006.00189.x.

Isma'ila, Yusuf. 2016. 'Electoral Malpractice and the Challenges of Democratic Consolidation in Nigeria's Fourth Republic'. In *Challenge of Ensuring Research Rigor in Soft Sciences*, vol. 14, 296–303, edited by B. Mohamad. European Proceedings of Social and Behavioural Sciences. Future Academy. https://doi.org/10.15405/epsbs.2016.08.42.

James, Toby S. 2019. 'Better Workers, Better Elections? Electoral Management Body Workforces and Electoral Integrity Worldwide'. *International Political Science Review* 40 (3): 370–90. https://doi.org/10.1177/0192512119829516.

James, Toby S. and Tyrone Jervier. 2017. 'The Cost of Elections: The Effects of Public Sector Austerity on Electoral Integrity and Voter Engagement'. *Public Money & Management* 37 (7): 461–68. https://doi.org/10.1080/09540962.2017.1351834.

Karp, Jeffrey A., Alessandro Nai and Pippa Norris. 2018. 'Dial 'F' for Fraud: Explaining Citizens Suspicions about Elections'. *Electoral Studies* 53 (June): 11–19. https://doi.org/10.1016/j.electstud.2018.01.010.

Kelley, Judith. 2009. 'D-Minus Elections: The Politics and Norms of International Election Observation'. *International Organization* 63 (4): 765–87. https://doi.org/10.1017/S0020818309990117.

Kerr, Nicholas. 2014. 'EMB Performance and African Perceptions of Electoral Integrity'. In *Advancing Electoral Integrity*, edited by Pippa Norris, Richard W. Frank and Ferran Martinez i Coma, 667–86. New York: Oxford University Press.

Kerr, Nicholas Nathan. 2018. 'Election-Day Experiences and Evaluations of Electoral Integrity in Unconsolidated Democracies: Evidence from Nigeria'. *Political Studies*. https://doi.org/10.1177/0032321717724932.

Kirişçi, Kemal. 2018. 'How to Read Turkey's Election Results Brookings Institution blog, https://www.brookings.edu/blog/order-from-chaos/2018/06/25/how-to-read-turkeys-election-results/.

Kuo, Didi and Jan Teorell. 2017. 'Illicit Tactics as Substitutes: Election Fraud, Ballot Reform, and Contested Congressional Elections in the United States, 1860–1930'. *Comparative Political Studies*. https://doi.org/10.1177/0010414016649481.

Lehoucq, Fabrice. 2003. 'Electoral Fraud: Causes, Types, and Consequences'. *Annual Review of Political Science* 6: 233–56. https://doi.org/10.1146/annurev.polisci.6.121901.085655.

Leveque, Christophe. 2018. 'Familism and Electoral Outcomes: The Case of French Municipal Elections'. *French Politics* 16 (4): 359–82. https://doi.org/10.1057/s41253-018-0072-y.

Levitsky, Steven and Lucan Way. 2010. *Competitive Authoritarianism: Hybrid Regimes after the Cold War*. Cambridge: Cambridge University Press.

Lindberg, Staffan. 2006. *Democracy and Elections in Africa*. Baltimore, MD: Johns Hopkins University Press.

Magaloni, Beatriz. 2008. 'Credible Power-Sharing and the Longevity of Authoritarian Rule'. *Comparative Political Studies*. https://doi.org/10.1177/0010414007313124.

Magar, Eric. 2012. 'Gubernatorial Coattails in Mexican Congressional Elections'. *The Journal of Politics* 74 (2): 383. https://doi.org/10.1017/s0022381611001629.

Mochtak, Michal. 2019. 'Electoral Violence under Different Contexts. Evidence from the Western Balkans'. *Nations and Nationalism*. https://doi.org/10.1111/nana.12484.

Norris, Pippa. 2013a. 'Does the World Agree about Standards of Electoral Integrity? Evidence for the Diffusion of Global Norms'. *Electoral Studies*. https://doi.org/10.1016/j.electstud.2013.07.016.

———. 2013b. 'The New Research Agenda Studying Electoral Integrity'. *Electoral Studies* 32 (4): 563–75. https://doi.org/10.1016/j.electstud.2013.07.015.

———. 2014. *Why Electoral Integrity Matters*. Cambridge: Cambridge University Press. https://doi.org/10.1017/CBO9781107280861.

———. 2015. *Why Elections Fail*. Cambridge: Cambridge University Press. https://doi.org/10.1017/CBO9781107280908.

———. 2016. 'Electoral Integrity in East Asia'. *Taiwan Journal of Democracy*.

———. 2018. 'Electoral Integrity'. In *The Routledge Handbook of Elections, Voting Behavior and Public Opinion*, edited by Justin Fisher, Edward Fieldhouse, Mark N. Franklin, Rachel Gibson, Marta Cantijoch and Christopher Wlezien, 220–31. Abingdon: Routledge. https://doi.org/10.4324/9781315712390-19.

———. 2019. 'Conclusions: The New Research Agenda on Electoral Management'. *International Political Science Review* 40 (3, SI): 391–403. https://doi.org/10.1177/0192512119829869.

Norris, Pippa, Sarah Cameron and Thomas Wynter, eds. 2018. *Electoral Integrity in America: Securing Democracy*. New York: Oxford University Press. https://doi.org/10.1017/s1537592719000550.

Norris, Pippa, Richard W. Frank and Ferran Martínez i Coma. 2013. 'Assessing the Quality of Elections'. *Journal of Democracy*. https://doi.org/10.1353/jod.2013.0063.

———. 2014. *Advancing Electoral Integrity*. Oxford: Oxford University Press.

———. 2015. *Contentious Elections: From Ballots to Barricades*. New York: Routledge. https://doi.org/10.4324/9781315723068.

Norris, Pippa, Holly Ann Garnett and Max Grömping. 2019. 'The Paranoid Style of American Elections: Explaining Perceptions of Electoral Integrity in an Age of Populism'. *Journal of Elections, Public Opinion and Parties* 30 (1): 105–25. https://doi.org/10.1080/17457289.2019.1593181.

Norris, Pippa and Max Grömping. 2019. *Electoral Integrity Worldwide*. Sydney: University of Sydney.

Norris, Pippa and Alessandro Nai. 2017. *Election Watchdogs: Transparency, Accountability and Integrity. Election Watchdogs: Transparency, Accountability and Integrity*. Oxford: Oxford University Press. https://doi.org/10.1093/acprof:oso/9780190677800.001.0001.

OSCE. 2018. 'Republic of Turkey Early Presidential and Parliamentary Elections 24 June 2018: ODIHR Election Observation Mission: Final Report'. Organization for Security and Co-operation in Europe, Warsaw.

Ostwald, Kai. 2017. 'Electoral Malpractice in Malaysia: The Methods and Costs of Entrenching Single-Party Dominance'. *SSRN Electronic Journal*. https://doi.org/10.2139/ssrn.3048551.

Otaola, Miguel Lara. 2018. 'To Include or Not to Include? Party Representation in Electoral Institutions and Confidence in Elections: A Comparative Study of Latin America'. *Party Politics* 24 (5): 598–608. https://doi.org/10.1177/1354068816686418.

Ottoway, M. 2003. *Democracy Challenged: The Rise of Semi-Authoritarianism*. Washington, DC: Carnegie Endowment for International Peace.

PACE Monitoring Committee. 2017. 'Statement on the Proposed Constitutional Reform in Turkey'. Strasbourg, France: Parliamentary Assembly of the Council of Europe. http://website-pace.net/documents/19887/3136217/20170126-StmtConstReform-EN.pdf/c4c15b85-9e13-46b2-a687-f25f07077183.

Pastor, Robert. 1998. 'Mediating Elections'. *Journal of Democracy* 9 (1): 154–68.

Reno, William. 2011. *Warfare in Independent Africa*. Cambridge: Cambridge University Press. https://doi.org/10.1017/CBO9780511993428.

Robbins, Michael D. H. and Mark Tessler. 2012. 'The Effect of Elections on Public Opinion Toward Democracy: Evidence From Longitudinal Survey Research in Algeria'. *Comparative Political Studies* 45 (10): 1255–76. https://doi.org/10.1177/0010414011434296.

Rose, Richard and William Mishler. 2009. 'How Do Electors Respond to an 'Unfair' Election? The Experience of Russians'. *Post-Soviet Affairs* 25 (2): 118–36. https://doi.org/10.2747/1060-586X.24.2.118.

Schedler, Andreas. 2002. 'The Menu of Manipulation'. *Journal of Democracy* 13 (2): 36–50. https://doi.org/10.1353/jod.2002.0031.

———. 2006. 'The Logic of Electoral Authoritarianism'. In *Electoral Authoritarianism: The Dynamics of Unfree Competition*, edited by Andreas Schedler. Cambridge: Cambridge University Press. https://doi.org/10.1017/S1537592708081024.

Simpser, Alberto. 2012. 'Does Electoral Manipulation Discourage Voter Turnout? Evidence from Mexico'. *The Journal of Politics* 74 (3): 782–95. https://doi.org/10.1017/s0022381612000333.

———. 2013. *Why Governments and Parties Manipulate Elections: Theory, Practice, and Implications*. Cambridge: Cambridge University Press. https://doi.org/10.1017/CBO9781139343824.

Skovoroda, Rodion and Tomila Lankina. 2017. 'Fabricating Votes for Putin: New Tests of Fraud and Electoral Manipulations from Russia'. *Post-Soviet Affairs*. https://doi.org/10.1080/1060586X.2016.1207988.

Steve, Amaramiro A., Matthew Enya Nwocha and Igwe Onyebuchi Igwe. 2019. 'An Appraisal of Electoral Malpractice and Violence as an Albatross in Nigerian's Democratic Consolidation'. *Beijing Law Review*. https://doi.org/10.4236/blr.2019.101005.

Toros, Emre. 2012. 'The Kurdish Problem, Print Media, and Democratic Consolidation in Turkey'. *Asia Europe Journal* 10 (4): 317–33. https://doi.org/10.1007/s10308-012-0336-0.

Toros, Emre and Sarah Birch. 2019a. 'Framing Electoral Impropriety: The Strategic Use of Allegations of Wrong-Doing in Election Campaigns'. *British Journal of Middle Eastern Studies*. https://doi.org/DOI:10.1080/13530194.2019.1566694.

———. 2019b. 'Who Are the Targets of Familial Electoral Coercion? Evidence from Turkey'. *Democratisation* 26 (8): 1342–61. https://doi.org/10.1080/13510347.2019.1639151.

Van Ham, Carolien and Staffan I. Lindberg. 2015. 'From Sticks to Carrots: Electoral Manipulation in Africa, 1986–2012'. *Government and Opposition*. https://doi.org/10.1017/gov.2015.6.

Wilkinson, Steven I. 2004. *Votes and Violence: Electoral Competition and Ethnic Riots in India*. Cambridge: Cambridge University Press. https://doi.org/10.1017/CBO9780511510458.

Zeid Ra'ad Al Hussein. 2018. 'State of Emergency Must Be Lifted for 'Credible Elections' in Turkey, Says UN Rights Chief'. *UN News*. https://news.un.org/en/story/2018/05/1009232.

2

ELECTORAL INTEGRITY IN TURKISH ELECTORAL HISTORY

In line with the framework described in Chapter One, this chapter focuses on Turkish electoral history and studies the electoral problems the country has experienced since the 1940s through the lens of electoral integrity. In the following sections I will first provide information on the political landscape of the relevant eras and then, by utilising the incident-based DIEV-T data, descriptively elaborate on the nature and intensity of the electoral issues. The chapter also portrays the evolution of the problems related to electoral integrity in Turkey, and the information provided in this chapter sheds further light on recent electoral issues that the country has experienced.

The Early Years: 1950–70

Although the story of the democratisation of Turkey started much earlier, it was during the 1940s that the Turkish political elite decided to alter the country's political system to a democratic parliamentary one. Even though this decision had multiple domestic and international reasons, it was mainly a response to a global flow as these values became the norm across the world's countries (Zürcher 2010, 206–9).

Against this background, the first multi-party elections in the Republic of Turkey took place on 21 July 1946. It was contested between the Cumhuriyet Halk Partisi (Republican People's Party, CHP) and the Demokrat Parti (Democrat Party, DP), founded by Adnan Menderes, Celal Bayar, Fuat

Koprulu and Refik Koraltan. They were former members of the CHP, and after its formation in January 1946, the DP gained ground rapidly and managed to win sixty-one seats in the election. According to Zürcher (2010, 212), the CHP was returned with a majority mainly because there had been massive vote-rigging. Indeed, the 1946 elections were held without impartial supervision and secrecy of voting was not guaranteed. Several allegations were made that electoral officials had destroyed the votes cast as soon as the results were declared, making any check impossible, and Turkish citizens waited another four years for the first completely free and openly contested election.

The election that was held on 14 May 1950 introduced truly competitive politics in Turkey and altered the government by bringing the DP to power and sending the CHP to the opposition. The DP's election victory was a crucial historical moment for the Republic since it represented electoral defeat of the elite who had shaped the sociopolitical power structure since 1918 (Zürcher 2010, 221–3).

It is important to note that several changes within the legal system, including the electoral law, provided the basis for this peaceful alteration. Just before the elections, in February 1950, the Turkiye Büyük Millet Meclisi (Turkish Grand National Assembly, TBMM) amended the Deputies Election Law No. 5545, providing judicial review and democratic standards for the upcoming polls (Tuncer 2010, 155–7). Four parties competed in the 1950 elections: CHP, DP, Millet Partisi (Nation Party, MP) and Milli Kalkınma Partisi (National Development Party, MKP). The DP, the eventual winner, deployed two dominant lines of argument during its campaign, underlining the oppressive nature of CHP rule. The first line was religious: if elected, the DP pledged to extend and guarantee religious freedoms during its period in office. The second focused on the economy. The party promised to establish an economically liberal system free of state intervention, accompanied by policies that would increase peasants' income. These arguments found favour with voters, and the party gained support from urban and rural populations (Keyder 1992, 54). The DP received 54 per cent of the votes and 408 seats in the parliament, while its main rival, the CHP, managed to secure only 40 per cent, leading to 69 seats in the parliament. Other than these parties, nine independents and one MP candidate made it to the TBMM.

Several studies tried to explain the unexpected landslide victory of the DP, and most of such studies utilised Shils' (1975) 'centre–periphery' approach.

Şerif Mardin was the first to apply the centre–periphery key to Turkish politics, arguing that the DP had managed to sweep out votes from the western part of the country since demographically wealthier districts and more impoverished villages were converging with each other, politically. When combined with the chance for the public to be a part of politics for the first time via multi-party elections, this convergence created a new political environment, which CHP cadres did not know how to handle (Mardin 1973). Working on the feelings of this new politically active periphery, which included inferiority, envy, and fear (A. E. Turan 2004, 29), the DP was quite successful in setting a 'democratic periphery' against a 'bureaucratic centre'. Özbudun (1976, 54), supporting Mardin's arguments, underlined the cultural differences between the centre and periphery that led to the victory of the DP. Tachau (2002) elaborated on the economic dimension of the election results and linked the triumph of the DP to the changing alliance structure within Turkish society. When wealthy landowners left the CHP and joined DP forces alongside a flourishing bourgeoisie, he argued that CHP lost a significant amount of its support. Tonak and Schick (1992, 385), agreeing with Tachau, evaluated the victory of the DP as the first example in Turkish politics of a class struggle that ended with a win. Lastly, commenting on the organisational aspect of the success of the DP, Sayarı (2014) underlined the success of the DP in establishing 'political machinery' in the rural areas of the country, where the party's administration delivered goods and services to its supporters.

During its first term in office, the DP managed to extend the limits of fundamental human rights such as freedom of assembly, of the press and travel abroad, all of which had been started during the CHP era. At the same time, it altered economic policies by drawing extensive aid and finances from abroad, which produced significant growth rates. However, after a couple of years this economic policy collapsed as the difference between the high levels of industrial investment and low production drove up the cost of living. More importantly, owing to this economic policy choice, intense mechanisation of farms deprived peasants of their livelihoods and drove them to migrate into cities (Karpat 2003, 73). As the main opposition party, the CHP tried to capitalise on these worsening conditions and launched a fierce campaign of criticism backed by the media. As a result, DP leaders decided to hold elections earlier than the Constitution obliged them to, in 1957 instead of in the summer of

1958 as initially scheduled. Simultaneously, the government adopted regulations directly related to electoral integrity, for the first time in the country's short multi-party experience.

Before 1950 the governments in power did not allow the judicial authorities legal powers to check the conduct of elections, or monitor them. In 1950 the YSK was established by Law No. 5545, which altered this situation (its infrastructure had been formed almost five years earlier). Once in office, the DP revised the Law to prevent the opposition from forming a coalition against the government and tighten the candidacy requirements. Like the 1950 and 1954 elections, the 1957 election took place under the supervision of local Election Boards. These boards were responsible to the YSK, the highest body of appeal on election matters. Although in general voting occurred peacefully, many irregularities were reported, including the disappearance of ballot boxes and the mishandling of voting registers (Karpat 2003, 94). According to some newspaper reports, votes were counted in secret, citizens known to support the opposition were refused registration and representatives of opposition parties were not permitted to participate in the counting. Even though such cases were rare, irregularities of this kind might have altered the election results, especially in the provinces where a few hundred votes could determine the outcome (Karpat 1961, 452). Criticisms of the integrity of elections increased after the results were announced. The opposition parties objected to the results in several constituencies, where they accused the DP government of fraudulent registration, multiple voting and intimidation of opposition voters. The YSK rejected the appeals because the cited violations of election procedure had not affected the final result (Karpat 2003, 96). These developments led to riots in provinces such as Kastamonu, Kayseri, Çanakkale, Samsun and Giresun, and fatalities in Gaziantep and Mersin. The CHP and the DP blamed each other for these events. The CHP argued these uprisings displayed voters' proper and justified reactions to the damage to election integrity; the DP blamed the opposition for fomenting and organising these events, to disguise their loss at the polls.

The rule of the DP continued until 27 May 1960. Owing to a series of critical controversies in economic and societal spheres, which, according to Tachau, were 'more than a fledgling democratic system could bear' (2002, 33–6), the military seized political power and appointed a constituent assembly. Military officers demanded a report on electoral processes from the YSK ('Seçim Kanunu Komisyonu Raporu' 1961). The report stressed that the majoritarian voting system was responsible for the DP gradually having become an authoritarian administration and underlined the disproportion between the votes received and the seats allotted in the 1950, 1954 and 1957 elections. In response the constituent assembly passed several laws, some regulating electoral processes. In one critical change, to replace the majoritarian system the new election law set up the d'Hont proportional system with regional thresholds for electing members to the lower house of the TBMM. Essentially, the assembly was trying to limit the executive's power and provide justice in representation (Cop 2018, 146).

When the military junta lifted the bans on political activity in late 1961, several new parties entered the political scene. The (now closed) Democrat Party was reunited under two new parties: Adalet Partisi (the Justice Party, AP) and Yeni Türkiye Partisi (the New Turkey Party, YTP). Additionally, Marxist groups formed İşçi Partisi (Labour Party, İP) under the leadership of Mehmet Ali Aybar, and nationalists formed Cumhuriyetçi Köylü Millet Partisi (the Republican Peasant Nation Party, CKMP) alongside the CHP. A newly revised constitution foresaw a bicameral legislative assembly. The new Law No. 298 on Basic Provisions on Elections and Voter Registers set two different electoral systems: the d'Hont proportional system for the lower house and a majoritarian system for the upper house. Although the military and intelligentsia supported CHP, the party could not win a sufficient majority to form an independent government after the parliamentary elections of 1961. These electoral results led to three successive coalition governments between 1961 and 1964, under the leadership of the CHP, before fresh elections were held in 1965.

During this period, local elections took place in 1963, the first local-level election after the 1960 military intervention. In 1961 a change in Law No. 307 let citizens elect local mayors directly, who had been selected by the elected city assemblies until then. The most controversial event related to this election was the removal from office by the YSK of an AP mayor elected in İstanbul (Girgin 2013, 202). The council argued that this mayor – Nuri Erdoğan, a civil servant – had contravened the law by not resigning from his position before the elections. Replacing Erdoğan, CHP's Haşim İşçan, who came second, was ratified as the mayor of İstanbul.

The next general elections took place in October 1965, following the resignation of the third coalition in February after a CHP-led alliance failed to obtain a vote of confidence. However, before going to the polls the CHP and its allies worked on a new election system to prevent the AP from forming a single-party government. They amended election law No. 5545 to implement a 'national remainder' system. Although the new electoral system worked well to set a better proportion between votes and seats, the AP won the elections with 53 per cent of the vote and formed a single-party government. Nonetheless, the existence of minor parties in the national assembly tied its hands to some extent, so the AP reinstituted the d'Hont system in 1968. Although the 1965 election presented no major issues of electoral integrity, the situation changed for the local elections in 1968. Electoral violence peaked, nineteen people were killed and several were wounded on election day (Ahmad and Turgay 1976, 347). Moreover, the ratification of results took considerable time in several locations after several appeals were lodged. Indeed, the YSK annulled the results in fourteen electoral districts in İstanbul, all of which had been won by AP candidates.

This summary of the pre-1970 period shows that problems related to electoral integrity have a long history in Turkey. Among other issues, it seems that electoral violence marked this era by constituting nearly half of the problems associated with electoral integrity. Figure 2.1 below shows the distribution of these problems.

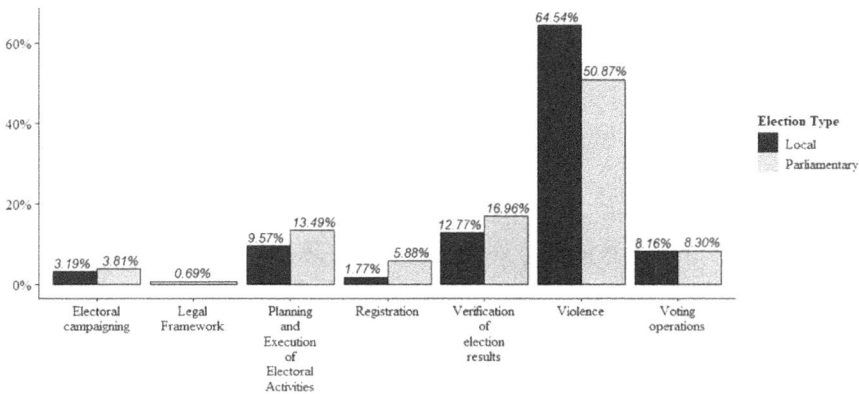

Figure 2.1 Distribution of electoral problems between local and parliamentary elections, 1950–70

Note: Owing to rounding, percentages do not add up to 100.00.

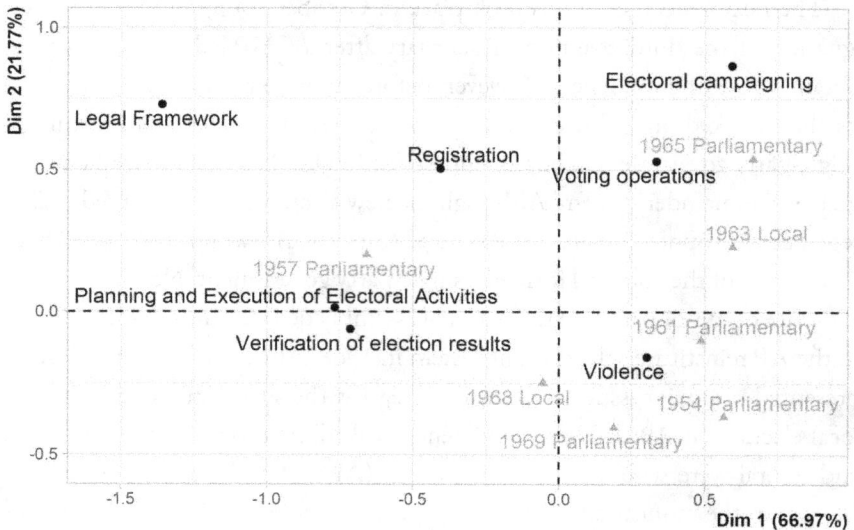

Figure 2.2 Correspondence analysis, electoral problems and election types, 1950–70

Figure 2.1. suggests that electoral violence was the most common problem in both local and parliamentary elections. It can be argued that local elections saw a greater share of electoral violence because of the clientelist nature of elections in Turkey, where the electoral race is usually between candidates of local grand families. This provides a base for high levels of polarisation, resulting in violence. The correspondence analysis presented in Figure 2.2 supports these arguments and further breaks down the association between particular elections and electoral problems.

The graph in figure 2.2 shows integrity problems relating to the legal framework, registration of voters, verification of election results and planning of electoral activities are associated with the 1957 Parliamentary elections (as stated in previous paragraphs), while violence was more visible during the 1954, 1961 and 1969 parliamentary and the 1968 local elections than during the other elections in this period.

The Years of Turbulence: 1970–90

On 14 October 1973, Turkish voters arrived at the polls once again. This election was particularly tense as it followed a second military intervention (on 12 March 1971), and many stakeholders were keen to assess whether previous electoral patterns persisted. Eight parties had entered the race, including some new ones. Alpaslan Türkeş's ultra-nationalist Milliyetçi Hareket Partisi (the Nationalist Action Party, MHP) on the far right, Birlik Partisi (the Unity Party, BP), which had taken on a new socialist cast on the left, and a new faction Milli Selamet Partisi (the National Salvation Party, MSP), which advocated social and economic justice with an emphasis on Islamic ideals, were among the new entrants alongside the main runners, the AP and the CHP. As in previous elections, the AP represented a centre-right coalition, seeking to gain a majority of the parliamentary seats as it had in the previous two elections. It was headed by Süleyman Demirel, who had resigned from his office as prime minister at the behest of the military in 1971. Opposing, the CHP was under the new and vigorous leadership of Bülent Ecevit.

The results represented a strong convergence of voters and parties, which had been signalled by the 1969 election. Although in 1969 the CHP had suffered one of its worst electoral losses, the party's weak performance in that election obscured a crucial shift in its electoral support. Starting from the late 1960s, the traditional strong support for the CHP from the less-developed provinces began to wane, and its support began to increase in the more-developed regions, particularly big cities (Özbudun and Tachau 1975). This trend intensified in 1973 and, coupled with a fall in support for the AP, the CHP won the most seats in the Grand National Assembly, albeit short of an absolute majority, which forced the party to form coalitions or minority governments throughout the 1970s. In January 1974, Ecevit managed to create a cabinet with Necmettin Erbakan's MSP. Although it was an unusual coalition, the government had a sizeable social base brought together by distrust of the power of Europe and America and of big business (Zürcher 2010, 216).

The government had only been in place for a few months when a crisis flared up in Cyprus, where the Greek junta plotted a *coup d'état* against Makarios on the island, to proclaim *enosis*. Ecevit called for intervention by the forces that had assured the independence of Cyprus, but the UK and Greece, the warrantor countries, rejected this demand. Acting independently, Turkish troops landed in northern Cyprus on 20 July, and two days later a truce was negotiated. However, since communal violence against Turkish Cypriots continued, the Turkish troops interfered again, and approximately 40 per cent of the island was brought under Turkish rule. Ecevit decided to use his new popularity to win an absolute majority in a snap election, and resigned on 16 September 1974. Other parties in the parliament knew that Ecevit had a competitive advantage and tried to postpone the election as long as possible, while Ecevit's resignation created an *impasse*: no government existed for 241 days. After months of negotiations, Demirel finally formed a coalition that called itself Milliyetçi Cephe (the Nationalist Front, MC). This move ended the possibility of an early general election, and the MC partners used this opening to seize the apparatus of state (Ahmad 2003, 142).

The first MC government remained in power until parliamentary elections in 1977. These elections were held in an environment of growing violence and economic turmoil and produced a return to the pre-1970s two-party system led by CHP and the AP. In 1977 the CHP, benefiting from Ecevit's personal popularity, won 41.4 per cent of the vote, the highest share the party ever won in a free election. Conversely, the AP received 36.9 per cent of the votes, which unfortunately led to yet another *impasse* for the political system. Ecevit's first attempt to form a coalition between his party and independents failed. Demirel then formed the 'Second MC', in which MSP and MHP held greater power than in the previous version. The second MC government did not last long; the coalition dissolved when several resignations took place from the AP. Those who resigned from the AP were rewarded by Ecevit; in January 1978 he established a CHP cabinet supported by some independents, giving cabinet posts to these 'resigners'. This government lasted until October 1979 without experiencing any significant success against the rising tide of violence across the country. When his attempts to restore order proved ineffective, and the criticism of the opposition became continuous, Ecevit resigned. Demirel returned to power with a minority government, supported by his party and some independents, but not the MSP or MHP. This last Demirel government survived until 12 September 1980, when the military intervened again.

The coalition governments of the 1970s were weak, and none were willing to take meaningful action to address the country's structural problems, including the growing political violence. The boom in political violence stemmed from a battle between extremist activists on the left and Bozkurtlar (the Grey Wolves, the paramilitary section of the MHP), in unison with other conservative organisations on the right. The number of victims of political violence in the country increased rapidly; more importantly, traditional conflicts like the Alevi–Sunni divide began to be expressed politically (Zürcher 2010, 263). The most dramatic event occurred in Kahramanmaraş in December 1978, when the Grey Wolves attacked Alevi neighbourhoods and killed more than 100 citizens. By the late 1970s, both camps began targeting public figures. The vice-president of the MHP, Gün Sazak, was assassinated in May 1980, preceded in July by former prime minister Nihat Erim and Kemal Türkler, a prominent figure of the Turkish left.

The extensive political violence in the country, perpetrated mainly by right-wing extremists, had also shaped the electoral campaigns of 1973 and 1977. During the CHP's 1973 campaign, a group of 200 people attacked Ecevit's convoy in Isparta, the homeland of his main rival, Demirel. The attackers stabbed one party member, destroyed the electoral material and injured many. Similarly, in Gerede, an important district in central Anatolia, when Ecevit was rallying for the 1975 interim elections, a gunman fired into the crowd from the minaret of a mosque. It has been reported that more than fifty people were injured, and several shops were damaged during the incident. The pace of political violence accelerated and reached its peak during the 1977 May Day festivities. A massive demonstration arranged by the Turkish left in Taksim Square in İstanbul turned into a massacre after shots were fired into the crowd, causing thirty-four deaths. Many thought state-supported rightist factions had organised the May Day shootings to scare voters (Ahmad 2003, 143). When such political violence began to combine with Kurdish separatism, Islamic fundamentalism, deadlocked democratic institutions and a shattered econ-omy, the military once again intervened and seized power in the morning of 12 September 1980, for the third time in the country's short democratic history.

The military mindset behind the 1980 *coup d'état* was different from previ-ous ones. The commanders tried to engineer a new political system for Turkey, which they thought would be the way to solve the many social and political problems just mentioned. This mindset accused political parties and leaders of the social rift in the country, economic recession, instability and never-ending violence. Accordingly, the military decided to reform the structure of the par-liament by introducing a new constitution, disqualifying existing politicians and parties and establishing a powerful control mechanism on democratic politics via new institutions. After reaching an acceptable level of law and order, in October 1981 the junta formed an advisory committee to draft a new constitution and submitted this to the citizens in a referendum in November 1982. The new constitution, unlike its predecessor, curbed the autonomous civil bureaucratic institutions and denied the functions of the higher tribunals. The military further pinned its role within the political sphere through institutions like the Milli Güvenlik Komitesi (National Security Council, MGK), an 'advisory board' to the government (Heper 1990). With 91.37 per cent of the valid vote, the citizens endorsed the new constitution, most probably with the hope of returning to civilian rule (Ahmad 2003, 166).

After the constitution's approval, a new law regulating political parties and elections also took effect, on 24 April 1983. Setting the rules for the forthcoming October 1983 elections, this law increased the number of MPs to be returned by small and middle-sized constituencies: 68 per cent of the seats were assigned to 45 per cent of the population, living in less densely populated areas of the country (Aleskerov, Ersel and Sabuncu 2010, 149). The new law also introduced an enormous 10 per cent national threshold and even higher constituency thresholds, denying candidates election unless their party received votes exceeding the percentage obtained by dividing the number of valid votes by the number of deputies to be elected from that district. In practice, this regulation led to thresholds that varied from 14.2 to 50 per cent, depending on the size of the constituency. These changes introduced by the new law aimed to stabilise the system, considerably increasing the difficulty for small parties across the ideological spectrum to gain representation.

With the new constitution and election law in place, the junta approved only three parties to contest at the polls: Turgut Özal's Anavatan Partisi (Motherland Party, ANAP), Necdet Calp's Halkçı Parti (People's Party, HP) and Turgut Sunalp's Milliyetçi Demokrasi Partisi (Nationalist Democracy Party, MDP). ANAP, which pledged a rapid return to civilian rule and democracy, won the election on 6 November 1983, receiving 45.15 per cent of the popular vote, ahead of the HP and MDP, which received 30.46 and 23.27 per cent, respectively.

As one of its first actions, the ANAP government introduced legislation creating a new administration level in Turkey called the 'metropolitan municipalities' under Act No. 3030. This act changed the face of local elections in Turkey henceforward, by increasing the importance of local elections. It granted enhanced authorisation to provide civic services to the fast-growing urban communities of İstanbul, Ankara, İzmir and Adana. Although shared with the central government, these extend to authorising land development and building, collection of property and environmental taxes, and transport, which conveyed on local authorities large budgets to manage and extensive resources to distribute. Accordingly, metropolitan mayors became influential political figures, and many of them continued their political careers at the national level.

Moreover, the 1984 local elections assumed additional significance. Three parties that were not permitted to compete in the 1983 national elections met the formalities to qualify for inclusion in the local elections (Doğru Yol Partisi, True Path Party, DYP; Sosyal Demokrasi Partisi, Social Democracy Party, SODEP; and the Refah Partisi, Welfare Party, RP). Accordingly, voters had the opportunity to choose between six parties. The elections took place in March 1984 and, leading the others, ANAP received 41.5 per cent of the vote. Following ANAP, the newcomers SODEP and DYP won 23.4 per cent and 13.2 per cent, respectively; HP won 8.8 per cent, MDP 7.1 per cent and the other newcomer, RP, received 4.4 per cent of the vote. These results show that, although voters had accepted ANAP as a legitimate political entity, that was not the case for the opposition parties in the TBMM, the HP and MDP. The result of the elections created a paradox for these two opposition parties, as they seemed to have lost the electoral bases they had briefly enjoyed in the less competitive climate of the 1983 national elections (Turan 1988, 77).

Following these two elections, further developments took place on the electoral scene. In August, SODEP and the Populist Party merged to form the Sosyal Demokrat Halkçı Parti (Social Democratic Populist Party, SHP), which provided parliamentary representation for SODEP. Similarly, on the right the MDP disbanded, and 20 of the party's MPs joined ANAP. These developments reshaped the role of the DYP, under the leadership of Demirel's loyal ally Husamettin Cindoruk, as the main right-wing opposition. The by-elections of 28 September 1986, in which twelve parties participated, marked another step for the democratic transition. If we analyse the content of the media's messages we find that the ten right-wing parties that competed in these elections had significant religious and nationalist themes, combined with

ANAP's positive promises of a rosy future (Unat 2015, 25). These elections displayed signs of further need for new electoral regulations, especially in the domains of registration, propaganda and finance, which eventually led to the constitutional amendment referendum of 6 September 1987.

The 1987 referendum was about restoring the political rights of former politicians who had been subjected to five- and ten-year suspensions from a range of political activities including the right to run for election. This issue was significantly elevated in the political agenda after the DYP received 23.6 per cent of the vote in the 1986 by-elections, placing second behind ANAP. The DYP, like other opposition parties, was led from the shadows by politicians who had been suspended; the DYP by Süleyman Demirel. The party's insistence on early elections and Özal's desire to comply with the demands to establish full democracy as a precondition for Turkey's access to full membership in the European Community were decisive in taking the decision to hold a referendum. The result favoured lifting the suspensions, but with only a slim margin between Yes and No votes, 50.16 per cent and 49.8 per cent respectively. Right after the referendum, Özal, assessing the Yes votes as an outcome of a joint move by all the opposition parties, interpreted 49.8 per cent as a vote of confidence and called a snap election. His calculation was based on three factors. First, he wanted to benefit from the unexpectedly high 'No' vote. Second, he and his allies controlled sufficient seats in the TBMM to pass a new electoral law that rearranged the boundaries of electoral constituencies, based on a new calculation that favoured the ANAP. And third, he wanted to leave the shortest time possible for opposing political leaders to develop programmes and organisation. As expected, the reform in the electoral law worked in favour of the ANAP. The party gained 65 per cent of the seats from only 36.3 per cent of the vote, owing to the introduction of 'quota seats' assigned to the strongest party. This change transformed the proportional system into a pseudo-majoritarian system and gave ANAP a 3/5 majority in parliament, sufficient to pass a constitutional amendment (Sabuncu 2006, 194).

The elections of the 1980s were more peaceful than the previous decade's, when evaluated in terms of electoral integrity. Even so, elections during the 1980s displayed some new problems of electoral integrity, especially in the campaign domain. Starting with the 1983 general elections, the importance of TV coverage of electoral campaigns increased. It became crucial in the 1987 elections, since the period allocated for campaigning was very short. When combined with the diminishing importance of mass gatherings, the decreasing influence of the press and tight regulations on opinion-forming centres of society, TV became the only tool that provided large-scale access to the public (Unat 2015, 35).

The following figures provide a look at the distribution of problems related to electoral integrity between 1970 and 1990.

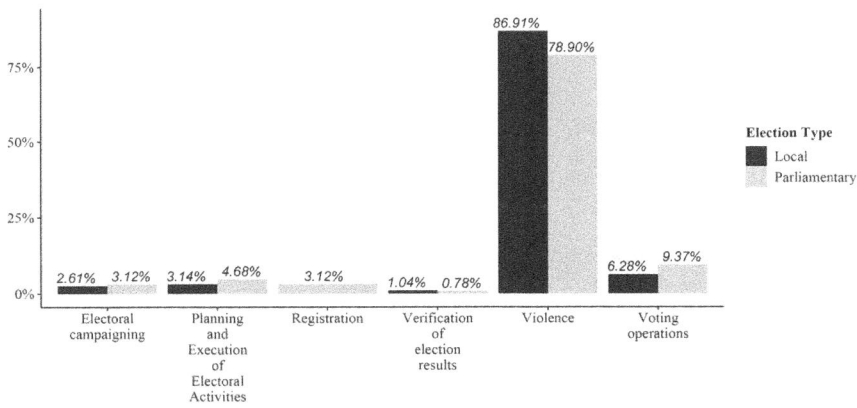

Figure 2.3 Distribution of electoral problems, parliamentary and local elections, 1970–80

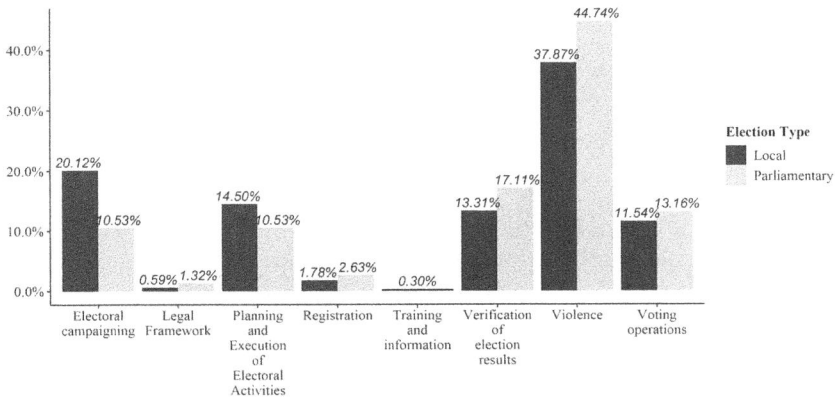

Figure 2.4 Distribution of electoral problems, parliamentary and local elections, 1980–90

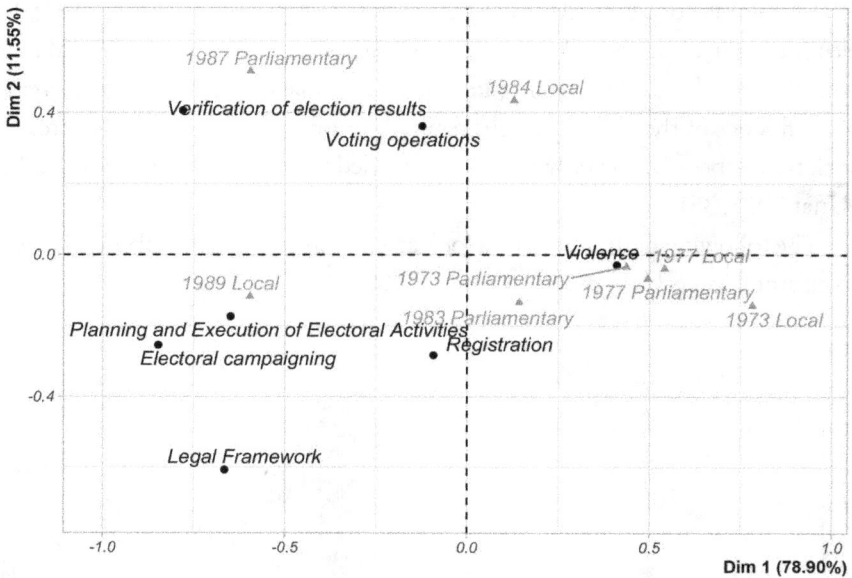

Figure 2.5 Correspondence analysis, electoral problems and election types, 1970–90

These graphs support the summary of this era. Most electoral problems were related to violence during the 1970s, as shown in Figure 2.3. Unsurprisingly, elections and electoral processes were affected by the storm of political violence the country experienced across the whole era. Newspapers reported only a fraction of other issues, primarily focusing on the problems related to voting operations. Even so, the distribution of electoral problems changed shape during the 1980s. Although electoral violence remained the most common problem in this decade, issues became visible in other areas, such as electoral campaigning, voting operations, verification of results and planning. These resulting from the systemic political and social change that followed the 1980 coup. The correspondence analysis in Figure 2.5 supports this argument, showing pre-1980 elections united around the issue of violence on the right-hand side of the graph and post-1980 elections grouped around other problems on the left-hand side, respectively. Lastly, the correspondence analysis shows the issues related to planning and execution, legal framework, registration and campaigning grouped around the 1983 parliamentary and 1989 local elections. This finding parallels the discussion above, which underlines the changes in the electoral system introduced before these elections.

Years of Transition: 1990–2009

The ANAP government took steady steps to liberalise the political system between 1989 and 1991. It announced several reforms between 1989 and 1991, which made multiple changes to the Constitution affecting the electoral system, such as increasing the number of MPs in the TBMM and lowering the voting age to 18. The reforms also included improvements in human rights. The TBMM allowed the Kurdish language to be used in private schools and accepted the annulment in the criminal code of Articles 141, 142 and 163, which forbade political activity based on ethnicity or religion.

These changes did not pass without criticism. Immediately after the 1987 elections the opposition parties began pointing out that the government's majority in the assembly resulted from a flawed electoral law and putting on pressure for early elections. These criticisms increased when the ANAP government lost popularity, especially after the party suffered a significant loss in the 1989 local elections. The government could not resist the demands coming from the opposition and began to hint that elections would be called early, in 1990, by announcing generous wage increases for civil servants and high agricultural guarantee prices for farmers. In due course, elections took place on 20 October 1991 and, as predicted, the primary competitor of the ANAP, Demirel's DYP, won the highest share of the vote, 27 per cent. ANAP was second with 24 per cent, which was a surprising result, twice as high as any polls had forecast. With 20 per cent of the vote, SODEP had a disappointing result, especially after its success in the 1989 local elections. Moreover, this vote share included votes for the Kurdish Halkın Emek Partisi (the People's Labour Party, HEP), whose candidates had run in SODEP lists. Of the other parties, Erbakan's RP fared the best with 17 per cent, thanks to its coalition with the Turkish ultra-nationalists MHP. In the meantime, Özal became the eighth president of the Turkish Republic, only the second civilian (after Celal Bayar) to hold that post, when Kenan Evren's term ended in November 1989.

One significant political development during this period was the deepening of polarisation between secularists and Islamists, which had begun in the late

1980s. On the Islamist side, radical groups linking to Erbakan's RP became more visible, including İBDA-C (İslamî Büyük Doğu Akıncıları Cephesi, the Muslim Great East Raiders) and the Hizbullah. In January 1993, a car bomb killed Uğur Mumcu, a prominent secular journalist writing extensively on the relations between these fundamentalist groups and Iran and Saudi Arabia. This assassination brought the secularist masses out on the streets, criticising the feeble efforts by police and state prosecutors to find the killers. In this environment, the sudden death of Özal in the spring of 1993 triggered several changes in the political system. Demirel filled the post of president, which created a power vacuum at the top of the DYP. Tansu Çiller, who had served as the economy minister in Demirel's cabinet, became the new party leader. In the same year, there was also a change in the leadership of the coalition partner SODEP when Erdal İnönü retired from politics and was succeeded by Murat Karayalçın, the former mayor of Ankara.

The other central political problem of the 1990s was the Kurdish problem. This had two dimensions: violence and representation. Relating to the first dimension, the Kurdish movement in the country turned to guerrilla warfare, guided by the Partiya Karkeran Kurdistan (Workers' Party of Kurdistan, PKK), which Abdullah Öcalan had established in November 1978. PKK's terrorist attacks peaked during this decade, causing thousands of fatalities, including civilians. The Kurdish population had the chance to be represented in the TBMM with eighteen MPs, when the HEP joined forces with SODEP for the 1991 elections. However, six Kurdish SODEP MPs were expelled from the party after attending a conference in Paris as representing 'Kurdistan', a tremendously taboo word at the time. In protest, nine other Kurdish SODEP representatives resigned from the party and reunited under the HEP, but in July 1993 the Constitutional Court banned the HEP on the grounds of separatism. Although the elected MPs of the party reunited under a new party, the Demokrasi Partisi (Democratic Party, DeP), to keep their representation at the TBMM, the destiny of DeP was no different from that of HEP. One DeP MP, Mehmet Sincar, was murdered in September 1993, and in February 1994 the party's headquarters in Ankara was attacked. In December 1993, prosecutors opened a case at the Constitutional Court to close the DeP, and in March 1994 the immunity of the remaining DeP MPs was lifted. The DeP MPs were arrested, received prison sentences of up to fifteen years, and the party was closed in June 1994. The closed party formed a successor, Halkın Demokrasi Partisi (People's Democracy Party, HADEP), which did very well in the 1995 elections in the south-east but failed to win over the Kurdish electorate in the big cities. Unlike its precursors HADEP was not banned but, in June 1997, many of its leading members were sentenced to lengthy prison terms.

Lastly, one should mention the rise of political Islam during the 1990s. Presenting itself as the only solution to the corruption of political functioning, the Islamist RP tripled its vote share throughout the decade. In the 1994 local elections, although the DYP just managed to remain the biggest party, with 21.4 per cent, the actual winner was the RP, which scored 19.1 per cent. As a result, the party took over six of the fifteen largest Turkish cities, including İstanbul and Ankara. The RP continued its success in the 1995 general elections, again receiving 21.4 per cent of the vote, and became the leading party. The ANAP came second with 19.7 per cent, and Çiller's DYP, doing much better than expected, won slightly fewer votes than ANAP (19.2 per cent) but gained more seats than its rival. The parties on the left received 25 per cent of the vote. Still, only former prime minister Ecevit's Demokratik Sol Parti (Democratic Left Party, DSP) managed to pass the 10 per cent threshold, winning 14.7 per cent of the vote. The re-opened CHP under the leadership of Deniz Baykal passed the national threshold with a slight margin and won forty-nine seats. A coalition of the far-right MHP and the pro-Kurdish HADEP failed to pass the national threshold.

The following five years were quite chaotic. An alliance between ANAP and DYP seemed to be the obvious way to keep the Islamist RP from government. Still, personal disagreements between ANAP's Mesut Yılmaz and DYP's Çiller made this alliance extremely difficult. Under tremendous pressure from the military and the business community, ANAP and DYP managed to form a reluctant coalition, which ended after only four months when the ANAP joined forces with the RP for a parliamentary inquiry into suspected wrongdoing by Çiller. In response, Çiller pulled DYP out of the coalition. This move opened the way for her to form a new alliance with the RP and retain power. In consequence, DYP and RP formed a cabinet on 28 June 1996, appointing Erbakan prime minister for the next two years. Predictably, this coalition raised eyebrows, especially among the military. Allying with the Islamist RP also caused a fissure among the DYP, and MPs who resigned from the party formed Demokrat Türkiye Partisi (the Democratic Turkey Party, DeTP). In the meantime, putting immense pressure on the DYP-RP coalition through several mechanisms (Zürcher 2010, 323–9), the military achieved its goal, forced Erbakan to resign his office in 1997. President Demirel appointed ANAP's Yılmaz to form a government, and Yılmaz managed to establish a coalition with Ecevit's DSP and Hüsamattin Cindoruk's DeTP. In the interim, prosecutors lodged files against Erbakan and other leading RP leaders, demanding another party be closed. In due course, the Constitutional Court closed the RP, and Erbakan was officially barred from politics for five years, a punishment that later increased to a life ban. The prosecutors also opened a case against Istanbul's RP Mayor, Recep Tayyip Erdoğan, who was sentenced to ten months in prison. After a series of economic and social crises, Yılmaz's government did not last very long, and he resigned on 25 November 1998, announcing new elections for April 1999.

On 15 April 1999, national and local elections were held on the same day for the first time in Turkish political history. The elections took place in a political climate shaped by the significant changes in Turkish politics discussed above, especially by ongoing conflicts between secular and Islamist movements and the Kurdish problem. The voters were asked to choose parliamentary parties and candidates, regional councils, mayors, local councils and mayors for the fifteen greater municipalities in the country. National and local election participation rates were high and varied only marginally, at 87.1 and 85.2 per cent, respectively. Although Islamists founded the Fazilet Partisi (Virtue Party, FP) to replace the closed RP for the 1999 elections, they lost nearly a quarter of their share of the vote. Even so, the newly founded FP came third in the national elections with 15 per cent of the vote, after Ecevit's DSP and the MHP, which received 22 and 18 per cent, respectively. The remaining parties of the centre-right, ANAP and DYP, received 13 and 12 per cent. The CHP, which had been in a state of decline, suffered another electoral blow by failing to pass the national 10 per cent threshold. The same was true of HADEP which, despite a substantial share of votes cast in the eastern and south-eastern provinces, did not send any delegates to the TBMM in Ankara after failing to pass the national threshold. The government formed after the elections consisted of DSP, MHP and ANAP, headed by veteran Bülent Ecevit. It might seem shocking that an alliance could combine the ultra-right and the progressive left. Still, there was much intellectual common ground since both DSP and MHP were aggressively nationalistic and believed in a strong state.

The most striking characteristic of the 1999 elections was their impact on changing the relationship between national and local elections in Turkey. Unlike their past behaviour, in 1999 Turkish electors appeared to split their votes when asked to cast their ballots for municipal and parliamentary elections (İncioğlu 2002, 82). For the first time in Turkish history, the outcomes of local elections did not precisely parallel national electoral trends, which was clearly shown in votes for the FP. Although, as mentioned above, the party did not perform well at the national level, it came first in the metropolitan and the district mayor elections. These disparities in votes for political parties were a significant new development in Turkish electoral politics; from 1999 onwards, local elections in Turkey ceased to be purely a product of national voting trends. The deterioration of the connection between national and local electoral norms underscores the increasing importance of the standard of regional government and the success of individual mayors in influencing voter preferences. The pervasive dissatisfaction with and declining level of confidence in the centrist political parties was another aspect that influenced the evolving trends.

The tension between secularists and Islamists, the August 1999 earthquake and economic crises marked the years until the next elections, in 2002. During these years, the Constitutional Court outlawed the FP on 22 June 2001, accusing the party of being a direct successor to the Welfare Party. This decision prompted argument within the Islamist movement, between 'conservatives' who advocated a rigid Islamist line and 'modernists' who wanted to convert the party into a centre-right one with less emphasis on Islamist rhetoric. On 14 August 2001, the modernists split from the conservatives under the leadership of Abdullah Gül and Tayyip Erdoğan. They founded the Adalet ve Kalkinma Partisi (Justice and Development Party, AKP) and the remaining conservatives united under the Saadet Partisi (Felicity Party, SP).

As mentioned above, Ecevit's coalition government struggled with the financial crises and the human and material cost of the earthquake in subsequent years. However, when his health deteriorated, coupled with these problems,

Ecevit called early elections. On 3 November 2002, the polls took place, and the results were impressive. Except for AKP and CHP, no party passed the 10 per cent election threshold. In such conditions, AKP, which took around 34 per cent of the vote, secured an absolute majority at the TBMM. The only other party to gain seats in the assembly was Deniz Baykal's CHP, with just over 19 per cent of the vote. Ecevit's popularity had fallen by 95 per cent, along with that of other centre-right parties, the ANAP and DYP, which failed to win enough votes to gain seats. The election results indicate that traditional political loyalties had almost entirely evaporated, and people were willing to support any-one who could give them hope. Gül headed the AKP government since Erdoğan was still in prison. Viewed through the lens of electoral integrity, the 2002 elections were comparatively peaceful – except for one very controversial issue, which will be discussed in Chapter Five – and only a few incidents were reported across the country. However, in a significant development, the annulment of elections in the constituency of Siirt opened the way for Erdoğan to become an AKP MP and, eventually, the prime minister.

The following election, in 2007, consolidated the power of the AKP: the party increased its share of the vote to 46.5 per cent. The CHP followed the AKP with 21 per cent, and MHP also managed to cross the threshold at 14 per cent. However, AKP was assigned fewer seats (341) despite the increase in its vote share. The closed HADEP re-united under the newly formed Demokratik Toplum Partisi (Democratic Society Party, DTP). To bypass the threshold set for parties, the DTP candidates ran as independent candidates, and the party managed to send twenty-seven MPs to the parliament. So by using a loophole in the electoral law that allowed independents to be elected without crossing a threshold, the Kurdish population again managed to find the chance to be represented at the national level.

Starting from the early years of the decade, numerous allegations were made that related to the integrity of elections, especially in eastern and south-eastern constituencies. These allegations included vote-rigging and voter intimidation strategies aiming to prevent a possible win by HADEP. The 'Mersin incident' in the 1999 elections proved that these allegations were not unfounded. When the Türkiye Radyo Televizyon Kurumu (Turkish National Radio and Broadcast Agency, TRT) broadcast the news that the Kurdish HADEP had won the elections in Mersin, counting the votes was suddenly suspended without any reason. After a recount, the victorious HADEP wsa placed third behind the DSP and CHP Mersin Metropolitan Municipality.

Other than these singular events, however, electoral problems decreased during the elections between 2000 and 2007. The following graphs provide an overview of the distribution of problems related to electoral integrity between 1990 and 2000.

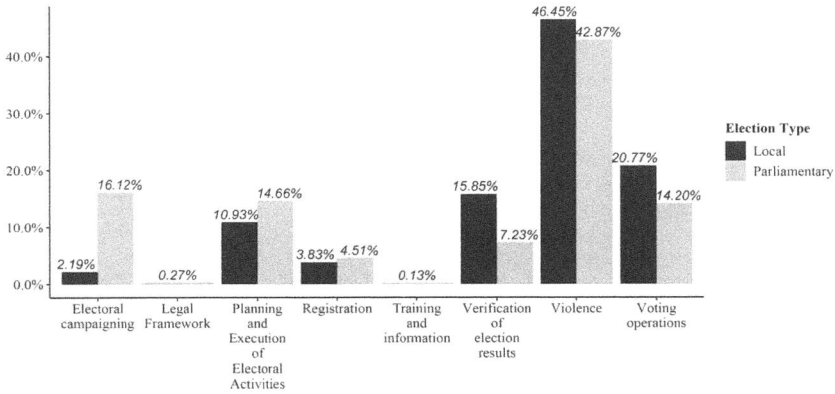

Figure 2.6 Distribution of electoral problems, parliamentary and local elections, 1990–2000

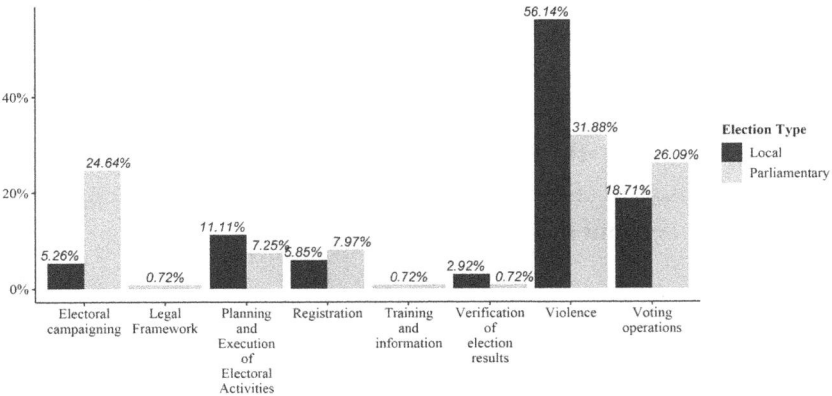

Figure 2.7 Distribution of electoral problems, parliamentary and local elections, 2000–7

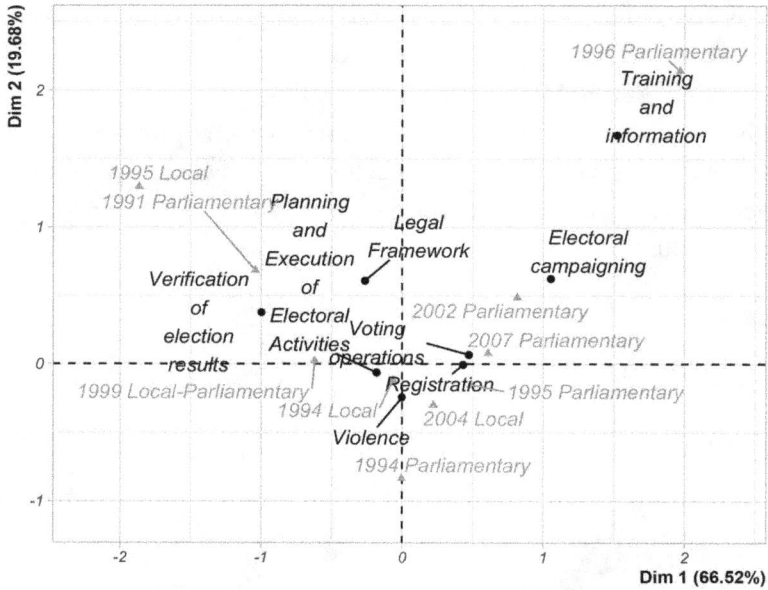

Figure 2.8 Correspondence analysis, electoral problems and election types, 1990–2007

Conclusion

Keeping with the framework given in the introduction, this chapter provided a summary of Turkey's political developments and electoral history up to 2010. It aimed to identify the electoral challenges that the country has experienced since the 1940s via the prism of electoral integrity. The analysis portrays electoral violence as the most common electoral problem between 1940 and 2010. Analyses based on the DIEV-T data also point to other problems of integrity which became visible after changes in electoral laws and regulations. Last but not least, the material offered in this chapter provides more insight into recent concerns with elections that the nation has been expressing.

References

Ahmad, Feroz. 2003. *Turkey: The Quest for Identity*. Oxford: Oneworld Publications.
Ahmad, Feroz and Bedia Turgay. 1976. *Türkiye'de Çok Partili Politikaların Açıklamalı Kronolojisi 1945–1971*. Ankara: Bilgi Yayınevi.
Aleskerov, Fuad, Hasan Ersel and Yavuz Sabuncu. 2010. *Seçimden Koalisyona*. 2nd edn. İstanbul: Efil Yayınevi.

Cop, Burak. 2018. *Türkiye'de Seçim Sistemleri*. İstanbul: Tekin Yayınevi.

Girgin, Ozan Kerem. 2013. *Türkiye Seçim Tarihi*. İstanbul: Sokak Kitapları.

Heper, Metin. 1990. 'The State, Political Party and Society in Post-1983 Turkey.' *Government and Opposition* 25 (3): 321–33.

İncioğlu, Nihal. 2002. 'Local Elections and Political Behaviour.' In *Politics, Parties and Elections in Turkey*, edited by Sabri Sayarı and Yılmaz Esmer, 73–90. Boulder, CO: Lynne Rienner Publishers.

Karpat, Kemal H. 1961. 'The Turkish Elections of 1957.' *The Western Political Quarterly* 14 (2): 436–59. https://doi.org/10.2307/443599.

———. 2003. *Studies on Turkish Politics and Society: Selected Articles and Essays*. Leiden, , Netherlands: Brill Academic Publishers.

Keyder, Çağlar. 1992. 'Türk Demokrasisinin Ekonomi Politiği.' In *Geçiş Sürecinde Türkiye*, edited by Irvin C. Schick and Ahmet E. Tonak, 38–75. İstanbul: Belge Yayınları.

Mardin, Şerif. 1973. 'Center–Periphery Relations: A Key to Turkish Politics?' *Daedalus* 2: 169–90.

Özbudun, Ergun. 1976. *Social Change and Political Participation in Turkey*. Princeton, NJ: Princeton University Press.

Özbudun, Ergun and Frank Tachau. 1975. 'Social Change and Electoral Behavior in Turkey: Toward a "Critical Realignment"?' *International Journal of Middle East Studies* 6 (4): 460–80.

Sabuncu, Yavuz. 2006. 'Seçim Barajları ve Siyasal Sonuçları.' *Anayasa Yargısı*. Ahlatlıbel, İncek Şehit. Savcı Mehmet Selim Kiraz Bulvarı Numara: 4, 06805 Çankaya/Ankara: T. C. Anayasa Mahkemesi.

Sayarı, Sabri. 2014. 'Interdisciplinary Approaches to Political Clientelism and Patronage in Turkey.' *Turkish Studies*. https://doi.org/10.1080/14683849.2014.985809.

'Seçim Kanunu Komisyonu Raporu.' 1961.

Shils, Edward. 1975. *Center and Periphery: Essays in Macrosociology*. Chicago: University of Chicago Press.

Tachau, Frank. 2002. 'An Overview of Electoral Behavior: Toward Protest or Consolidation of Democracy?' In *Politics, Parties and Elections in Turkey*, edited by Sabri Sayarı and Yılmaz Esmer, 33–54. Boulder: Lynne Rienner Publishers.

Tonak, Ertuğrul Ahmet and Irvin Cemil Schick. 1992. 'Uluslararası Boyut: Ticaret, Yardım ve Borçlanma.' In *Geçiş Sürecinde Türkiye*, edited by Irvin C. Schick and Ahmet E. Tonak, 354–85. İstanbul: Belge Yayınları.

Tuncer, Erol. 2010. *1950 Seçimleri*. Ankara, Turkey: TESAV.

Turan, Ali Eşref. 2004. *Türkiye'de Seçmen Davranışı: Önceki Kırılmalar ve 2002 Seçimi*. İstanbul: İstanbul Bilgi Üniversitesi Yayınları.

Turan, İlter. 1988. 'Political Parties and the Party System in Post-1973 Turkey.' In *State, Democracy and the Military: Turkey in the 1980s*, edited by Metin Heper and Ahmet Evin, 63–80. Berlin and New York: de Gruyter.

Unat, Nermin Abadan. 2015. 'Legitimacy, Participation and Restricted Pluralism: The 1987 Elections in Turkey.' *Ankara Üniversitesi SBF Dergisi* 44 (1).

Zürcher, Erik J. 2010. *Turkey : A Modern History*. 3rd edn. London: I. B.Tauris.

3

PUTTING TURKEY IN PERSPECTIVE

This chapter continues the discussion in Chapter Two with a particular focus on the last two decades, when electoral integrity problems rose to the top of the political agenda in Turkey. It sets a functional classification of electoral integrity problems and operationalises this classification, primarily focusing on formal and informal institutions – such as electoral management bodies (EMBs) – and media structures. Finally, it locates the current Turkish case within this framework.

The Troubled Years: 2009–19

As Chapter Two indicated, examples of damage to electoral integrity can be observed as far back as the 1950s. However, the incidents have significantly increased during the last two decades, an era marked by the successive victories of the Adalet ve Kalkınma Partisi (Justice and Development Party, AKP), with the danger of institutionalising this damage. While the AKP had effectively established itself as the dominant party in Turkey by 2010, the power struggle behind this outcome further damaged Turkey's democratic functioning, eventually affecting fundamental rights and freedoms enjoyed in the country, including the domain of electoral integrity. The accelerated personalisation of authority in the governing party by its leader Recep Tayyip Erdoğan has generated sustaining political crises. These crises peaked when he announced his intention to replace the parliamentary structure of

Turkey with a presidential system in 2011. Many scholars have interpreted these developments as a shift to competitive authoritarianism (Akkoyunlu 2017, 55; Yardımcı-Geyikçi 2015; Esen and Gumuscu 2016; 2018), indicating a system where elections are regularly held without substantive problems but, at the same time, where incumbents systematically manipulate state resources and refuse media coverage to the opposition, attack and abuse opposition candidates and supporters, and abuse electoral results (Levitsky and Way 2002). In the Turkish case, indeed, elections have allowed the incumbent AKP to create a system based on populist single-party rule mainly driven by personalities. Since the AKP's political hegemony depends on winning elections, the party has resorted to a variety of tactics ranging from using the government's administrative resources to media restrictions (OSCE 2015). The following paragraphs will discuss some of the most controversial problems related to electoral integrity during the period since 2010.

The series of events that raised doubts about the integrity of elections started during the 2011 national elections when the Supreme Electoral Council (YSK) ordered 69 million extra ballots to be printed, nearly 40 per cent more than the actual number of voters. As Turkey's highest authority on elections, this unexpected ruling paved the way for serious allegations of electoral fraud. Although the opposition parties raised many official questions about the purpose of these extra printed ballots, related state offices provided only inconsistent comments and responses and failed to dispel the conspiracy theories (Toker 2014, 119–20).

Following these controversial elections, problems of electoral integrity rose to the top of the political agenda with the 2014 local elections. As an overt example of gerrymandering, the government introduced a new law just before the elections, which reset the electoral boundaries and doubled the number of cities in the metropolitan areas. This move aimed to give more weight to the rural vote, which has always favoured conservative and Islamist parties (Aygül 2016, 183), including the AKP. The problems associated with the 2014 local elections were not confined to pre-election arrangements. Numerous accusations referred to various types of rigging, including 'losing' ballot papers, ballot-box tallies that did not carry legally required stamps and signatures, high numbers of invalid votes in constituencies that were likely to have close races, power blackouts and electoral violence (Toros and Birch 2019). I quoted the explanation offered by AKP's minister of energy Taner Yıldız at the head of Chapter One. After the elections, the debate shifted to the number of votes declared invalid. Meyersson (2014) has demonstrated an unusual relationship between the percentage of invalid ballots and the increase in the voting share of the AKP. Especially in Ankara and İstanbul, this relationship was robust across districts and voting stations. Moreover, the relationship was found in areas with more support for the opposition.

The problems of electoral integrity continued during the general elections that took place in 2015. The AKP emerged in first place from the June election, with a 40 per cent share of the vote. Cumhuriyet Halk Partisi (the Republican Peoples Party, CHP) and Milliyetçi Hareket Partisi (the Nationalist Action Party, MHP) followed AKP with 25 and 16 per cent of the vote, respectively. Halkların Demokratik Partisi (the People's Democratic Party, HDP), the precursor to HADEP, decided to run as a party instead of as independent candidates, receiving 13 per cent of the votes and earning a record number of eighty parliamentary seats, surpassing most expectations. The results turned the Türkiye Büyük Millet Meclisi (Turkish Grand National Assembly, TBMM) into a hung parliament since the AKP did not have an overall majority, so could not form a single-party government. Since the party was also reluctant to enter a coalition government, president Erdoğan called for fresh elections in November instead of delegating the task to the next-largest party, CHP, which would have been conventional practice. The AKP regained its legislative majority in the November re-election with a 49.5 per cent share of the vote, and the party again returned to power as a single-party government.

These double elections of 2015 were quite problematic when scrutinised through the lens of electoral integrity. The opposition parties made numerous allegations of electoral fraud and abuse, especially during and after the June 2015 elections. To start with, even though this had been severely criticised in 2011, the YSK again decided to print extra ballots, ordering 17 million more ballot papers than strictly required for the 2015 June elections. Although the opposition parties questioned this action and raised the issue in the TBMM, the YSK did not provide conclusive responses. Second, the opposition parties also accused the incumbent AKP of abusing state resources for their own ends. Erdoğan himself organised rallies in various provinces in preparation for the general election and endorsed the AKP, although he was under oath to stay neutral as president. The HDP's appeal to the YSK in this matter was rejected.

There were severe allegations about media censorship. On 7 April 2015, the state authorities blocked Twitter, Facebook, YouTube and 166 other websites for sharing photographs related to a hostage incident. Since this decision was taken only weeks before the elections, it prompted charges of increasing government censorship of the opposition (Kasapoglu 2015). Other criticisms targeted the state-owned Türkiye Radyo Televizyon Kurumu (Turkish National Radio and Broadcast Agency, TRT), a constitutional institution mandated to impartial broadcasting. Despite this, during the pre-election period the TRT did not broadcast a single opposition party election rally, instead focusing entirely on AKP rallies. TRT also decided not to air a CHP campaign advertisement because it was perceived to be openly critical of the governing AKP. The advert featured a cat walking near a transformer, referring to Yıldız's explanation for the nationwide electricity cuts during the 2014 local elections. These actions were taken to court by the CHP on several occasions, producing no satisfactory results.

Many also criticised SEÇSİS, the computer-aided electoral informatics system used to facilitate electoral procedures such as registration and voting during the 2015 elections. Most criticisms focused on vulnerability to external manipulation. These concerns were brought to the Constitutional Court, where AKP politicians were accused of manipulating the system for electoral advantage. The CHP also raised the issue for investigation, and the YSK, after eight months of investigation, accepted that the SEÇSİS system lacked a security certificate, meaning that its operations were open to undetected manipulation.

The incumbent AKP, the primary addressee of these allegations, counterattacked by accusing the opposition parties of resorting to violent tactics during the election campaign. On 23 April 2015, during an armed attack on the AKP election centre in Batman, the son of a former AKP MP had been killed. AKP officials blamed the opposition parties for the incident, although their guilt was never proven. Likewise, when AKP parliamentary candidates were greeted with hostility by residents in Van – a heavily Kurdish-populated city – the AKP delegate accused the HDP of organising the incident. On 2 May 2015, AKP officials accused CHP supporters of attacking their election van during their canvassing work in İstanbul. AKP district heads in Kurdish-populated Van and Ağrı also accused the HDP of using force and coercion against voters and village heads via the Partiya Karkeran Kurdistan (Workers' Party of Kurdistan, PKK). Conversely, several violent incidents were reported in which opposition parties were attacked. For example, on 18 April 2015, two people were taken into custody for an armed assault on the HDP headquarters in Ankara. HDP chairman Selahattin Demirtaş claimed that forty-one HDP election offices had been subject to similar violent attacks. Similarly, on 30 April, the HDP election offices in Uşak were attacked by a group; several people were injured during the fight, while electoral materials belonging to the party were destroyed. Another example of an attack on the HDP happened in Kırşehir on 14 May 2015, when a group of Turkish nationalists began harassing HDP supporters, who had joined Selahattin Demirtaş in his visit to the city. Again, several people were injured, and the police used water cannon to break up the crowd.

After the turbulent elections in 2015, Turkish citizens once again went to the polls to vote on a constitutional referendum in 2017. After winning the 2015 elections, by establishing an unexpected alliance with the MHP under the name of Cumhur İttifakı (People's Alliance, Cİ), Erdoğan and the AKP found an oppportunity to transform the country's parliamentary democracy into a presidential system, a policy he had been pursuing for a long time. Since the AKP could not by itself provide the necessary majority for constitutional changes, which require the backing of two-thirds of the MPs at the TBMM, the matter was put to the electorate. The referendum result opened the way to the most important constitutional change since the Turkish republic was proclaimed in 1923, with only a small majority – 51 per cent of the votes were cast in favour of the presidential system.

Once again, electoral integrity matters were on the agenda during and after the referendum. As voting was taking place, the YSK lifted the law requiring each ballot to carry an official stamp. Instead, it ruled that votes not carrying the official stamp of the council must be considered legitimate unless there is a suspicion that they were fake, since the ballots carry logos and other protective measures (YSK 2017). Large-scale demonstrations in protest at the decision of the YSK erupted after the election results were announced, since nearly 1.5 million unstamped blank ballots were counted as valid. Although opposition parties demanded the annulment of the election results, all their appeals were rejected. The Organization for Security and Co-operation in Europe (OSCE) and the Parliamentary Assembly of the Council of Europe (PACE) raised this issue in reports, both organisations alleging unfairness during the campaign and declaring the YSK's decision illegal (OSCE 2017; Preda 2017).

Once again, media bias was quite visible during the referendum. According to one report, live television broadcasts during the period 1–20 March dedicated 169 hours to Erdoğan, 301.5 hours to the ruling AKP and 15.5 hours to its small partner MHP, which was supporting the 'Yes' campaign, while CHP received 45.5 hours of coverage and the HDP was given none (Caliskan 2017). Commenting on this matter, the Venice Commission reported that 'the extremely unfavourable environment for journalism and the increasingly impoverished and one-sided public debate that prevail in Turkey at this point question the very possibility of holding a meaningful, inclusive democratic referendum campaign' (Barrett et al., 2017).

Additionally, opposition parties and other organisations reported several incidents of electoral violence during the campaign, in which the AKP government and the police were accused of using methods intended to restrict the capacity of 'No' supporters to lobby, such as prosecutions, media monitoring and electoral censorship. For example, Meral Akşener, the leader of the İyi Parti (Good Party) and one of the most popular campaigners for the 'No' bloc, was prevented from speaking in Yalova and Edirne shortly before her meetings had been due to start. On another occasion, while she was delivering a speech at a hotel in Çanakkale, the venue suffered a sudden power cut. After initially being obstructed by riot police, attendees at the conference used the torches in their mobile phones to light the venue and allow the event to continue.

The storm of elections in Turkey continued in 2018 following the ratification of the constitutional amendments in the 2017 referendum. Turkish citizens went to the polls to elect the president and the MPs on the same day, knowing that the elected candidate would be both head of state and head of the Government of Turkey, taking over the office of prime minister. The incumbent president, Erdoğan, announced his candidacy for the Cİ. The opposition ran three alternates: the CHP's Muharrem Ince, a member of parliament known for his combative criticism and buoyant anti-Erdogan speeches, the HDP's imprisoned former chairman Selahattin Demirtaş and the İyi Party's Meral Akşener. In addition to these candidates Temel Karamollaoğlu, leader of the Saadet Partisi (Felicity Party, SP), and Doğu Perinçek, leader of the Vatan Partisi (Patriotic Party, VP), declared their candidacy and gathered the 100,000 signatures needed for the nomination.

Although several controversies arose during the 2018 elections, holding an election while a state of emergency was in force dominated the others. On 20 July 2016, five days after a coup had failed, the government proclaimed a state of emergency, allowing the administration to rule the country by decree, circumvent the parliament and, most importantly, restrict several civil liberties. Additionally, many interpreted the government's decision to extend the state of emergency to include the electoral cycle as a pretext for suppressing the opposition. When PACE raised its concern at the situation and recommended postponement, since the elections would not meet European standards for democratic accountability, the Turkish government called its declaration 'politicised, unequal, unjust and beyond limits'.

Throughout the campaign period, the tone of the political speeches and literature was highly aggressive, parties accusing each other of supporting terrorism. During the campaign, several violent incidents occurred: opposition parties, notably the CHP, the HDP, the SP and İyi, reported several attacks on their offices, vehicles and electoral materials coupled with obstruction of meetings in several cities. The most controversial event occurred on 14 June, when a shooting incident between AKP campaigners and local shopkeepers in the south-eastern village Suruç, some of whom were HDP supporters, left four people dead and eight injured.

The following graphs provide an overview of the problems related to electoral integrity between 2009 and 2000.

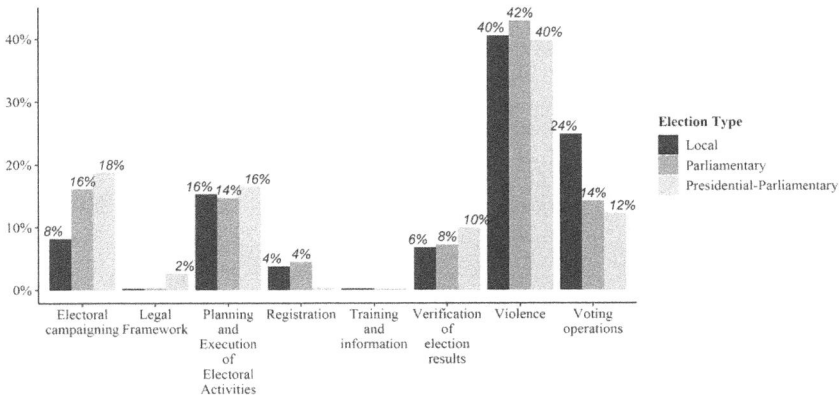

Figure 3.1 Distribution of electoral problems, parliamentary, local and presidential-parliamentary elections, 2009–18

Note: Owing to rounding, percentages do not add up to 100.

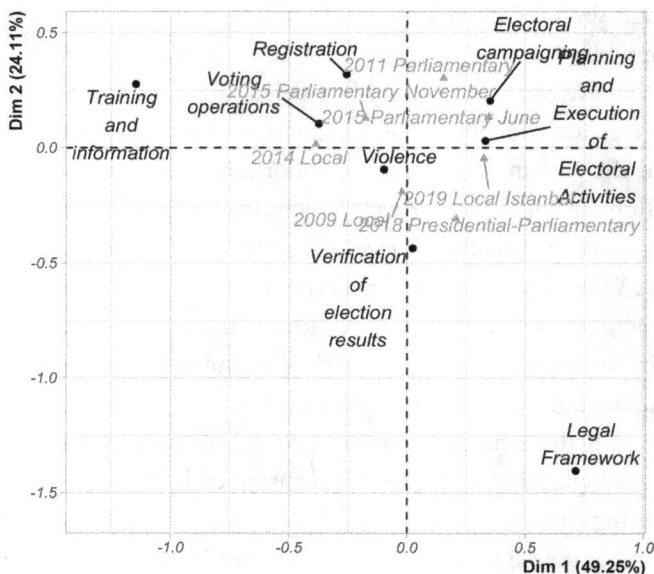

Figure 3.2 Correspondence analysis, electoral problems and election types, 2009–18

These graphs above display the changing nature of the problems with electoral integrity during the second decade of this century. Although violence still tops the list, according to the DIEV-T data, it is accompanied by high levels of problems related to campaigns, planning and voting operations. This era was also marked by the issues associated with the verification of election results, which had not been an issue in previous periods. Legal arrangements also came onto the scene because of the radical systemic change which replaced the parliamentary system with a presidential one. The correspondence analysis supports these arguments, showing pre-2018 elections united around these new electoral integrity problems. The following sections will further elaborate on these issues from a comparative perspective, drawing on other data sources.

Turkey in Comparative Perspective

The following paragraphs, using Turkey as the focal case, will further deepen the discussion to identify primary problematic areas and introduce data tools and concepts that will be discussed in the remaining parts of this book.

Electoral Malpractice

Although elections are given the highest priority and consideration, they frequently face several problems that threaten their integrity. Throughout the world, incidents of electoral abuse and violence, incompetent and unfair EMBs, biased media structures, under-representation of women and minority candidates, and cybersecurity attacks have caused elections to fail to produce legitimate results. Norris (2013) classifies these problems as first- and second-order problems. The former are different types of substantial electoral malpractice. According to Birch (2011, 27), such problems take three primary forms: manipulation of the legislative framework behind elections, of individual voters' choices and of the administrative voting process. The latter describes issues like lack of technical capacity and unintentional human error. Whether planned or accidental, first- or second-order, problems during elections have significant impact on democratic systems, including deterioration of trust in the democratic regime and its institutions, and violence. As mentioned in Chapter One, electoral integrity is an umbrella term for defining the ideal practical and normative context for elections (Norris 2018, 220). Thus, an election having integrity should be based on the democratic values of universal suffrage and political equality and function across the electoral cycle in an unbiased and transparent way, throughout its planning and administration. Accordingly, electoral integrity necessitates some critical features that operate in formal and informal domains. These features include competent and independent institutions such as unbiased EMBs that handle the formal domain of the election in an open and trustworthy manner. Similarly, electoral integrity requires structures such as free and impartial media to ensure fair competition and thereby strengthen democracy on the informal level. Above all, electoral integrity must be underpinned by a rule of law that guarantees a democratic system.

Using the World Values Survey Wave 7 (WVS7) database, figure 3.3. provides a recent portrait of the levels of electoral integrity in several countries.

Figure 3.3. reveals that the Scandic region – Denmark, Finland, Norway, Sweden and Iceland – accompanied by New Zealand, Germany, the Netherlands, Switzerland and Austria, have held polls with the highest credibility ratings for electoral integrity. It is worth noting that these are prosperous, post-industrial countries with consensus-based economies and progressive welfare

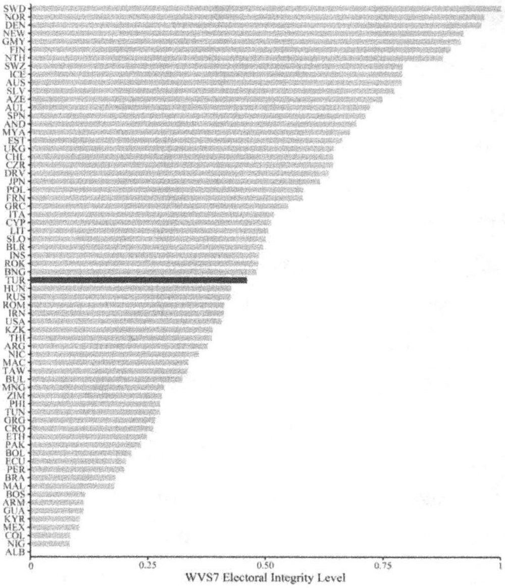

Figure 3.3   Levels of electoral integrity

Note: Values are the mean of eight questions on electoral integrity, standardised and rescaled between 0 and 1

Source: WVS seventh wave

states that experience only minor problems related to human rights and the rule of law. The United Kingdom, Slovakia, Spain and Estonia, and other consolidated democracies like Australia and Japan, follow this leading group, displaying very similar characteristics to that group.

Following this top rank, Turkey is ranked below the 0.5 mark, primarily owing to the series of problematic elections that took place after 2010. As detailed earlier in this chapter, by the end of 2019 Turkey had held four parliamentary, two presidential and three local elections (including the İstanbul repeat elections), and a constitutional referendum, making ten elections in nine years. Allegations of fraud, undue influence and violence were made in all of these elections, casting doubt on Turkey's claim to be an established democracy (Akkoyunlu 2017; Toros and Birch 2019). These allegations reached a climax in 2018 during the combined presidential and parliamentary election, which the *Economist* described as 'the most unfair election in Turkey in decades' (*Economist* 2018). The 2018 elections took place after a short but tense campaigning period, but more importantly, under a state of emergency. The state of emergency laws prompted the integrity of the 2018 elections to be questioned since these measures affected the judiciary, police, military, civil service, local authorities, academia, the media and the business community, shutting down more than 1,000 institutions and private companies and transferring their assets to public institutions (PACE Monitoring Committee 2017). International organisations, including the United Nations, underlined the severity of the situation. They noted that 'protracted restrictions on the human rights to freedom of expression, assembly and association are incompatible with the conduct of a credible electoral process' (Zeid Ra'ad Al Hussein 2018). Although the government tried to overcome these criticisms by announcing that the election had been conducted transparently, the atmosphere was hardly conducive to a level playing field for many reasons, including the opposition's limited access to the media and state resources (Kirişçi 2018). Agreeing with this argument, the OSCE election observation report cited violations of electoral procedure, limitations on media freedom, intimidation and numerous violent attacks on candidates and partisans (OSCE 2018). Figure 3.4 depicts the deterioration in standards of electoral integrity in Turkey.

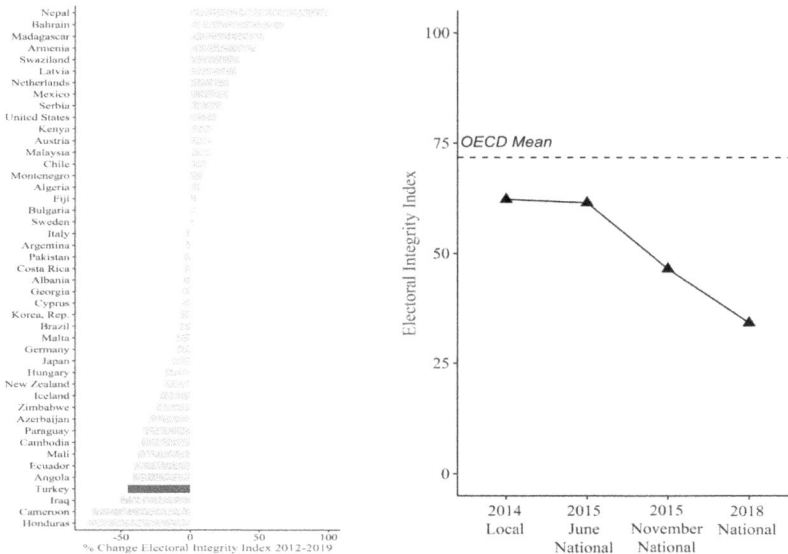

Figure 3.4 Falling levels of electoral integrity in Turkey

Note: The data estimate the quality of electoral integrity on a standardised 100-point scale

Source: Perceptions of Electoral Integrity (PEI) expert survey V7.0 data

As Figure 3.4 shows, Turkey's electoral integrity record has deteriorated significantly, remaining well below the OECD mean. When compared at the country level, joining Iraq, Cameroon, and Honduras, Turkey is among the four countries with the worst figures for backsliding electoral integrity.

The WVS data, which tracks perceptions of electoral integrity in a number of countries, provides finer-grained evidence. The questions used in the WVS are intended to probe electoral problems and include questions on the perceptions of fairness in vote-counting, whether voters are offered genuine political alternatives, whether wealthy people shape the election results by buying votes, and whether voters are threatened with violence. A multi-item battery also aims to assess perceptions of malpractice.

Electoral malpractice necessitates three main types of manipulation differentiated by purpose: of the legislative framework for elections, of individual electors' choices and of the administrative process (Birch 2011, 29). Such manipulation can happen before, during and after the elections. For example, manipulating the legal framework that rules elections would normally occur before elections are launched. Conversely, actions aiming to influence electoral administration usually occur closer to the announcement of the result. Lastly, manipulation of vote choice usually takes place between these two other types, perhaps through intimidating voters at the ballot box. Figure 3.5 displays the results of the electoral malpractice index across countries.

Electoral Management Bodies

The following paragraphs will focus on the components of different types of malpractice to produce a more comprehensive picture of the phenomenon. In political science, it is well documented that formal institutions shape political results by specifying limitations and setting incentives for the actors (Dahl 1971; Helmke and Levitsky 2004). In that sense, as the formal institutions that are chiefly responsible for the management of elections, EMBs are vital institutions for ensuring not only the integrity of elections but also for democratisation and democratic sustainability (Elklit and Reynolds 2005; Norris 2015; 2019a; James et al. 2019; Garnett 2019; van Ham and Garnett 2019). Since elections mobilise many people, EMBs exercise multiple, complex tasks like safeguarding electoral and campaign laws, building and staffing polling stations, administering ballots, creating and reviewing voter lists, counting votes and distributing

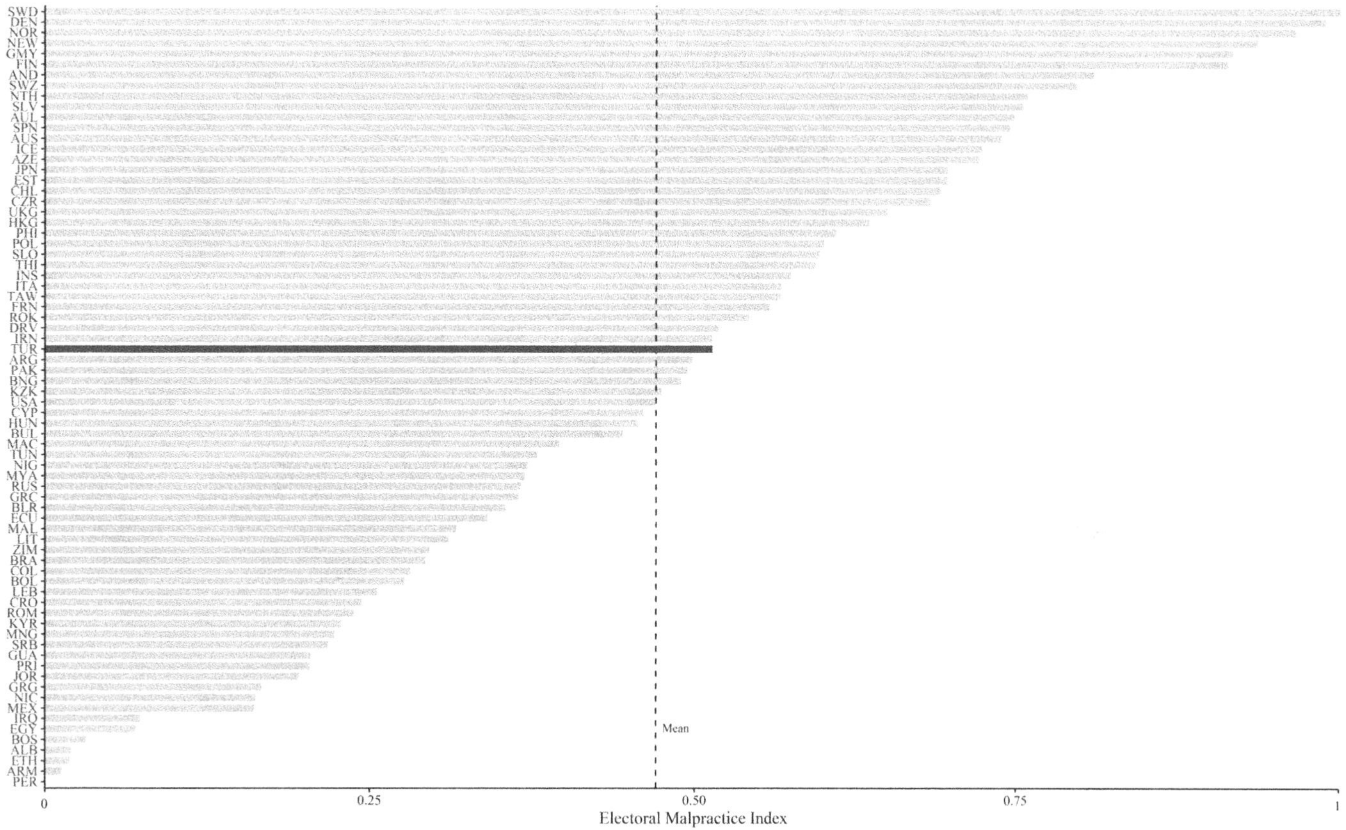

Figure 3.5 Electoral malpractice index

Note: Values are the mean of the malpractice component of the battery on electoral integrity, standardised and rescaled between 0 and 1; high scores denote low malpractice

Source: WVS seventh wave

information (Elklit and Reynolds 2002). Despite this, there are many examples of formal institutions tasked with electoral administration struggling to meet these demands. As Mozaffar (2002) points out, elections have always had an 'error margin', depending on the degree of inaccuracies and shortcomings. However, what is essential is that the magnitude of this error margin depends on the EMBs' ability to coordinate, staff, and organise the electoral process.

Though EMBs differ significantly in administration, composition and procedures, there are three sets of tasks that they all share: planning, tracking and certifying elections (James et al., 2019). Focusing on these tasks, studies on EMBs commonly scrutinise issues like the importance of staffing (James 2019), budgeting (Clark 2019) and, most often, autonomy (Mozaffar 2002; Birch 2008; Kerr and Lührmann 2017). Oher studies have underlined the latent functions of the EMBs for democratic systems. The most common of those is the role of EMBs in shaping the legitimacy of elections and hence democratic functioning. Research shows that doubts relating to the practical uncertainties of free and fair elections are removed only when the capability of an EMB is high (Birch 2011; Norris 2019a). That is to say, if EMBs cannot coordinate elections effectively, there follows a lack of faith in the electoral process and a loss of credibility for state institutions. These studies find that EMBs have essential effects on the quality of elections and democracy. Hence, improving EMB performance and independence is now regarded as a critical development goal (Lundstedt and Edgell 2020). Figure 3.6 illustrates the relationship between change in EMB capacity using two indicators of democratic functioning.

Norris (2019a) describes three conditions – organisational structure, functional capacity and the administrative ethos of EMBs – that she considers vital for establishing the legitimacy of elections. She argues that it would be best if electoral authorities were formed as autonomous regulatory bodies that could limit governments' ambition to intervene in election processes. Although I agree, there is a difference between the *de facto* and *de jure* autonomy of EMBs. As figure 3.6 indicates, although the capacity of the Turkish EMB, the YSK, has grown over the years, the Council has not contributed to either the cleanness of elections or liberal democracy in the country. Van Ham and Garnett (2019) provide similar evidence and suggest that although *de jure* independence is a must for electoral integrity, *de facto* independence matters. *De facto* autonomy can also be related to the administrative ethos of particular contexts. Elections are more likely to follow international norms where an unbiased and

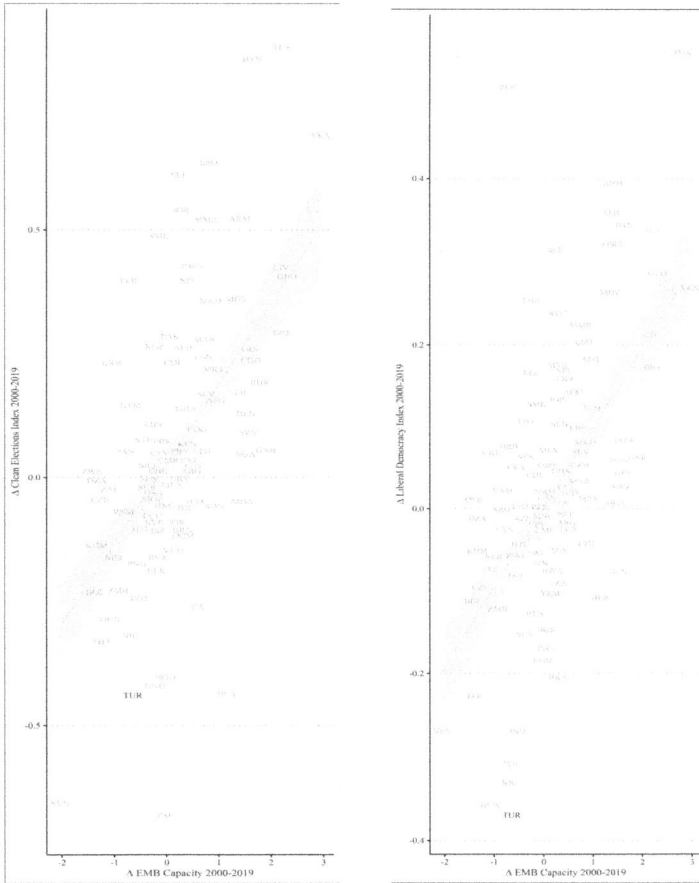

Figure 3.6 EMB capacities, clean elections and liberal democracy
Note: Data from Clean Elections and Liberal Democracy indices and EMB capacity
Source: Varieties of Democracy project V10

competent administrative tradition prevails among public sector officers, setting the requirements for an impartial service (James 2019).

The election administration in Turkey is a four-level structure, and the YSK sits at the top. It was established in 1950 by Law No. 5545 on Parliamentary Elections, to guarantee the safety of elections by applying pre-determined procedures backed up by judicial control. The related regulations set functions for the YSK to implement in order to ensure fair and orderly elections, from announcement to outcome. The YSK also conducts investigations and takes final decisions, during and after elections, on all irregularities, complaints and objections concerning electoral matters and receives the records of elections of the members of the TBMM and the president. The Council regulates 81 Provincial Election Boards, 1,436 District Electoral Boards and roughly 174,240 Ballot Box Committees across the country, and its rulings cannot be appealed to any other court. As well as the primary responsibilities just described, the YSK regulates a broad spectrum of activity, including examining all corruption charges or other complaints and objections related to election issues during and after the election, providing information and controlling radio and television broadcasts that facilitate voting abroad.

The Council is a permanent body composed of eleven senior judges (seven principal and four substitute members) who are appointed for six-year terms. Six members are elected by the General Board of the High Court of Appeals, and the General Board of the Council of State elects the other five. Even though only seven judges are regular YSK members, while the remaining four are substitutes, YSK takes decisions at sessions where all eleven members vote. The four political parties that received the most votes in the previous parliamentary elections can appoint non-voting members to the YSK.

Although *de jure* YSK is an independent and impartial body when performing its duties and exercising its powers, especially after the 2017 constitutional reform necessary safeguards of the judicial independence of the board were severely damaged. Amendments to the relevant laws gave the president of the republic and the government authority to appoint members to the Council of Judges and Prosecutors. That Council chooses the members of the General Board of the High Court of Appeals and the General Board of the Council of State, which, as mentioned before, appoint the members of the YSK. Although it seems unrelated, this change politicised the YSK to a great extent and led to controversial decisions that were seen as inconsistent, partial and favouring the government. According to a report by the Congress of Local and Regional Authorities, the YSK President has confirmed that the body is under immense pressure from a range of actors (Dawson 2019).

The Media

For electoral integrity, fair coverage of elections across a range of media is another vital issue. The media, an indispensable source of information through which citizens obtain knowledge of politics, has crucial potential to shape perceptions of elections. For this reason, candidates, parties and organisations should be provided with equal opportunities to put across their plans and proposals. If the field is not level, this will damage transparency and fairness at different stages of the electoral cycle (Norris 2014), and have significant consequences for the election results. Since citizens assess politics and elections by reference to the information they gather via different media sources, it is essential to understand whether access and use of media practices achieve the standards of electoral integrity mentioned earlier in this chapter.

Although several kinds of media outlet exist in Turkey, traditional media are likely to have a more beneficial impact on the accuracy of citizens' views of electoral legitimacy in countries with a free flow of information. However, in countries where freedom of the press is restricted, the traditional media function under state regulation and put out one-sided, censored information (Levitsky and Way 2002). In such countries, alternative media channels, perhaps tools available on the internet, are becoming essential sources of information, especially where the state goes further than simple censorship and seeks to control information. In such countries, the information accessible online provides a range of views on elections, making them more credible than the state's official line. In countries with high standards of press freedom, on the other hand, all media outlets are expected to provide complete and reliable reports on elections that will underpin the standards of electoral integrity.

Evaluations of the quality of elections are known to contribute to feelings of political legitimacy. These evaluations influence the degree to which people participate in the political system, and how they participate. It has been documented that perceptions of electoral malpractice can mobilise protest actions and violent confrontation, while favourable perceptions of electoral integrity raise the probability of participation in elections (Birch 2010). Consequently, the media become a vital source of knowledge for people to shape their views on elections and are expected to affect the accuracy of citizens' opinions of the electoral process (Coffé 2017). Accordingly, to harness the power of the media, governments around the world try to regulate or manipulate them, with varying success. In most illiberal contexts, state-controlled media provide one-sided accounts to inspire confidence in the government and elections, even where independent national and international observers argue the opposite (Norris and Inglehart 2010). In these contexts, since citizens usually remain misinformed and unaware of critiques of the existing regime, access to media outlets will have a negative influence on the accuracy of citizens' views of electoral integrity. Where the media are relatively free, however, this enhances the accountability of the whole system by allowing fairly independent commentators to keep a more or less careful eye on the political actors. In such a media climate, where conventional media offer an accessible and varied analysis of political issues, the level of traditional media consumption is likely to align favourably with the consistency of citizens' views of electoral integrity (Coffé 2017). Figure 3.7 displays the relationship between media freedom, electoral integrity and liberal democracy.

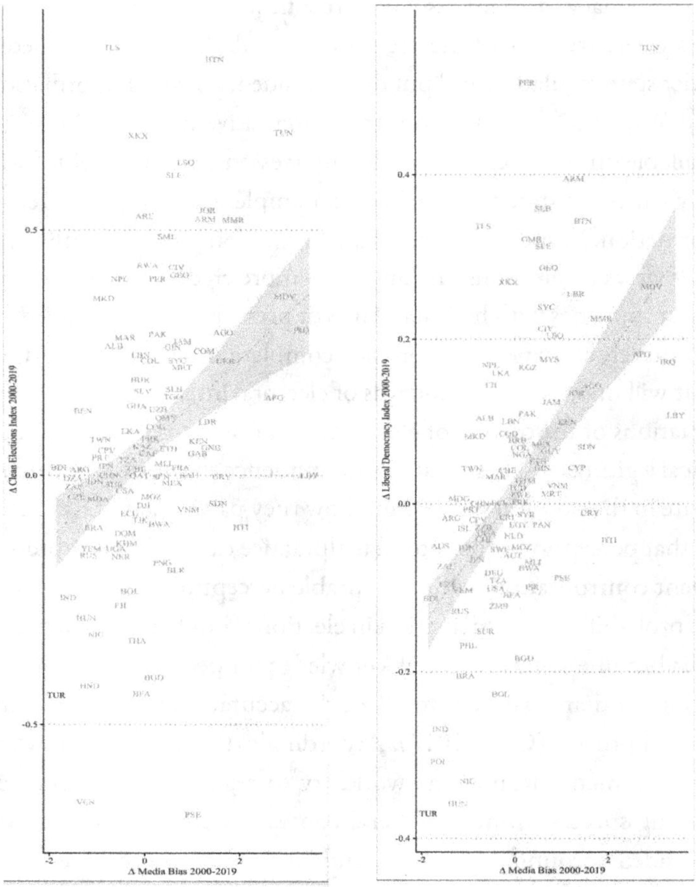

Figure 3.7   Free media, clean elections and liberal democracy
Note: Data from Clean Elections and Liberal Democracy indices and free media
Source: Varieties of Democracy project V10

Conclusion

The first three chapters illustrate the state of electoral integrity in Turkey since the 1940s. Following the proposed structure in Chapter One, the second chapter analysed the elections that the nation has undergone since the 1940s through the lenses of electoral integrity and electoral participation. It demonstrates the nature and severity of the difficulties linked to electoral integrity in Turkey and the development of the problems related to electoral integrity in the country, via the use of DIEV-T data. The material offered in the present chapter provided more insight into the country's recent election challenges, which were introduced in Chapter Two.

Lastly, the topic of electoral integrity in Turkey is further developed in a comparative context. Accordingly, this chapter has drawn on a range of datasets, including WVS, PEI and V-Dem, to provide global comparisons and a more recent picture of the two most recent decades. This chapter also contains introductory information about the EMB and the media in Turkey, which will be covered in more depth in the following chapters.

References

Akkoyunlu, Karabekir. 2017. 'Electoral Integrity in Turkey: From Tutelary Democracy to Competitive Authoritarianism'. In *Authoritarian Politics in Turkey: Elections, Resistance, and the AKP*, edited by B. Başer and A. E. Öztürk, 47–63. London: I. B. Tauris.

Aygül, Cenk. 2016. 'Electoral Manipulation in March 30, 2014 Turkish Local Elections'. *Turkish Studies*. https://doi.org/10.1080/14683849.2015.1135061.

Barrett, Richard, Veronika Bílková, Sarah Cleveland, Jean-Claude Scholse, Hanna Suchocka, and Kaarlo Tuori. 2017. 'Opinion to the Amendments to the Constitution Adopted by the Grand National Assembly on January 21 201 and to Be Submitted to a National Referendum on April 16 2017'. https://www.venice.coe.int/webforms/documents/default.aspx?pdffile=cdl-ad(2017)005-e.

Birch, Sarah. 2008. 'Electoral Institutions and Popular Confidence in Electoral Processes: A Cross-National Analysis'. *Electoral Studies* 27 (2): 305–20. https://doi.org/10.1016/j.electstud.2008.01.005.

———. 2010. 'Perceptions of Electoral Fairness and Voter Turnout'. *Comparative Political Studies*. https://doi.org/10.1177/0010414010374021.

———. 2011. *Electoral Malpractice*. Oxford: Oxford University Press. https://doi. org/10.1093/acprof:oso/9780199606160.001.0001.

Caliskan, Mehmet Emin. 2017. 'With Media Muzzled, Turkish "no" Voters Seek Alternative Channels'. *Reuters*. https://www.reuters.com/article/ turkey-referendum-no-campaign/rpt-with-media-muzzled-turkish-no-voters-seek-alternative-channels-idUSL8N1HK112.

Clark, Alistair. 2019. 'The Cost of Democracy: The Determinants of Spending on the Public Administration of Elections'. *International Political Science Review* 40 (3, SI): 354–69. https://doi.org/10.1177/0192512118824787.

Coffé, Hilde. 2017. 'Citizens' Media Use and the Accuracy of Their Perceptions of Electoral Integrity'. *International Political Science Review* 38 (3): 281–97. https://doi.org/10.1177/0192512116640984.

Dahl, Robert. 1971. *Polyarchy: Participation and Opposition*. New Haven, CT: Yale University Press.

Dawson, Andrew. 2019. 'Local Elections in Turkey and Mayoral Re-Run in Istanbul'. https://rm.coe.int/local-elections-in-turkey-and-mayoral-re-run-in-istanbul-committee-on-/1680981fcf.

Economist, The. 2018. 'Recep Tayyip the First', 28 June.

Elklit, Jørgen and Andrew Reynolds. 2002. 'The Impact of Election Administration on the Legitimacy of Emerging Democracies: A New Comparative Politics Research Agenda'. *Commonwealth & Comparative Politics* 40 (2): 86–119. https://doi. org/10.1080/713999584.

Elklit, Jørgen and Andrew Reynolds. 2005. 'Judging Elections and Election Management Quality by Process'. *Representation* 41 (3): 189–207. https://doi. org/10.1080/00344890508523311.

Esen, Berk and Sebnem Gumuscu. 2016. 'Rising Competitive Authoritarianism in Turkey'. *Third World Quarterly*. https://doi.org/10.1080/01436597.2015.1135732.

———. 2018. 'Building a Competitive Authoritarian Regime: State–Business Relations in the AKP's Turkey'. *Journal of Balkan and Near Eastern Studies*. https://doi.org /10.1080/19448953.2018.1385924.

Garnett, Holly Ann. 2019. 'Evaluating Electoral Management Body Capacity'. *International Political Science Review* 40 (3): 335–53. https://doi.org/10.1177/ 0192512119832924.

Helmke, Gretchen and Steven Levitsky. 2004. 'Informal Institutions and Comparative Politics: A Research Agenda'. *Perspectives on Politics* 2 (4): 725–40. https:// doi.org/10.1017/S1537592704040472.

James, Toby S. 2019. 'Better Workers, Better Elections? Electoral Management Body Workforces and Electoral Integrity Worldwide'. *International Political Science Review* 40 (3): 370–90. https://doi.org/10.1177/0192512119829516.

James, Toby S., Holly Ann Garnett, Leontine Loeber and Carolien van Ham. 2019. 'Electoral Management and the Organisational Determinants of Electoral Integrity: Introduction'. *International Political Science Review* 40 (3): 295–312. https://doi.org/10.1177/0192512119828206.

Kasapoglu, Cagil. 2015. 'Turkey Social Media Ban Raises Censorship Fears'. *BBC News*. https://www.bbc.com/news/world-europe-32204177.

Kerr, Nicholas and Anna Lührmann. 2017. 'Public Trust in Manipulated Elections: The Role of Election Administration and Media Freedom'. *Electoral Studies*. https://doi.org/10.1016/j.electstud.2017.08.003.

Kirişçi, Kemal. 2018. 'How to Read Turkey's Election Results'. Brookings Institution blog, https://www.brookings.edu/blog/order-from-chaos/2018/06/25/how-to-read-turkeys-election-results/.

Levitsky, Steven and Lucan Way. 2002. 'Elections without Democracy: The Rise of Competitive Authoritarianism'. *Journal of Democracy*. https://doi.org/10.1353/jod.2002.0026.

Lundstedt, Martin and Amanda B. Edgell. 2020. 'Institutions of Electoral Integrity and Clientelism: The Role of Electoral Management Bodies'. Stockholm. https://v-dem.net/media/publications/wp_108_final.pdf.

Meyersson, Erik. 2014. 'Trouble in Turkey's Elections'. Blog post. https://erikmeyersson.com/2014/04/06/trouble-in-turkeys-elections/.

Mozaffar, Shaheen. 2002. 'Patterns of Electoral Governance in Africa's Emerging Democracies'. *International Political Science Review* 23 (1): 85–101. https://doi.org/10.1177/0192512102023001005.

Norris, Pippa. 2013. 'The New Research Agenda Studying Electoral Integrity'. *Electoral Studies* 32 (4): 563–75. https://doi.org/10.1016/j.electstud.2013.07.015.

———. 2014. *Why Electoral Integrity Matters*. Cambridge: Cambridge University Press. https://doi.org/10.1017/CBO9781107280861.

———. 2015. *Why Elections Fail*. Cambridge: Cambridge University Press. https://doi.org/10.1017/CBO9781107280908.

———. 2018. 'Electoral Integrity'. In *The Routledge Handbook of Elections, Voting Behaviorand Public Opinion*, edited by Justin Fisher, Edward Fieldhouse, Mark N. Franklin, Rachel Gibson, Marta Cantijoch and Christopher Wlezien, 220–31. Abingdon: Routledge. https://doi.org/10.4324/9781315712390-19.

———. 2019a. 'Conclusions: The New Research Agenda on Electoral Management'. *International Political Science Review* 40 (3, SI): 391–403. https://doi.org/10.1177/0192512119829869.

———. 2019b. 'Do Perceptions of Electoral Malpractice Undermine Democratic Satisfaction? The US in Comparative Perspective'. *International Political Science Review* 40 (1): 5–22. https://doi.org/10.1177/0192512118806783.

Norris, Pippa and Ronald Inglehart. 2010. 'Limits on Press Freedom and Regime Support'. In *News Media and Governance Reform*, edited by Pippa Norris, 193–220. Washington DC: The World Bank.

OSCE. 2015. 'Turkey, Early Parliamentary Elections, November 1 2015: Statement of Preliminary Findings and Conclusions'. Organization for Security and Co-operation in Europe, Warsaw.

———. 2017. 'Turkey, Constitutional Referendum, April 16 2017: Final Report'. OSCE, Warsaw.

———. 2018. 'International Election Observation Mission: Republic of Turkey – Early Presidential and Parliamentary Elections – June 24 2018'. OSCE, Warsaw.

PACE Monitoring Committee. 2017. 'Statement on the Proposed Constitutional Reform in Turkey'. Strasbourg, France. http://website-pace.net/documents/19887/3136217/20170126-StmtConstReform-EN.pdf/c4c15b85-9e13-46b2-a687-f25f07077183.

Preda, Cezar Florin. 2017. 'Observation of the Referendum on the Constitutional Amendments in Turkey (April 16 2017)'. https://pace.coe.int/en/files/23746.

Toker, Cem. 2014. 'Elections in Turkey: Fair or Fraud-Ridden?' *Turkish Policy Quarterly*, Winter: 115–23.

Toros, Emre and Sarah Birch. 2019. 'Framing Electoral Impropriety: The Strategic Use of Allegations of Wrong-Doing in Election Campaigns'. *British Journal of Middle Eastern Studies*. https://doi.org/DOI:10.1080/13530194.2019.1566694.

Van Ham, Carolien and Holly Ann Garnett. 2019. 'Building Impartial Electoral Management? Institutional Design, Independence and Electoral Integrity'. *International Political Science Review* 40 (3): 313–34. https://doi.org/10.1177/0192512119834573.

Yardımcı-Geyikçi, Şebnem. 2015. 'Party Institutionalization and Democratic Consolidation: Turkey and Southern Europe in Comparative Perspective'. *Party Politics* 21 (4): 527–38. https://doi.org/10.1177/1354068813487110.

YSK. 2017. Yüksek Seçim Kurulu 573 *No'lu Kararı* [YSK Decision No 573].

Zeid Ra'ad Al Hussein. 2018. 'State of Emergency Must Be Lifted for "Credible Elections" in Turkey, Says UN Rights Chief'. *UN News*. https://news.un.org/en/story/2018/05/1009232.

Part 2

CAUSES FOR PERCEPTIONS OF DAMAGE TO ELECTORAL INTEGRITY

4

AN ACCOUNT OF INDIVIDUAL PERCEPTIONS OF DAMAGE TO ELECTORAL INTEGRITY

Introduction

Democratic elections need peaceful competition and voting, but problems frequently erupt throughout electoral processes in several societies, and Turkey is no exception. Although recent studies have clarified some of the causes of damage to electoral integrity at the individual level, we still have little understanding of the degree to which voters consider elections problematic. This chapter constructs and measures an informational model of perceptions that electoral integrity has been damaged, building on literature on perceptions of electoral justice, electoral violence and information processing. The basic argument is that sources of information are crucial in individual perceptions of electoral integrity, influencing common expectations of elections' integrity.

Although democratically run elections are the cornerstone of democracy, and most states in today's world conduct democratic elections, we hear plenty of news of flawed elections that exhibit manipulation and abuse. An increasing body of literature has followed this recent surge to try to understand public views of electoral integrity. Studies have recorded the circumstances in which people have faith in how their elections are conducted and which citizens are more vulnerable likely to be targeted by electoral misconduct (Barnes and Beaulieu 2014; Birch 2008; Bowler et al. 2015; Cantú and García-Ponce 2015; Flesken and Hartl 2018; Karp, Nai and Norris 2018; Kerr 2013; McAllister and White 2011; Norris, Frank and Martínez i Coma 2014; Rosas 2010). A variety of recent

comparative research has also analysed the impact of violence on electoral processes (Bhasin and Gandhi 2013; Birch and Muchlinski 2017; Daxecker 2012;
Fjelde and Höglund 2016; Taylor, Pevehouse and Straus 2017; van Ham and
Lindberg 2015; Salehyan and Linebarger 2015). Contributing to this literature,
this chapter introduces an additional individual-level correlate: popular perceptions of problems with electoral integrity. Although some studies have
shown which citizens are more likely to feel at risk of violence during elections
(Bratton 2008; Bekoe and Burchard 2017; Dercon and Gutiérrez-Romero 2012;
Gonzalez-Ocantos et al. 2020; von Borzyskowski and Kuhn 2020; Mares and
Young 2016), these studies concentrate on citizens' specific complaints about
being targeted; they do not discuss the degree to which people feel the political
structure of their nation is impaired by failures of democratic legitimacy in general. This is a crucial question since there is sufficient proof that perceptions of
damaged electoral integrity shape turnout and voting behaviour (Bratton 2008;
Bekoe and Burchard 2017; Höglund and Piyarathne 2009). Accordingly, the
aim here is to model how information sources shape perceptions of problems
with electoral integrity, using data from several sources, including the World
Values Survey (WVS) and the Electoral Integrity in Turkey (EI-T) database.
This should help us understand the micro-level foundations of perceptions that
electoral integrity has been damaged. Understanding how and why such devia-
tions are perceived will help us tease out the factors that lead citizens to lose
confidence in the conduct of elections in their country and assess the conditions
under which citizens perceive electoral integrity to be problematic.

Given the growing body of literature that examines how the collection
and processing of knowledge influences citizen orientations against electoral
behaviour (Kerr and Lührmann 2017; Norris, Frank and Martínez i Coma
2014; Reuter and Szakonyi 2015), it is plausible to argue that matters related
to electoral integrity are also influenced by the informational lenses which
people use. Individuals depend on the knowledge they gain from observation
within their immediate context. For measures of electoral integrity, people also
depend upon knowledge gathered from media and internet sources they trust.
To the degree that cognitively competent people derive well-founded information from trustworthy news outlets, their assumptions regarding electoral
integrity would match the actual level of problems related to electoral integrity,
to a great extent. To the degree that the information sources on which citizens

make their decisions are skewed, their perceptions of electoral integrity may be influenced by critically limited evidence and subjective distrust (or overtrust) in those sources. Public opinion on elections can be assumed to be influenced by three sets of variables that serve as lenses through which citizens perceive and assess information about election quality:

(a) a citizen's cognitive ability to assimilate and assess information about electoral processes against abstract standards of good practice;
(b) the availability of accurate information about election quality; and
(c) the citizen's willingness to trust the sources through which information about election quality is conveyed to them.

If this is so, it follows that opinion may be affected by different conditioning procedures. If someone gets reliable statistics but distrusts their origins, the information can negatively impact their view of election quality. Conversely, where a citizen obtains reliable data from a trustworthy source but cannot interpret and make sense of them, that citizen may lack the cognitive capacity to assess how open, equal and peaceful an election is. To go further, if citizens trust the details but obtain them from an imperfect source those citizens may develop an inaccurate perception of the electoral process.

Cognitive capacity is connected to schooling, which ought to teach people the democratic values related to elections. Previous analyses of electoral fairness have shown that citizens with higher educational qualifications tend to view elections as having higher levels of integrity (Birch 2008; Cantú and García-Ponce 2015; Karp, Nai and Norris 2018; Rosas 2010). In the domain of electoral violence, there are conflicting findings *vis-à-vis* the role of education in influencing personal fear. In a study of Nigeria using Afrobarometer statistics, Bratton (2008) found citizens with lower education levels to be more likely to encounter electoral violence directly. However, in a comparative African study using the same data sources, Burchard (2018) found more highly trained voters reported becoming victims of violence at election time more frequently than other voters. This finding might be attributed to the greater average involvement in politics of the more highly trained, rather than to education levels *per se*. Participation and engagement in politics may be anticipated to raise personal fear of becoming subject to abuse.

The delivery of reliable information on electoral integrity relies on the accuracy of the public and private information outlets accessible to voters and voters' willingness to access this information. The availability of reliable public information is a function of freedom and absence of bias in the mass media, and the level of media freedom varies among polities. Leaders who are tempted to manipulate information experience a dilemma in the electoral arena: the free distribution of information via transparent and impartial news media provides them with crucial hints as to their actual success (Egorov, Guriev and Sonin 2009). However, at the same time, the free flow of accurate, honest evidence often plays an essential role in allowing the opposition to keep officials responsible for corruption and mobilising efforts to unseat incumbents, or to collect sufficient factual information regarding wrong-doing (Beaulieu 2014; Fearon 2011; Hyde and Marinov 2012; Magaloni 2006; 2010). Thus, governments that want to manipulate elections try to obstruct the free flow of information through media repression, and to suppress free expression and independent voices. Supporting this argument, Varieties of Democracy data show that, at the country level, there is a correlation of 0.703 between the indicators of media bias and electoral intimidation and a correlation of 0.812 between the indicators of the abuse of journalists and electoral intimidation. Also, opposition actors try to manipulate elections and disseminate misleading indications of the scale of electoral fraud if they are about to lose an election (Birch and ElSafoury 2017; Schedler 2013 chp. 9). Previous studies have also demonstrated that political actors use the media to highlight claims of electoral impropriety, as a tool to manipulate credibility in various contexts (Blaydes 2011; Toros and Birch 2019b). These findings indicate that transparent and objective media could increase public access to knowledge of electoral malpractice, thereby making people more inclined to believe that elections are flawed, a supposition for which studies by Coffé (2017) and Kerr and Lührmann (2017) both find justification. On the other hand, voters are less likely to learn of wrong-doings during elections if the incumbent controls the media.

Lastly, I argue that voters' evaluation of the integrity of elections depends on how far they trust sources of information. In contexts where problems with electoral integrity are common, people might have reasons to be wary of media messages regarding elections. Moreover, levels of trust also depend on other variables, such as partisanship (Anderson et al., 2005; Flesken and Hartl 2018). Motivated reasoning (Kunda 1990; Kim, Taber and Lodge 2010) may lead pro-incumbent partisans to assume that pro-government sources are more reliable than pro-opposition sources. Additionally, where prejudice is exhibited in public news outlets and restrictions are placed on pro-opposition media, when assessing electoral activity opposition supporters may resort to private sources of knowledge as a supplement to public information in which they may have little confidence (Coffé 2017; Reuter and Szakonyi 2015). This knowledge often passes in interactions with friends and relatives, or via social networking and other online sources that the government cannot block entirely (Bennett 2012). Given their opinions on electoral integrity, citizens' views of the issue would be more likely to be influenced by knowledge of this sort if they refrain from receiving news from public sources.

Two other crucial control variables are expected to have a comparable influence on how electoral integrity is viewed: demographics and political ideologies. For example, previous research on the subject shows that women and those on lower incomes (Burchard 2018; Gonzalez-Ocantos et al. 2020; Mares and Young 2016) are more likely than other citizens to suffer electoral violence. It also seems sensible to use per capita GDP as a control variable, as Kerr and Lührmann (2017) observed that GDP per capita is associated with expectations of electoral integrity. This particular attempt shifts away from personal experiences and thus explores general expectations that elections conducted in a nation have suffered or are likely to suffer from electoral integrity problems. However, we can still expect personal experience to condition general perceptions, so the studies just cited offer reasons to expect citizen demographic characteristics to relate to perceptions of integrity. Political factors that have been shown in previous research to be connected to fear of electoral violence, which is perhaps one of the most common problems related to integrity, include partisanship (Toros and Birch 2019a; von Borzyskowski and Kuhn 2020), with opposition supporters typically more afraid of electoral violence than government supporters; and engagement in politics. Likewise, Burchard (2018) considers interest in politics to be an indicator of fear of electoral violence. Several studies have found interest in politics to be strongly associated with expectations of electoral integrity (Flesken and Hartl 2018; Kerr 2013).

The Turkish Media Scene

The Turkish context can be considered as highly relevant for a case study based on the theoretical arguments described above. As described in Part One, in

Turkey electoral quality has deteriorated in recent years (Akkoyunlu 2017; Esen and Gumuscu 2016; Öktem and Akkoyunlu 2016), including problems of vote-buying (Çarkoğlu and Aytaç 2015), fraud and electoral violence (Toros and Birch 2019b). The 2018 elections, which are the empirical focus of the current study, saw an uptick in violence, especially in the south and southeast of the country; this was accompanied by media harassment and numerous journalists were jailed (*Economist* 2018).

The media atmosphere in Turkey revolves around numerous inconsistencies. While dedicated professional reporters are willing to do their jobs against considerable odds, the system is seriously lacking in integrity on many levels, and increasingly is failing to serve the public interest and fulfil democratic functions (Tunç 2015). Especially during the 2010s, leading news organisations started to convey only content praising government actions, and have increasingly become a 'government mouthpiece' (Reporters without Borders 2021). Media outlets and journalists who decided not to do this and retained a critical stance have been punished in several ways. According to the Reporters without Borders report just cited, twenty journalists were convicted for 'offences' amounting to criticising or making allegations against the government, and have been sentenced to fines or to sentences that add up to thirty-eight person-years in prison.

According to a recent report, 2,474 daily newspapers, 3,650 magazines, 899 radio stations and 196 TV channels are active in Turkey (TÜİK, 2018). As of 2021, four media groups served a total of 71 per cent of all media followers, including TV, radio, print media and online web portals. Among these, Turkuvaz/Kalyon Group was dominant, with investments in all four sectors and a share of 30 per cent of the total followers. With a share of 15 per cent each, the Ciner and Demiören Groups followed Turkuvaz/Kalyon. The Doğuş Group was the fourth, with 11 per cent of the audience share (Reporters without Borders, 2021).

Television continues to be the most popular media platform in Turkey. Among the 196 television channels, 19 of which are national, 12 regional, and 165 local, the state-owned Turkish Radio and Broadcast Agency (TRT) owns 13 channels. The TRT, which held a monopoly in broadcasting until commercial television was introduced in the 1990s, has been criticised for pro-government broadcasting. In the private sphere, the concentration of media ownership increased significantly after the sale of the media assets of the Doğan Group to the Demirören Group in March 2018. With this change in ownership, five groups controlled seven of the ten TV channels that attract the most viewers. On the legal side, the Radio and Television Authority of Turkey (RTÜK), formed in 1994, is the legal entity that regulates Turkey's media ecosystem. RTÜK issues licences and audits broadcasters, and in 2018 it temporarily stopped the broadcast of sixty-seven TV programmes and issued eighty-five fines (Reporters without Borders 2021).

The following analysis uses individual-level surveys and aggregate country-level data to test these arguments. The cross-national component of the study draws on the electoral integrity battery included in Wave 6 of the WVS. The Survey brings together representative sample surveys from countries with different levels of democracy based on a standard questionnaire. Nine questions on electoral integrity were asked of the respondents to gauge different dimensions of election quality. Voters were asked to answer the question 'In your view, how often do the following things occur in this country's elections?' with response options including 'Very often', 'Fairly often', 'Not often' and 'Not at all often'. The original coding of these items was inverted for analysis, so that a higher score conveys greater likelihood of occurrence. The battery included an item 'Votes are counted fairly', which is the dependent variable. Other items included 'Voters are threatened with violence at the polls', 'Opposition candidates are prevented from running', 'TV news favours the governing party', 'Voters are bribed', 'Journalists provide fair coverage of elections', 'Election officials are fair', 'Rich people buy elections' and 'Voters are offered a genuine choice in the elections'. The item 'Voters are threatened with violence at the polls' is used as a dependent variable in the analyses presented below, while 'TV news favours the governing party' and 'Journalists provide fair coverage of elections' are employed as independent variables. The analysis used control variables for gender, age, education, income, interest in politics and media consumption based on WVS survey items. The Turkish data come from the EI-T dataset, which repeated the WVS electoral legitimacy battery and incorporated party partisanship and ethnicity covariates.

Cross-national Evidence and the Turkish Case

The WVS data give insight into overall perceptions of electoral integrity around the world. For those familiar with electoral integrity patterns worldwide, these figures will come as little surprise; the countries where citizens are most concerned about counting the votes are Peru, Mexico, Nicaragua, Iraq and Ethiopia.

But there are also some unexpected figures here, including the puzzling finding that 7.7 per cent and 6.7 per cent of US and French citizens, respectively, believe that fairly often votes are not counted properly in their country. One of the most noteworthy aspects of these figures is the wide variation in individual countries' views. Dispersion is highest in those countries where violence is a problem, which include Lithuania and Mexico, where citizen assessments are roughly evenly divided among the four available response categories. Thus, people in countries affected by problems with electoral integrity have different understandings of the severity of the problem. Figure 4.1 provides a snapshot of these results.

The following analysis uses a series of logit models to test the arguments outlined in the previous section. The first model includes demographic indicators for gender, age, education, income and interest in politics coupled with respondents' sources of information. Information sources are tapped through a suite of variables designating the frequency of accessing public sources of information, such as newspapers, magazines, television news, radio news and the internet, and private sources such as mobile phones, email and personal contacts. Since the EI-T questionnaire of 2018 replicated the WVS battery, the data allows us to analyse perceptions of electoral integrity in this context. In addition to partisanship, one important contextual factor in Turkish electoral politics is ethnicity, because regions where the Kurdish population is densest frequently experience problems related to electoral integrity; knowledge of the Kurdish language is thus a crucial feature for the study of this topic (Toros and Birch 2019a).

In Turkey, concerns about electoral integrity were relatively serious in 2018, consistent with the V-Dem expert analysis that the election had been marred by 'some' instances of electoral intimidation, the midpoint on the five-point scale underlying this variable (Coppedge et al. 2019). One-third of the EI-T survey respondents stated that votes are not counted fairly. Table 2 presents binary logit models of electoral integrity perceptions based on the question with the same wording as that in the WVS survey. Model 1 was run first, using the demographic and media consumption variables (for convenience, political interest is included with the demographic variables). The findings for Model 1 indicate that being female and having low income levels are associated with perceiving highly problematic electoral integrity, once other factors are taken into consideration. Respondents who use public information sources such as TV and radio news showed a lower propensity to view elections as being at

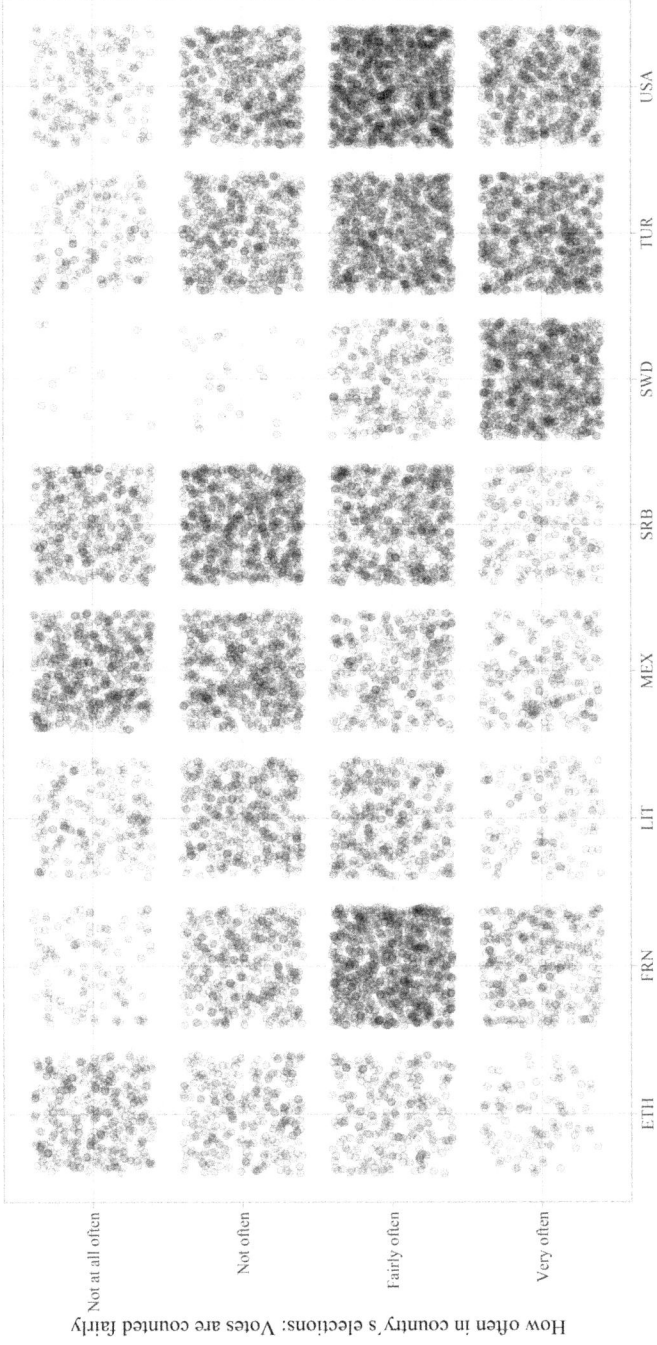

Figure 4.1 How often are votes counted fairly in your country's elections?

risk, while those most likely to obtain information from the internet are more likely to perceive elections as having integrity problems.

Model 2 adds perceptions of TV news bias and journalistic coverage of electoral campaigns. The coefficients of this model show that the respondents who perceived more problems related to electoral integrity tended to think that TV favoured the government party and journalists did not provide fair coverage of elections. This was also found by model 4, where the analysis included the party id(entification) variable. The model found that those who thought TV news coverage of the election was biased in favour of the ruling party (AKP) were considerably more likely to believe that there are problems with the integrity of elections, while those who thought journalistic coverage of the election was fair were significantly less likely to believe this to be the case. Models 3 and 4 both included the party id and use of Kurdish language variables (use of language was taken to be a proxy for ethnicity); model 3 did not include the perceptions variables. All the variables introduced were found to be significant; support for the ruling AKP party and the nationalist MHP is associated with a lower propensity to see elections having problems with integrity.

In contrast, adherents of the opposition CHP and HDP evaluated the situation almost diametrically differently. Kurdish speakers were more likely than average to perceive elections as having problems with integrity, as might be expected because a disproportionate number of the violent events in recent Turkish elections have been in areas heavily populated by ethnic Kurds. These findings confirm that partisanship is a powerful shaper of perceptions of electoral integrity in the Turkish context. They also suggest that the variables capturing citizen assessments of the fairness of electoral coverage may well be proxies for partisanship, especially the question about TV news bias favouring the ruling party. Once partisanship and language use are considered, the only significant information variable is internet usage. This indicator may be a proxy for insertion in the digital world and, thus, an indicator of cognitive sophistication beyond formal education. In sum, in the Turkish context, partisanship appears to provide an essential channel through which information is processed and a cueing device through which voters may assess the integrity of elections. Simultaneously, citizens who depend to a great extent on private information who are also cognitively engaged (i.e. use the internet) also appearrd to rely on this information source to form their views of electoral integrity.

Table 4.1 Binary logit models of perceptions of electoral integrity

	Model 1	Model 2	Model 3	Model 4
Demography				
(Intercept)	0.83 (0.51)	−0.10 (0.78)	−0.29 (0.75)	−0.40 (0.99)
Gender (Female)	−0.42 * (0.15)	−0.51* (0.21)	−0.49* (0.21)	−0.63** (0.24)
Age	−0.00 (0.01)	0.00 (0.01)	0.01 (0.01)	0.01 (0.01)
Education	−0.06 (0.06)	−0.02 (0.07)	−0.00 (0.08)	−0.03 (0.09)
Income	0.09 * (0.04)	0.14* (0.05)	0.09 (0.05)	0.15* (0.06)
Interest in politics	−0.11 (0.08)	−0.08 (0.11)	−0.15 (0.11)	−0.13 (0.13)
Information sources				
TV	0.29*** (0.08)	0.12 (0.11)	0.23 (0.12)	0.10 (0.13)
Radio	0.15** (0.06)	0.12 (0.07)	0.03 (0.08)	0.01 (0.09)
Internet	−0.17** (0.06)	−0.20* (0.08)	−0.14 (0.08)	−0.15* (0.09)
Newspapers	−0.02 (0.05)	−0.05 (0.07)	−0.01 (0.07)	−0.04 (0.08)
Magazines	0.15 (0.08)	0.21 (0.11)	0.26 (0.11)	0.27 (0.13)
Mobile phone	−0.02 (0.06)	−0.08 (0.08)	−0.10 (0.08)	−0.09 (0.09)
Email	−0.02 (0.05)	0.04 (0.07)	−0.02 (0.07)	−0.01 (0.08)
Friends	−0.08 (0.06)	−0.09 (0.09)	−0.07 (0.09)	−0.08 (0.10)
Perceptions				
TV favours government party		−0.72*** (0.11)		−0.51*** (0.13)
Journalists provide fair coverage of elections		1.33*** (0.10)		0.79*** (0.12)

(contd)

Table 4.1 Binary logit models of perceptions of electoral integrity (*contd*)

	Model 1	Model 2	Model 3	Model 4
Party ID				
AKP			3.52*** (0.33)	2.90*** (0.39)
CHP			−0.86** (0.27)	−0.51* (0.32)
MHP			2.41*** (0.43)	1.96*** (0.50)
HDP			−0.49* (0.43)	−0.33* (0.51)
Kurdish speaker			−0.79* (0.33)	−0.82 * (0.38)
Observations	1070	1019	1061	1011
R^2 Tjur	0.060	0.478	0.520	0.622
Deviance	1240.632	716.947	690.664	536.382
AIC	1269.030	749.490	729.394	579.316
Log-likelihood	−620.316	−358.474	−345.332	−268.191

Cell contents are log-odds coefficients (standard errors), *$p<0.05$ **$p<0.01$ ***$p<0.001$

All in all, these findings provide ample evidence that the media impacts on perceptions of electoral integrity. Most notable are the effects of citizen trust in the media. The information available to voters and their assessment of this information play essential roles in conditioning their evaluation of electoral processes and the potential threats they carry.

Conclusion

Although research into electoral integrity is on the rise among scholars and practitioners alike, enquiries into popular perceptions of electoral integrity have received less attention and there have been only a few systematic studies of the factors that condition popular perceptions of this phenomenon. What is aimed at here is to set out the principal variables that appear to induce citizens to believe their elections experience problems with integrity. The analysis shows that education, media consumption patterns and trust in media sources at the individual level, and media quality and level of economic development, shape perceptions of electoral integrity. The Turkish context also points to the role of partisanship in conditioning perceptions of electoral integrity and indicates that controlling for partisanship does not entirely eliminate the role played by sources of information.

Several studies have found a free media to be one of the strongest determinants of electoral integrity (Birch and van Ham 2017; Birch 2011; Norris 2015; Schedler 2013). However, the evidence presented here suggests that a skewed media environment favouring the government makes it more likely that people will perceive elections as problematic. Inasmuch as fear of electoral violence has been found to lower turnout, this suggests that the lack of a level media playing field could depress trust in elections, a worrying possibility. From a methodological point of view, one of the main implications of this analysis is the substantive distinction between objective levels of electoral integrity and popular perceptions of how electoral integrity is damaged. Although there is indisputably a relationship between these two variables, they are clearly not the same since voter perceptions are influenced by several factors, as demonstrated here. The findings presented here also raise interesting questions that require further analysis, including the role of public and private media sources in conditioning perceptions of electoral violence and the possible role of local and regional factors in shaping how the media landscape conditions people's understanding of the problems associated with elections.

References

Akkoyunlu, Karabekir. 2017. 'Electoral Integrity in Turkey: From Tutelary Democracy to Competitive Authoritarianism'. In *Authoritarian Politics in Turkey: Elections, Resistance, and the AKP*, edited by B. Başer and A. E. Öztürk, 47–63. London: I. B. Tauris.

Anderson, Christopher J., André Blais, Shaun Bowler, Donovan Todd and Ola Listhaug. 2005. *Losers' Consent: Elections and Democratic Legitimacy*. Oxford: Oxford University Press.

Barnes, Tiffany D. and Emily Beaulieu. 2014. 'Gender Stereotypes and Corruption: How Candidates Affect Perceptions of Election Fraud'. *Politics and Gender* 10 (3). https://doi.org/10.1017/S1743923X14000221.

Beaulieu, Emily. 2014. *Electoral Protest and Democracy in the Developing World*. Cambridge: Cambridge University Press.

Bekoe, Dorina A. and Stephanie M. Burchard. 2017. 'The Contradictions of Pre-Election Violence: The Effects of Violence on Voter Turnout in Sub-Saharan Africa'. *African Studies Review*. https://doi.org/10.1017/asr.2017.50.

Bennett, W. Lance. 2012. 'The Personalization of Politics: Political Identity, Social Media, and Changing Patterns of Participation'. *Annals of the American Academy of Political and Social Science*. https://doi.org/10.1177/0002716212451428.

Bhasin, Tavishi and Jennifer Gandhi. 2013. 'Timing and Targeting of State Repression in Authoritarian Elections'. *Electoral Studies*. https://doi.org/10.1016/j.electstud.2013.07.011.

Birch, Sarah. 2008. 'Electoral Institutions and Popular Confidence in Electoral Processes: A Cross-National Analysis'. *Electoral Studies* 27 (2): 305–20. https://doi.org/10.1016/j.electstud.2008.01.005.

———. 2011. *Electoral Malpractice*. Oxford: Oxford University Press. https://doi.org/10.1093/acprof:oso/9780199606160.001.0001.

Birch, Sarah and Fatma ElSafoury. 2017. 'Fraud, Plot, or Collective Delusion? Social Media and Perceptions of Electoral Misconduct in the 2014 Scottish Independence Referendum'. *Election Law Journal: Rules, Politics, and Policy*. https://doi.org/10.1089/elj.2016.0393.

Birch, Sarah and David Muchlinski. 2017. 'Electoral Violence'. In *Electoral Integrity and Political Regimes: Actors, Strategies and Consequences*, edited by Holly Ann Garnett and Margarita Zavadskaya, 110–113. Abingdon: Routledge. https://doi.org/10.4324/9781315315126-6.

Birch, Sarah and Carolien van Ham. 2017. 'Getting Away with Foul Play? The Importance of Formal and Informal Oversight Institutions for Electoral Integrity'. *European Journal of Political Research*. https://doi.org/10.1111/1475-6765.12189.

Blaydes, Lisa. 2011. *Elections and Distributive Politics in Mubarak's Egypt*. Cambridge: Cambridge University Press.

Bowler, Shaun, Thomas Brunell, Todd Donovan and Paul Gronke. 2015. 'Election Administration and Perceptions of Fair Elections'. *Electoral Studies* 38. https://doi.org/10.1016/j.electstud.2015.01.004.

Bratton, Michael. 2008. 'Vote Buying and Violence in Nigerian Election Campaigns'. *Electoral Studies*. https://doi.org/10.1016/j.electstud.2008.04.013.

Burchard, Stephanie M. 2018. 'Get out the Vote – or Else: the impact of fear of election violence on voters'. *Democratization*, 27: 1–17. https://doi.org/10.1080/13510347.2019.1710490.

Cantú, Francisco and Omar García-Ponce. 2015. 'Partisan Losers' Effects: Perceptions of Electoral Integrity in Mexico'. *Electoral Studies* 39: 1–14. https://doi.org/10.1016/j.electstud.2015.03.004.

Çarkoğlu, Ali and S. Erdem Aytaç. 2015. 'Who Gets Targeted for Vote-Buying? Evidence from an Augmented List Experiment in Turkey'. *European Political Science Review* 7 (4): 547–66. https://doi.org/10.1017/S1755773914000320.

Coffé, Hilde. 2017. 'Citizens' Media Use and the Accuracy of Their Perceptions of Electoral Integrity'. *International Political Science Review* 38 (3): 281–97. https://doi.org/10.1177/0192512116640984.

Coppedge, M., J. Gerring, C. H. Knutsen, J. Krusell, J. Medzihorsky, J. Pernes, S.-E. Skaaning, N. Stepanova, J. Teorell, E. Tzelgov, S. L. Wilson and S. I. Lindberg. 2019. 'The Methodology of "Varieties of Democracy" (V-Dem) 1'. *Bulletin of Sociological Methodology/Bulletin de Méthodologie Sociologique* 143 (1): 107–33. https://doi.org/10.1177/0759106319854989.

Daxecker, Ursula E. 2012. 'The Cost of Exposing Cheating: International Election Monitoring, Fraud, and Post-Election Violence in Africa'." *Journal of Peace Research* 49 (4). https://doi.org/10.1177/0022343312445649.

Dercon, Stefan and Roxana Gutiérrez-Romero. 2012. 'Triggers and Characteristics of the 2007 Kenyan Electoral Violence'. *World Development*. https://doi.org/10.1016/j.worlddev.2011.09.015.

Economist, The. 2018. 'Recep Tayyip the First', 28 June.

Egorov, Georgy, Sergei Guriev and Konstantin Sonin. 2009. 'Why Resource-Poor Dictators Allow Freer Media: A Theory and Evidence from Panel Data'. *American Political Science Review* 103 (4). https://doi.org/10.1017/S0003055409990219.

Esen, Berk and Sebnem Gumuscu. 2016. 'Rising Competitive Authoritarianism in Turkey'. *Third World Quarterly*. https://doi.org/10.1080/01436597.2015.1135732.

Fearon, James D. 2011. 'Self-Enforcing Democracy'. *Quarterly Journal of Economics* 126 (4). https://doi.org/10.1093/qje/qjr038.

Fjelde, Hanne, and Kristine Höglund. 2016. "Electoral Institutions and Electoral Violence in Sub-Saharan Africa." *British Journal of Political Science*. https://doi.org/10.1017/S0007123414000179.

Flesken, Anaïd and Jakob Hartl. 2018. 'Party Support, Values, and Perceptions of Electoral Integrity'. *Political Psychology*. https://doi.org/10.1111/pops.12431.

Gonzalez-Ocantos, Ezequiel, Chad Kiewiet de Jonge, Carlos Meléndez, David Nickerson and Javier Osorio. 2020. 'Carrots and Sticks: Experimental Evidence of Vote-Buying and Voter Intimidation in Guatemala'. *Journal of Peace Research* 57 (1). https://doi.org/10.1177/0022343319884998.

Höglund, Kristine and Anton Piyarathne. 2009. 'Paying the Price for Patronage: Electoral Violence in Sri Lanka'. *Commonwealth and Comparative Politics*. https://doi.org/10.1080/14662040903090807.

Hyde, Susan D. and Nikolay Marinov. 2012. 'Which Elections Can Be Lost?' *Political Analysis* 20 (2). https://doi.org/10.1093/pan/mpr040.

Karp, Jeffrey A., Alessandro Nai and Pippa Norris. 2018. 'Dial "F" for Fraud: Explaining Citizens Suspicions about Elections'. *Electoral Studies* 53 (June): 11–19. https://doi.org/10.1016/j.electstud.2018.01.010.

Kerr, Nicholas. 2013. 'Popular Evaluations of Election Quality in Africa: Evidence from Nigeria'. *Electoral Studies* 32 (4). https://doi.org/10.1016/j.electstud.2013.02.010.

Kerr, Nicholas and Anna Lührmann. 2017. 'Public Trust in Manipulated Elections: The Role of Election Administration and Media Freedom'. *Electoral Studies*. https://doi.org/10.1016/j.electstud.2017.08.003.

Kim, Sung-youn, Charles Taber and Milton Lodge. 2010. 'A Computational Model of the Citizen as Motivated Reasoner: Modeling the Dynamics of the 2000 Presidential Election'. *Political Behavior* 32 (1): 1–28. https://doi.org/10.1007/s11109-009-9099-8.

Kunda, Ziva. 1990. 'The Case for Motivated Reasoning'. *Psychological Bulletin* 108 (3). https://doi.org/10.1037/0033-2909.108.3.480.

Magaloni, Beatriz. 2006. *Voting for Autocracy: Hegemonic Party Survival and Its Demise in Mexico*. Cambridge: Cambridge University Press.

———. 2010. 'The Game of Electoral Fraud and the Ousting of Authoritarian Rule'. *American Journal of Political Science* 54 (3). https://doi.org/10.1111/j.1540-5907.2010.00458.x.

Mares, Isabela and Lauren Young. 2016. 'Buying, Expropriating, and Stealing Votes'. *Annual Review of Political Science* 19: 267–88. https://doi.org/10.1146/annurev-polisci-060514-120923.

McAllister, Ian and Stephen White. 2011. 'Public Perceptions of Electoral Fairness in Russia'. *Europe–Asia Studies* 63 (4): 663–83. https://doi.org/10.1080/09668136.2011.566429.

Norris, Pippa. 2015. *Why Elections Fail*. Cambridge: Cambridge University Press. https://doi.org/10.1017/CBO9781107280908.

Norris, Pippa, Richard W. Frank and Ferran Martínez i Coma. 2014. *Advancing Electoral Integrity*. Oxford: Oxford University Press.

Öktem, Kerem and Karabekir Akkoyunlu. 2016. 'Exit from Democracy: Illiberal Governance in Turkey and Beyond'. *Journal of Southeast European and Black Sea*. https://doi.org/10.1080/14683857.2016.1253231.

Reporters without Borders. 2021. 'Media Ownership Monitor: Turkey'. https://rsf.org/en/country-türkiye.

Reuter, Ora John and David Szakonyi. 2015. 'Online Social Media and Political Awareness in Authoritarian Regimes'. *British Journal of Political Science* 45 (1): 29–51. https://doi.org/10.1017/S0007123413000203.

Rosas, Guillermo. 2010. 'Trust in Elections and the Institutional Design of Electoral Authorities: Evidence from Latin America'. *Electoral Studies* 29 (1): 74–90.

Salehyan, Idean and Christopher Linebarger. 2015. 'Elections and Social Conflict in Africa, 1990–2009'. *Studies in Comparative International Development*. https://doi.org/10.1007/s12116-014-9163-1.

Schedler, Andreas. 2013. *The Politics of Uncertainty: Sustaining and Subverting Electoral Authoritarianism*. Oxford: Oxford University Press.

Taylor, Charles Fernandes, Jon C. W. Pevehouse and Scott Straus. 2017. 'Perils of Pluralism: Electoral Violence and Incumbency in Sub-Saharan Africa'. *Journal of Peace Research*. https://doi.org/10.1177/0022343316687801.

Toros, Emre and Sarah Birch. 2019a. 'Who Are the Targets of Familial Electoral Coercion? Evidence from Turkey'. *Democratisation* 26 (8): 1342–61. https://doi.org/10.1080/13510347.2019.1639151.

Toros, Emre and Sarah Birch. 2019b. 'Framing Electoral Impropriety: The Strategic Use of Allegations of Wrong-Doing in Election Campaigns'. *British Journal of Middle Eastern Studies*. https://doi.org/DOI:10.1080/13530194.2019.1566694.

Tunç, Aslı. 2015. 'Media Integrity Report: Media Ownership and Financing in Turkey'. Southeastern Media Observatory Group. https://mediaobservatory.net/radar/media-integrity-report-media-ownership-and-financing-turkey.

TÜİK. 2018. 'Yazılı Medya İstatistikleri, 2018'. Türkiye İstatistik Kurumu Raporları. https://data.tuik.gov.tr/Bulten/Index?p=Yazili-Medya--Istatistikleri-2018-30593.

Van Ham, Carolien and Staffan I. Lindberg. 2015. 'From Sticks to Carrots: Electoral Manipulation in Africa, 1986–2012'. *Government and Opposition*. https://doi.org/10.1017/gov.2015.6.

von Borzyskowski, Inken and Patrick M. Kuhn. 2020. 'Dangerously Informed: Voter Information and Pre-Electoral Violence in Africa'. *Journal of Peace Research* 57 (1). https://doi.org/10.1177/0022343319885166.

5

ELECTORAL MANAGEMENT BODIES AS ESTABLISHERS OF ELECTORAL INTEGRITY

W hat do voters think about electoral officers and electoral management bodies (EMBs), and how do these thoughts build to become perceptions associated with electoral integrity? How do the decisions of EMBs relate to electoral integrity? Recently, the growing number of electoral problems worldwide has brought these issues under the spotlight. Accordingly, we observe increasing attempts to understand the role of electoral officers and EMBs in building or damaging electoral integrity. In this respect, this chapter examines the problem that the link between electoral integrity and EMBs presents by discussing the issue on a global comparative level and relocating the discussion to the Turkish context by providing a historical outlook on the Turkish EMB, the Supreme Election Council (YSK).

According to a report by the United Nations Development Programme (UNDP), in 53 per cent of all democracies elections are run by electoral commissions (López-Pintor 2000). The general tendency worldwide is toward establishing electoral authorities as long-term commissions independent of the government, having representatives of political parties sit on them, and mostly staffing them with professionals in the field. It is also known that in most cases, especially in Latin America and Africa, constitutions govern the legal status of such electoral authorities to keep them autonomous from ordinary law or the executive. Observers, analysts and people who work in the field agree that elections run by independent electoral bodies are better than those run by the executive and that permanent electoral administrations are more cost-effective than temporary ones (Carothers 1997). International organisations like the United Nations, the European Union, the Organization for Security and Co-operation in Europe (OSCE) and the British Commonwealth support the idea that EMBs should encourage all political parties to participate in elections, promote transparency at all stages of the process, be accountable to the legislature and the public and spread voter information and civic education (Joseph 2021). This autonomy is also needed to deal with the massive reach of elections and make it easier to organise local elections, which happen in almost every democracy today. The issue also has an international dimension. In many new democracies, technical and financial help from other countries has made a big difference in setting up electoral management bodies and running elections. Accordingly, EMBs have become more organised and efficient over time, and their need for administrative, management and operational support from the international community has decreased. However, many of them still need technical advice, especially financial help. In parallel with these developments, several regional and international associations of electoral authorities have been established in the last few years to network and promote standards of good practice and exchange professional expertise. As discussed below, recent field research shows that citizens have started to relate performance of the EMB to how well the democracy is functioning.

Fuelled by these critical developments and as a neglected area within electoral integrity research, a comprehensive analysis of the regulations governing EMBs seems crucial for several reasons. As the organisations responsible for implementing elections, evaluating the impact of their decisions would help us comprehensively perceive the problems related to electoral integrity. Although EMBs worldwide seem to follow international democratic standards on paper, we still have scarce evidence on whether and how the decisions of EMBs relate to problems with electoral integrity. In that respect, the initial research on the link between electoral integrity and EMB behaviour emphasised the organisational independence of the EMBs from governments and compared the level of independence of EMBs around the world as a benchmark for electoral integrity (López-Pintor 2000). Subsequently, scholars have continued to examine the problem and have demonstrated examples of the role of EMBs in protecting or endangering electoral integrity (Van Ham and Lindberg 2015; Norris,

Frank and Martínez i Coma 2014a; Orji 2017). A line of research shows that public trust in election administration is directly related to how independent the electoral authority is perceived to be (Bowler et al. 2015; Kerr 2013; Norris, Frank and Martínez i Coma 2014b).

More recently, James et al. (2019) formulated a framework to analyse how institutional design, organisational performance and electoral integrity are related; Clark (2019) linked electoral spending levels to the administrative and organisational capacity of EMBs; Garnett (2019), with an innovative tool, investigated the capacity of EMBs to perform their tasks; James (2019), focusing on EMB workforces, found that those offering better opportunities for employees to be involved in decision-making processes perform better. Commenting on these studies, Norris (2019b) concluded that additional research is needed to focus on the institutional structures and processes of electoral management, and especially for 'determining the impact of electoral management on broader indicators of democratic performance'. Lastly, in line with these studies, Ruiz-Rafino and Birch (2020) have theorised a link between electoral administration and electoral violence. They argue that a significant factor for electoral credibility is the independence of the EMBs from governments and show that *de facto* autonomy matters for impartiality and freedom from political interference.

These findings show that decisions of electoral administration organisations can play a critical role in establishing electoral integrity. However, how their decisions damage electoral integrity in other contexts remains unknown. The following paragraphs will try to solve this puzzle, utilising Turkey as a case study.

Worldwide Perceptions of EMBs

The following analysis will check citizens' perceptions of EMBs by linking these to their perceptions of electoral integrity and electoral malpractice. It is logical to expect that citizens think the electoral officials are fair will hold more positive perceptions of electoral integrity. In contrast, citizens will perceive majormalpractice if they believe the electoral officers do not act impartially. This chapter utilises World Values Survey (WVS) data to check whether these hypotheses hold. The analysis will provide the opportunity to compare evidence from consolidated democracies with well-known, high standards of electoral procedure with the grey zone democracies and autocracies, where elections are alleged to be more problematic.

The two most recent waves of the WVS (Six and Seven) include batteries on electoral integrity and malpractice. The questions on integrity are designed to elicit perceptions of elections by asking whether citizens think votes are counted fairly, whether voters are given legitimate alternatives, whether wealthy people buy elections and whether voters are threatened with violence at the polls. In a similar vein, public concerns about malpractice are measured by combining questions, to tap into citizens' evaluations of different electoral qualities. After reviewing the survey responses, I decided to apply two levels of analysis to these dimensions by combining the answers to the integrity and malpractice questions then, following a logic similar to Norris (2019a), averaging them, standardising them and rescaling between 0 and 1 for easy comparison. This process generated two independent variables, electoral integrity and malpractice respectively. The dependent variable was set using the question that probes the fairness of the electoral officers.

Figure 5.1 show a clear link between positive perceptions of electoral officers' fairness and electoral integrity at the national level. Citizens perceive high levels of electoral integrity and low levels of malpractice in countries where they also think that electoral officers act impartially. Scandinavian countries, including Norway, Sweden, Denmark and Finland, are examples of such countries.

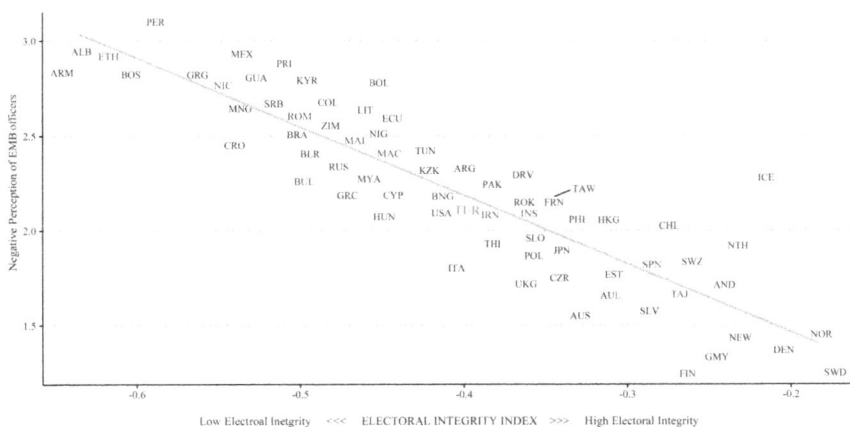

Figure 5.1 Fairness of electoral officers and electoral integrity indices

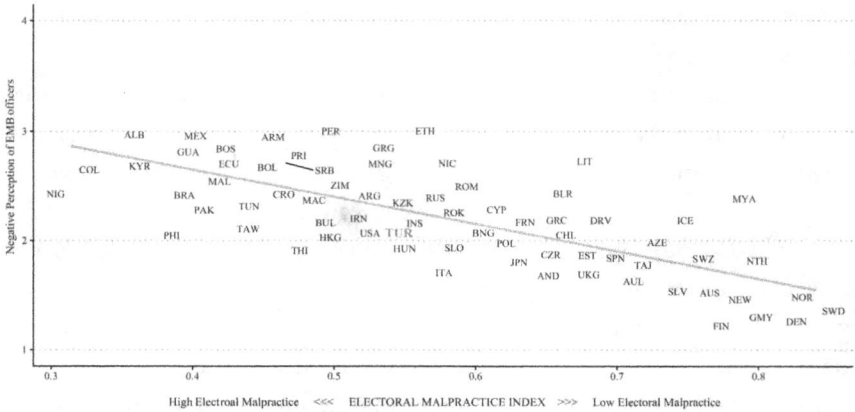

Figure 5.2 Regime types, fairness of electoral officers and electoral malpractice indices

At the other end of the spectrum, where citizens perceive low levels of electoral integrity, the perception of electoral officers' impartiality tends to come under question. Countries like Peru, Ethiopia, and Albania are good examples of such countries. It is also interesting to see some outliers, such as Iceland and the Netherlands. Although citizens perceive high levels of electoral integrity in these countries, they still seem to doubt the fairness of electoral officers.

Below, using the PEI's Electoral Integrity 7.0 data, Figure 5.2. portrays a similar finding. Additional to the graphs based on public opinion above, these data based on expert opinion show the link between types of regime and perceived electoral malpractice: the perception of electoral officers' fairness is relatively high in established liberal democracies and low in more illiberal settings.

The Turkish Context

As discussed above, numerous boards and institutions monitor the conduct and establish the integrity of elections around the world. Undoubtedly, among these institutions the EMBs are the most important as they typically hold the highest rank in electoral mechanisms, and in Turkey Yüksek Seçim Kurulu (the Supreme Electoral Council, YSK) is no exception, in that sense. Although Turkish law gives some serious levels of authority to the county provincial and county election boards, the YSK's decisions are definitive. Interestingly, however, the YSK and its many controversial decisions have become a central issue of elections during the second decade of this century.

A series of events have impacted on YSK as it has evolved to reach its current structural and operational status. The precise manifestation of these changes of structural and functional position, and the specific needs and particular political perspectives that drove them, are of great importance in evaluating the Council's current status accurately. It is highly valuable to examine how these changes emerged after particular political and legal incidents or decisions, to lay out the reason behind them.

The council has held different places in the country's political structure during Turkish political history. However, when changes and demands for change in its structural position are considered, we can separate its historical development into three periods: 1950–60, 1960–90 and the period from 1990 onwards (Güler 2020). Even though the Council was established on a legal basis for the first time during the 1950s, it gained full authorisation with amendments to the law in 1954 and its constitutional base with the 1961 Constitution.

In the early years of the Turkish Republic, until 1942, there were almost no legal regulations concerning the elections, and all the polls were conducted and monitored under the Act of Deputy Elections (İntihab-ı Mebusan Kanun-ı Muvakkatı) dated 20 July 1908. However, no duty or authorisation had been given to specific judicial authorities concerning the implementation or monitoring of elections. Act of Deputy Elections No. 4320 dated 14 December 1942 did not regulate election boards clearly; however, it gave authorisation to them, set out their duties during elections and established inspection committees. Act of Deputy Elections No. 4918 dated 6 June 1946 repealed Act No. 4320 and gave regulation, execution and monitoring functions to election boards for the first time. Since these boards are presided over by local mayors, it would be almost impossible to say they had successfully conducted and monitored electoral activities correctly. These facts demonstrate that, although the YSK was established with Act No. 5545, the infrastructure it built on had been formed almost five years earlier. It can be argued that, to some extent, discussions of today's conduct and monitoring system need to take account of the developments of the early 1950s (Güler 2020).

The first multi-party elections took place on 21 July 1946 after the foundation of the Demokrat Parti (Democrat Party, DP) on 7 January 1946. The Democrat Party contested no other elections until the general elections of 14 May 1950, as the party expressed concerns about electoral integrity. This boycott led to extensive social and political pressure on the Cumhuriyet Halk Partisi (Republican People's Party, CHP), which was already planning to establish a genuine multi-party system in the country (Sönmez 2014). The DP expended a considerable amount of effort towards the propaganda aim of achieving judicial surveillance of an election. To that end, the party continuously underlined that election legislation enforced between 1946 and 1950 had failed to achieve the fair and honest conduct of elections in a safe environment, and therefore to accurately reflect the authentic will of the citizens. Discussions were prolonged and, in 1948, although the DP had already announced to the public that the principles of judicial surveillance and monitoring had been conceded to ensure election safety, the CHP proved unwilling to put judicial monitoring in place, reasoning that the judiciary should not be involved in any practices outside its strict purview. The issue also found a place in the government programme. Government officials announced that a new election law would be drafted for the 1950 elections, to assure every citizen that the country was benefiting from science and experience.

A strong case can be made that Act No. 5545 is a product of a democratic maturity and negotiating culture far in advance of contemporary understanding. Some further developments should be noted, such as the publication of a pink book summarising the views of English, French and Belgian lawyers on the changes made in 1948 to Act No. 4918 and on a *corpus* that combined the election legislation that had been enforced since 1876. An independent committee composed of officials from the Ministry of Justice and the Ministry of the Interior prepared a draft of the electoral law along similar lines. Another expert group, the 'Science Committee', also worked on this draft; this committee included representatives from the Supreme Court, the Council of State, the Bar and some universities. It identified itself as 'an exclusively scientific, completely autonomous think-tank organisation with a wide authorisation that is compatible with its impartial responsibility'. The Science Committee officially asked the existing political parties to supply ideas, reviews and suggestions about the election law under drafting. The free and independent working environment of the Science Committee, enabling freedom of speech and ideas, is a striking example of a democratic approach during a period of one-party government under the CHP (Güngör 2014). Since the political parties were given the opportunity to present their ideas, the discussions in the

TBMM began to relax. Drafting moved forward more quickly than usual in the Assembly Commission. The Election Act No. 5545 was recognised on 16 February 1950 at the Grand Assembly and entered into force on 21 February 1950, when it was published in the *Official Gazette*. However, this new law was not free from flaws: it granted the TBMM authority to rescind electoral records, which provided a tool that a majority in the assembly could misuse against its opponents (Güler 2020).

Positive developments continued in subsequent years, when DP governments amended Act No. 5545 to increase democracy and transparency in the election system. The first amendment aimed to alter the right of rescission mentioned above by relocating authority to annul records of deputies' election to the YSK, taking it away from the Grand Assembly. The second amendment, Law No. 6272 of 1954, considerably expanded the membership of the YSK. It was agreed that the Council should now consist of one president and ten members, and that the president of the High Court of Appeals (president of the Supreme Court) should preside over the YSK. Council members were to be designated by lot from among the members of the Supreme Court and the Council of State (each designating five regulars and three substitutes), and reserve members were to be appointed to the board based on seniority. The change embodied in the first amendment, it was reasoned, demanded a larger committee with relatively high levels of representation and expertise; this was also why the presidency was assigned to the president of the Supreme Court.

Today's disputes about whether the Council should be regarded as a judiciary body or as a court go back to this period. Although the Science Committee that drafted Act No. 5545 in 1950 envisaged this board being a Supreme Court of Election, the CHP, using its parliamentary majority, amended the law to establish a Supreme Election Council, over the objections of the DP. The political atmosphere of the period was harsh and challenging for both ruling and opposition parties. However, the regulations governing pre-election processes, with the potential to directly affect election outcomes, should be regarded as a positive step towards democratisation.

In subsequent periods, the responsibilities of the YSK changed, mainly in consequence of constitutional amendments. For example, during the early 1960s Milli Birlik Komitesi (the National Unity Committee, MBK), which seized power after the 1960 *coup d'état*, altered the Council's responsibilities.

The drafts prepared for this purpose contained two opposing views of the YSK's responsibilities for monitoring elections. One position argued that resolution of electoral problems should be left to the Constitutional Court, while the other left the conduct and monitoring of elections to the TBMM. In the end, the YSK and its duties to conduct and monitor elections gained constitutional legitimacy in the 1961 Constitution and were sustained in the 1982 Constitution. The Constitution Commission, responsible for drafting a new constitution after the 1980 coup, reported that '[a]s one of the best functioning provisions of 1961 Constitution, it has been found right that the rules on the conduct and monitoring of elections are to be exactly protected in terms of a constitutional rule' (Güler 2020). The 1982 Constitution also conveyed additional duties on the YSK, such as monitoring referenda of any kind, and the provision making its decisions final gained constitutional status. As a result, the YSK became the authority solely responsible for carrying out functions to ensure the fair and orderly conduct of elections from beginning to end. The Council's duties now included investigating and taking final decisions on all irregularities, complaints and objections raised about electoral matters during and after elections, and no appeal could be made to any authority against its decisions.

The 1982 Constitution also altered the composition of the council, to seven regular members and four substitutes. Six of these members would be elected by the General Board of the High Court of Appeals, and the other five by the General Board of the Council of State, from amongst their members, in both cases by the absolute majority vote of the all members of those Boards through secret ballot. The eleven members so elected would elect a chairperson and a vice-chairperson from amongst their number, again by absolute majority and secret vote. Two each of the members elected to the YSK by the High Court of Appeals and by the Council of State would be designated substitute members, by lot. The president and vice-president of the YSK would not participate in the drawing of lots.

As one might quickly notice, several amendments have marked the development of the Council and related laws. Among other articles, No. 14, regulating the authority of the Council, has been amended nine times; No. 52, regulating radio and television propaganda, eight times; No. 30, regulating the General Directorate of the Electoral Register, seven times; and No. 182, regulating payments and fees, also seven times (Güler 2020). Although codes and laws are prone to amendment, ideally the electoral law that embodies principles and rules on a constitutional level should be drafted with minimal vulnerability and scope for influence. Frequent changes in electoral laws may cause severe problems since every new provision opens the way for new interpretations, resulting in ongoing vagueness and unclarity. In Turkish electoral law an attempt was made to consolidate organisational procedures, trials and norms under Act No. 298 of 1961; nevertheless, the law now appears disorganised again. Act No. 298 has been in operation for more than sixty years but is now readily open to new arguments after so many disruptions to its system.

These concerns and the resulting need for reform have also drawn the attention of legislators and political parties. As an example of this attention, Act No. 7062 of 30 December 2017 aimed to consolidate specific provisions contained in Act No. 298. However, the new act contains only fifteen articles; one is provisional, two relate to execution and enforcement, another two define aims, scope and definitions, and one is a repetition of the Constitutional provisions. Four repeat the provisions from Act No. 298, so only five articles have brought novelty. These represent some steps to diminish the problems, but the drawbacks and deficits in the regulations have shown scant progress (Güler 2020). Beside Act No. 7062, there have also been some positive developments: a 'Supreme Election Council Officer Examination, Assignment, Relocation and Transportation Regulation' and a 'Supreme Election Council Personnel Promotion and Title Change Regulation' were published in the *Official Gazette* on 18 June 2018, and these are highly important as they govern the specialist careers of the election bureaucracy.

Current Problem Areas

During the second decade of this century, several controversial issues have been observed in the areas where the YSK has regulatory authority. The first relates to the Council's power to ban the political parties from participating in elections, or allow them to do so. This authority becomes critical for early or snap elections held before the date envisaged in the constitution or election laws. Taking part in elections, along with the possibility of winning them, brings a set of other rights and obligations for political parties, such as putting their ppolicies across via the press, communication tools and/or the internet; gaining representation in the YSK, provincial and district election boards, opening an election office and preparing and submitting voter lists. These rights and duties have been granted only to those political parties that are participating in the election. Since the YSK acts as the sole authority to determine which political parties may take part in the elections under the criteria specified by the legislator, the decisions taken in performance of this duty directly impact on the results of elections.

According to current regulations in force, the criteria for the participation of political parties in elections are set in the Parliamentary Election Act, the Basic Provisions of Elections, the Electoral Registers Act and, finally, in the Political Parties Act. These regulations grant the legislator significant power, making the participation process challenging and complicated (Güler 2020).

Article No. 36 of Act No. 2820 requires political parties wishing to participate in elections to have established an organisation in at least half of the provinces or have a group in the TBMM, and to hold a general congress at least six months before the voting day. A provincial organisation must have an establishment in at least one-third of the districts of that province, including the central district. As mentioned, the duty of designating the political parties that may contest an election belongs to the YSK. However, no information or document in the YSK database covers parties' organisations in districts and provinces; the council requests this information and documents to support it from the Office of the Chief Public Prosecutor at the Supreme Court. Not surprisingly, this procedure has created many problems during the process of designating and announcing the policies of political parties that would like to participate in elections. Since 1990, in more than a dozen cases the YSK has had to amend an initial decision not to let parties compete in elections because they could not meet the necessary conditions.

Among other examples, that of the Demokratik Halk Partisi (Democratic People's Party, DEHAP) shows how critical this task can be in terms of potential political ramifications. In 2002, just after the decision of the TBMM to hold a snap election, the YSK requested the Office of the Chief Public Prosecutor to provide it with details of the organisational status of the political parties. That Office replied that the DEHAP was established in sixty-three provinces, and on this information the Council listed the party among those authorised to contest the elections. Even though it had supplied this information, the Chief Public Prosecutor appealed to the YSK, noting that the DEHAP had organisations only in a few cities, naming Ankara, İzmir, Hakkari and Adıyaman, and that it had no other provincial organisations, and demanding annulment of the party's participation in the elections. YSK rejected the appeal as no concrete and legally valid information was supplied to necessitate the annulment. However, the Office of the Chief Public Prosecutor to the Supreme Court filed another complaint against the party managers of DEHAP on 16 October 2002, right after the YSK handed down this ruling. The court that first heard the case found some party managers guilty of forgery of official documents, giving incorrect information about the organisation to provincial governorships and the Chief Public Prosecutor's Office, and this ruling was upheld by Supreme Court decree. Although this ruling meant that DEHAP did not have the legal right to take part in the elections, it did so and received 2 million votes (6.2 per cent).

This chaos continued after the election. Since a decree by the 6th Penal Chamber provided the necessary legal grounds to appeal, six parties that had failed to meet the 10 per cent national threshold in the general election used the opportunity and appealed to the YSK, demanding the annulment and rerunning of the election. In addition, Doğru Yol Partisi (the True Path Party, DYP), which would have been assigned sixty-six deputies if DEHAP's votes were deemed invalid, also appealed to the YSK. On 4 October 2003, nearly one year after the election, the YSK rejected all appeals. If the votes of DEHAP had been deemed invalid, the two-party parliament that the YSK upheld – split between the Adalet ve Kalkınma Partisi (Justice and Development Party, AKP) and the CHP – would have been replaced by another – 44 seats assigned to AKP and 22 seats assigned to the CHP would have had to transfer to the DYP. Such a distribution in the TBMM in 2002 would have had very different political consequences.

As a second crucial problematic area, it would be appropriate to mention the problems relating to the registration of voters. An honest and accurate registration of the voters is of great importance for both citizens planning to vote in elections and the candidates hoping to win election, and can directly affect the integrity of elections (Lijphart 1997; Rosenstone and Wolfinger 1978; Mann and Bryant 2020; Minnis and Shah 2020; Aydin and Sunar 2018). Electoral registries and lists are the official records of citizens who have the right to vote and against whom no obstacles to voting have been found, identifying citizens qualified to vote and registering the voters' residences among other information. Although updating electoral records raises numerous issues, the primary task is determining who is eligible to vote and removing from the register those who do not meet the conditions. Although preferences and methods for keeping electoral registration records differ among countries and electoral systems, the aim is to keep the registry up-to-date by constantly supervising the changes.

The YSK uses a computerised system called Seçim Bilgi Sistemi (Electoral Information System, SEÇSİS) to keep the electoral registration records of Turkish voters. Since the early years of its use, parties have regarded SEÇSİS as an efficient and well-functioning system despite some minor problems. Commenting on the November 2015 elections, OSCE examiners generally expressed confidence in the accuracy of the voter list (OSCE 2015). In addition, for the same election, only four parties applied to the YSK to obtain a copy of electoral rolls, and registrations were found to be safe by all authorised to share them. None of the parties has filed any complaint about the accuracy of the rolls.

SEÇSİS provides the designation as voters of all Turkish citizens aged 18 or over, prepares voter lists and removes duplicate records, and provides an easy and fast voting process. Domestic voter lists are shared electronically with political parties before and after the announcement of the lists (after the lists are finalised) and after ballot boxes have been assigned. SEÇSİS also creates a structure that allows safe and rapid transmission of electoral results from districts to centres, and announcements of electoral results to the public, and produces all kinds of information and documents related to election work and voting transactions. IT specialists and politicians are also agreed that SEÇSİS complies with the standards and that no internet access to SEÇSİS is provided, preventing external interference or hacking. In addition, it is generally agreed that there are no unauthorised users within the system, and that all transactions and data changes in the system can be monitored instantly (Güler 2020).

When generating electoral rolls, YSK receives the required data from the General Directorate of Population and Citizenship Affairs, which is affiliated with the Ministry of the Interior, and finalises the list based on its 'Address-Based Registration System'. More recently, opposition parties have criticised this procedure, alleging that voters have been registered or 'assigned' in non-residential locations and that unusual population changes have been recorded in several provinces, districts and towns. Be that as it may, several reports by independent professional organisations have consistently emphasised that all system outputs are shared with political parties simultaneously and that all are open to objection within legislated periods. Civil society organisations that monitor electoral integrity provide similar reports. For example, after monitoring the 2018 parliamentary and presidential elections, Oy ve Ötesi (Vote and Beyond, OvÖ), which is the most prominent domestic voluntary organisation involved in election monitoring, found only minor inconsistencies between the election results based on SEÇSİS and manual records taken by volunteers, not affecting the overall results (Oy ve Ötesi 2018). However, some other studies have argued that, although the election results produced consistent outputs, there might have been corruption in individual elections (Meyersson 2015), but no evidence has been found to support these arguments. Moreover, there has been no flow of complaints about SEÇSİS that might justify doubts about the system's reliability.

The other crucial problematic area relates to the drawing-up of electoral rolls. As a rule, every Turkish citizen aged 18 years or over with legal residence has the right to vote and participate in elections. Nonetheless, the fifth paragraph of Article 67 of the Constitution states that members of the armed forces, including conscripts and non-commissioned officers, and military students are ineligible to vote, and those convicted of crimes attributable to negligence cannot vote while in penal institutions. Accordingly, to draw up the electoral roll, YSK cooperates with several state institutions and organisations to establish accurate registration of the voters, coordinating through SEÇSİS. The General Directorate of Electoral Rolls, a sub-branch of the YSK, provides information about those citizens of the Turkish Republic qualified to vote, with valid residential addresses supplied by the Ministry of the Interior, General Directorate of Civil Registration and Citizen Affairs. The General Directorate of Civil Registration and Citizen Affairs keeps (and supplies to SEÇSİS) records of who has lost citizenship and who has died. Similarly, the General Directorate of Recruitment, part of the Ministry of Defence, sends information about restricted citizens, such as soldiers, non-commissioned officers, military students and reserve officers in service on voting day. Lastly, the Ministry of Justice obtains information about convicts in penal institutions for non-negligent crimes, and others who are restricted from voting. YSK requests these data from these various institutions about three months before the election. Undoubtedly, changes may occur in these data, such as death, loss of citizenship or conviction for a crime, etc., during that period. The YSK requests lists of changes from the relevant institutions one week before the election, and updates the electoral roll accordingly.

These complex procedures inevitably lead to some serious errors. On many occasions, where it has found that restricted voters, citizens banned from public service and/or those not eligible to vote have been included in electoral rolls and cast votes, the YSK has annulled elections (Güler 2020). Güler (2020) also argues these drawbacks result from failures of capacity in the institutions transmitting the requested data. In a recent example, it has been revealed that the Ministry of Justice mistakenly included in electoral rolls data for 601 restricted citizens who do not have the right to vote.

Against this background, it becomes crucial to investigate the link between how the EMBs are perceived and overall electoral integrity. The following analysis uses the sixth wave of the World Values Survey to check the relationship between the perception of EMBs and electoral integrity, with related control variables including the perceptions of democracy, partisanship and demographic variables. Both the sixth and the seventh waves of the World Values Survey include batteries on electoral integrity and malpractice, including a specific question on perceptions of EMBs' fairness during the elections with the following wording: 'In your view, how often do the following things occur in this country's elections? Election officials are fair 1. Very often 2. Fairly often 3. Not often 4. Not at all often.' The other questions on integrity are designed to elicit perceptions of elections by asking whether citizens think votes are counted fairly, whether voters are given legitimate alternatives, whether wealthy people buy elections and whether voters are threatened with violence at the polls. In a similar vein, public concerns about malpractice are measured by combining questions by tapping into citizens' evaluations of different electoral qualities. As with the methods used to prepare figures 5.1 and 5.2, after reviewing the survey responses I applied two levels of analysis by combining the answers to the integrity and malpractice questions then, following a logic similar to Norris (2019a), averaging them, standardising them and rescaling between 0 and 1 for easy comparison. This process generated two independent variables, electoral integrity and malpractice respectively.

Table 5.1 provides evidence related to EMBs' fairness from a comparative perspective. As seen in Figure 5.2 above, across the globe there is an association between levels of perceived fairness of electoral officers and electoral integrity at the national level. Countries with consolidated democracies, such as Sweden, Denmark, Canada and Finland, constitute a category with the highest levels of perceived fairness of electoral officers, and also of integrity. The middle category, which includes Turkey, shows relatively low levels of perceived fairness of EMBs. In the third and last category, which primarily consists of illiberal countries, we observe low levels both of perceived fairness of EMBs and of electoral integrity. Accordingly, several different factors may cause the picture in Figure 5.2. To understand these factors, Table 5.1 below shows a cross-national analysis in

Table 5.1 Cross-national analysis: perceptions of the fairness of electoral officers

Predictors	Model 1 World std beta	Model 2 World std beta	Model 3 World disaggregated std beta
(Intercept)	1.80*** (0.01)	2.18*** (0.03)	1.60*** (0.03)
Integrity index	2.05*** (0.01)	1.84*** (0.01)	
Malpractice index	−0.75 *** (0.01)	−0.51*** (0.01)	
Importance of democracy		−0.02*** (0.00)	−0.01*** (0.00)
Income		−0.00*** (0.00)	−0.00** (0.00)
Age		−0.00*** (0.00)	−0.00*** (0.00)
Gender (female)		0.03*** (0.01)	0.02*** (0.01)
Education		−0.02*** (0.00)	−0.02*** (0.00)
Votes are counted fairly			0.36*** (0.00)
Journalists provide fair coverage of elections			0.25*** (0.00)
Opposition candidates are prevented from running			−0.04*** (0.00)
TV news favours the governing party			0.01*** (0.00)
Voters are bribed			−0.08*** (0.00)
Rich people buy elections			−0.03*** (0.00)
Voters are threatened with violence at the polls			−0.02*** (0.00)
Observations	79,279	79,279	79,279
R^2/R^2 adjusted	0.380/0.380	0.433/0.433	0.440/0.439

*$p<0.05$ **$p<0.01$ ***$p<0.001$, country fixed effects removed from the table*

which the perceived fairness of the EMBs is the dependent variable. The first model, the base model, checks the relationship between the constructed indices and fairness. The second model incorporates additional, mostly demographic, independent variables and controls. The third and final model uses the questions asked in the WVS in a disaggregated form.

The base model's findings suggest that public perceptions of electoral integrity and malpractice are strongly related to the perceived fairness of electoral officers. Both variables produced results in the expected directions: as electoral integrity increases, the perceived fairness of electoral officers increases, and as electoral malpractice increases, the perceived fairness of electoral officers decreases. The second model introduces five independent variables: the importance of democracy and respondent's income, parallel to the theoretical discussion above, combined with three demographic control variables. The statistically significant results show that high levels of income and education are associated with relatively low perceived fairness of the EMBs. Additionally, compared to others, citizens who attribute importance to democracy, who are male and/or who are older show higher levels of perceived fairness of electoral officers. The third and final model, which checks the robustness of these findings with the disaggregated items that made up the indices, displays a picture similar to the previous models.

Table 5.2, using an approach similar to that employed in Table 5.1, provides empirical evidence for the Turkish case. Like cross-national evidence, the base model confirms the significant link between electoral integrity and the perception of fairness among electoral officers. For both indices, the coefficients carried the expected sign: as the integrity score increases and the malpractice score decreases, the perceived fairness of electoral officers increases. We observe a different picture for the second model, which introduces the control variables. Although the importance of the democracy variable has the same sign and nearly the same magnitude as the coefficient for the cross-national model, the coefficients of the remaining controls – income, age, gender and education – are statistically insignificant in the Turkish case. And finally, in the third model, which introduces partisanship variables, none of the coefficients is found to be significant. This finding means that partisanship does not shape the relationship between the perception of the fairness of electoral officers and electoral integrity.

Table 5.2 Analysis of Turkey: perceptions of the fairness of electoral officers

	Model 1	Model 2	Model 3
Predictors	std beta	std beta	std beta
(Intercept)	−0.00	−0.00	−0.03
	(−0.03 to 0.03)	(−0.03 to 0.03)	(−0.08 to 0.02)
Integrity index	0.63***	0.63***	0.62***
	(0.60 to 0.67)	(0.59 to 0.66)	(0.58 to 0.65)
Malpractice index	−0.12***	−0.11***	−0.10***
	(−0.15 to −0.08)	(−0.15 to −0.08)	(−0.14 to −0.06)
Importance of democracy		−0.09***	−0.09***
		(−0.12 to −0.05)	(−0.13 to −0.06)
Income		0.00	0.01
		(−0.03 to 0.04)	(−0.03 to 0.04)
Age		−0.01	−0.01
		(−0.05 to 0.03)	(−0.04 to 0.03)
Gender (female)		0.00	0.00
		(−0.03 to 0.04)	(−0.03 to 0.04)
Education		0.02	0.01
		(−0.02 to 0.05)	(−0.02 to 0.05)
CHP voter			0.06
			(−0.03 to 0.15)
HDP voter			0.12
			(−0.01 to 0.26)
İyi voter			−0.02
			(−0.18 to 0.14)
MHP voter			0.09
			(−0.03 to 0.20)
Observations	1,845	1,845	1,845
R^2/R^2 adjusted	0.430/0.429	0.438/0.435	0.439/0.436

*p<0.05 **p<0.01 ***p<0.001

For Model 3, the base category is the AKP voter

Conclusion

The above findings show that voters' impressions of the electoral officers and electoral management bodies (EMBs) running the election can substantially influence the election's perceived integrity. Voters are more likely to feel that the election was handled with integrity if they have faith in the fairness and impartiality of these persons and organisations.

In that sense, the decisions of EMBs have a significant power to shape these perceptions since EMBs are in charge of various electoral-process operations, such as voter registration, ballot design, and addressing complaints or objections. If citizens view these efforts as fair, transparent, and unbiased, they can add to the election's overall perceived integrity. Conversely, questions about the fairness or impartiality of EMB decision-making can damage public trust in the election's legitimacy. Accordingly, to ensure public confidence in the integrity of the election, EMBs must be transparent and responsible in their decision-making procedures by giving transparent explanations for their actions and responding to voters' and other stakeholders' concerns. EMBs can assist in guaranteeing that elections are viewed to be handled with integrity, making them more likely to be accepted by the public.

Since the perceived integrity of an electoral process is necessary for a functioning democracy, if citizens lose faith in the fairness and impartiality of elections, it can erode the democratic process's legitimacy and lead to widespread mistrust in the political system. In that framework, partisanship may function as a threat since partisanship may alter the opinions related to the electoral management bodies in various ways, which can harm election integrity. Political parties and candidates, for example, may hold opposing opinions on the fairness and impartiality of EMBs and endeavour to influence public opinion about them. This can lead to a situation where the public's opinions of the election process are divided along party lines, with one side viewing the EMB through a skewed lens. Furthermore, voters who strongly support a specific political party or candidate are more likely to interpret EMBs via a partisan lens, further polarising perceptions of the voting process. This might lead to a perception that the election's credibility is based on whatever party or candidate is in power rather than the impartiality and fairness of the electoral process itself.

EMBs must be as neutral and fair as possible to retain public trust in the election process's integrity. This might be difficult in a politicised environment, but it is necessary for the credibility of the democratic process. EMBs should be open and responsible in their decision-making processes and sensitive to all stakeholders' concerns, including political parties and candidates. They can assist in guaranteeing that elections are regarded as being run with honesty, which is critical for the health and stability of any democracy.

References

Aydin, Nizamettin and Sinan Sunar. 2018. 'Seçimlerin Yönetimi Bağlaminda Seçmen Kütüklerinin ve Listelerinin Yerel Idareler Tarafindan Hazirlanmasi: Danimarka Örneği ve Türkiye'de Uygulanabilirliği'. *Selçuk Üniversitesi Adalet Meslek Yüksekokulu Dergisi* 1 (1).

Bowler, Shaun, Thomas Brunell, Todd Donovan and Paul Gronke. 2015. 'Election Administration and Perceptions of Fair Elections'. *Electoral Studies* 38. https://doi.org/10.1016/j.electstud.2015.01.004.

Carothers, Thomas. 1997. 'The Observers Observed'. *Journal of Democracy* 8 (3). https://doi.org/10.1353/jod.1997.0037.

Clark, Alistair. 2019. 'The Cost of Democracy: The Determinants of Spending on the Public Administration of Elections'. *International Political Science Review* 40 (3, SI): 354–69. https://doi.org/10.1177/0192512118824787.

Garnett, Holly Ann. 2019. 'Evaluating Electoral Management Body Capacity'. *International Political Science Review* 40 (3): 335–53. https://doi.org/10.1177/0192512119832924.

Güler, Fatih. 2020. 'Yüksek Seçim Kurulu'nun Yapisal Ve Işlevsel Sorunlarini Giderici Çözümler'. Doctoral dissertation, Uludağ University. https://acikerisim.uludag.edu.tr/bitstream/11452/15463/1/10338123.pdf.

Güngör, Süleyman. 2014. 'Seçim Kanunlarında Demokrat Parti'nin Yaptığı Değişiklikler ve Siyasal Anlamı'. *Mülkiye Dergisi* 29 (247): 100–101.

James, Toby S. 2019. 'Better Workers, Better Elections? Electoral Management Body Workforces and Electoral Integrity Worldwide'. *International Political Science Review* 40 (3): 370–90. https://doi.org/10.1177/0192512119829516.

James, Toby S., Holly Ann Garnett, Leontine Loeber and Carolien van Ham. 2019. 'Electoral Management and the Organisational Determinants of Electoral Integrity: Introduction'. *International Political Science Review* 40 (3): 295–312. https://doi.org/10.1177/0192512119828206.

Joseph, Oliver. 2021. 'Independence in Electoral Management'. Stockholm: IDEA. https://www.idea.int/sites/default/files/publications/independence-in-electoral-management.pdf.

Kerr, Nicholas. 2013. 'Popular Evaluations of Election Quality in Africa: Evidence from Nigeria'. *Electoral Studies* 32 (4). https://doi.org/10.1016/j.electstud.2013.02.010.

Lijphart, Arend. 1997. 'Unequal Participation: Democracy's Unresolved Dilemma. Presidential Address, American Political Science Association, 1996'. *American Political Science Review* 91 (1). https://doi.org/10.2307/2952255.

López-Pintor, Rafael. 2000. 'Electoral Management Bodies as Institutions of Governance' (New York: United Nations Development Programme).

Mann, Christopher B. and Lisa A. Bryant. 2020. 'If You Ask, They Will Come (to Register and Vote): Field Experiments with State Election Agencies on Encouraging Voter Registration'. *Electoral Studies* 63. https://doi.org/10.1016/j.electstud.2019.02.012.

Meyersson, Erik. 2015. 'Digit Tests and the Peculiar Election Dynamics of Turkey's November Elections'. Blog post, 4 November. https://Erikmeyersson.Com/2015/11/04/Digit-Tests-and-the-Peculiar-Election-Dynamics-of-Turkeys-November-Elections/.

Minnis, Terry A. and Niyati Shah. 2020. 'Voter Registration in Today's Democracy: Barriers and Opportunities.' *Human Rights* 45 (1).

Norris, Pippa. 2019a. 'Do Perceptions of Electoral Malpractice Undermine Democratic Satisfaction? The US in Comparative Perspective'. *International Political Science Review* 40 (1): 5–22. https://doi.org/10.1177/0192512118806783.

———. 2019b. Conclusions: The New Research Agenda on Electoral Management'. *International Political Science Review* 40 (3, SI): 391–403. https://doi.org/10.1177/0192512119829869.

Norris, Pippa, Richard W. Frank and Ferran Martínez i Coma. 2014a. *Advancing Electoral Integrity*. Oxford: Oxford University Press.

Norris, Pippa, Richard W. Frank and Ferran Martínez i Coma. 2014b. 'Measuring Electoral Integrity around the World: A New Dataset'. *PS – Political Science and Politics*. https://doi.org/10.1017/S1049096514001061.

Orji, Nkwachukwu. 2017. 'Preventive Action and Conflict Mitigation in Nigeria's 2015 Elections'. *Democratisation* 24 (4). https://doi.org/10.1080/13510347.2016.1191067.

OSCE. 2015. 'Republic of Turkey Parliamentary Elections 7 June 2015: OSCE/ODIHR Limited Election Observation Mission Final Report'. Organization for Security and Co-operation in Europe, Warsaw.

Oy ve Ötesi. 2018. '24 Haziran 2018 Tarihli Cumhurbaşkanı ve Milletvekili Genel Seçimleri Değerlendirme Raporu'. https://oyveotesi.org/wp-content/uploads/2021/12/24-Haziran-2018-Sec%CC%A7im-Raporu.pdf.

Rosenstone, Steven J. and Raymond E. Wolfinger. 1978. 'The Effect of Registration Laws on Voter Turnout'. *American Political Science Review* 72 (1). https://doi.org/10.2307/1953597.

Ruiz-Rufino, R. and S. Birch. 2020. 'The Effect of Alternation in Power on Electoral Intimidation in Democratizing Regimes'. *Journal of Peace Research* 57 (1): 126–39. https://doi.org/10.1177/0022343319885171

Sönmez, Naim. 2014. 'Seçim Sisteminin Demokratikleşmesinin Bir Aşaması:1950 Milletvekili Seçim Kanunu'. *Erzincan Üniversitesi Sosyal Bilimler Enstitüsü Dergisi* 6 (2).

Van Ham, Carolien and Staffan I. Lindberg. 2015. 'From Sticks to Carrots: Electoral Manipulation in Africa, 1986–2012'. *Government and Opposition*. https://doi.org/10.1017/gov.2015.6.

Part 3

CONSEQUENCES OF PERCEIVED DAMAGE TO ELECTORAL INTEGRITY

6

DOES ELECTORAL INTEGRITY MATTER FOR VOTE CHOICE?

Introduction

Following the previous chapter, this one also concentrates on the consequences of electoral problems, arguing that voters may change how they
decide to vote if they believe the election is seriously flawed. Although the electoral integrity literature has touched upon many dimensions of the phenomenon, we still have minimal knowledge of how citizens respond to failures of
electoral integrity when voting is considered. In which conditions does electoral manipulation work for the incumbent? Do citizens perceive these tactics
as manipulative or not? If yes, which factors shape these perceptions? Does
partisanship matter in these perceptions? How do these perceptions affect voting? To answer these questions, this chapter analyses the dynamics of the 2019
İstanbul repeat elections via the lens of electoral integrity.

The Context

In 2019 local elections were held against the background of a difficult economic
situation in Turkey and heated competition between two major party coalitions, the People's Alliance formed by Adalet ve Kalkınma Partisi (the Justice
and Development Party, AKP) and Milliyetçi Hareket Partisi (the Nationalist Action Party, MHP), both government parties, and the Nation Alliance of
the Cumhuriyet Halk Partisi (the Republican Peoples Party, CHP), İyi Party
(The Good Party, İyi), Saadet Partisi (the Felicity Party, SP) and Demokrat Parti

(the Democrat Party, DP). Halkların Demokratik Partisi (the People's Democratic Party, HDP) competed independently but had agreed with Nation's Alliance parties (primarily the CHP) not to run in each other's traditional strongholds, to maximise electoral gains relative to the People's Alliance. The local elections were held to elect provincial and municipal councillors, mayors of regular and metropolitan municipalities, such as İstanbul, Ankara and other major cities. The 2019 municipal elections were the second elections held in Turkey following the 2017 constitutional referendum that converted the country from a parliamentary to a presidential administration. These were the first elections held after full implementation of all the constitutional amendments agreed upon in the referendum. Unlike the presidential and parliamentary elections held soon after the referendum, in June 2018, the 2019 municipal elections were not held under the state of emergency that had been proclaimed after a failed coup attempt in July 2016.

As mentioned above, this chapter focuses on the annulment and rerun in İstanbul of the March elections. In İstanbul this took place on 31 March 2019 as part of country-wide local elections. Along with a mayor for the İstanbul metropolitan municipality, the city's thirty-nine districts went to the polls to choose mayors and councillors. On election night, early returns indicated that Binali Yıldırım, a candidate supported by the incumbent AKP and MHP, had a slim lead over the challenger, Ekrem İmamoğlu, who was backed by the Nation Alliance. However, İmamoğlu passed Yıldırım in the end, with a 0.2 per cent margin, and won the elections. The AKP challenged the result, alleging several election irregularities. The Yüksek Seçim Kurulu (Supreme Election Council, YSK) officials accepted AKP's requests for a complete recount of all votes in five of Istanbul's districts; the other thirty-four districts were instructed to recount invalid and blank ballots only.

After concluding the recount, which took sixteen days, İmamoğlu maintained his lead with around 14,000 votes, down from the 23,000 assigned to him in the original count. Challenging these results, the AKP filed an exceptional case to have the election annulled and rerun. The party's appeal to the YSK was based on a single report that voters had been registered unlawfully in Büyükçekmece, one electoral district in İstanbul, and irregularities in selecting the ballot-box committee presidents. At the same time, police had launched an investigation to find 'fake voters', and numerous electoral officials and public workers were arrested on allegations of fraud without solid evidence. Evaluating the AKP's appeal, the YSK ruled that the İstanbul mayoral election should be annulled and repeated on 23 June 2019. The rerun results indicated a significant swing in favour of İmamoğlu, who won the elections with 54.2 per cent of the vote against Yıldırım's 45.0 per cent, a margin of nearly 800,000 votes. To explain and understand this gap between the voting in two consecutive elections, this study hypothesises that the decision of the YSK was not welcomed by İstanbul voters, both AKP supporters and opposition voters. To test this hypothesis, this study employed a list experiment to tap voters' concerns about the YSK's repeat decision, which we have included in a representative survey of İstanbul. Findings indicate that both governing party supporters and other voters indeed thought that the decision had damaged the credibility of the elections. This finding contributes to the electoral integrity literature since the current literature usually categorises electoral malpractices as harmful to democratic functioning. However, in this instance the Turkish case demonstrates that electoral malpractices might also contribute to improve democratic functioning.

The Literature

Political actors resort to electoral manipulation with several purposes in mind. The first and most obvious reason is to win elections, and many tools can help with this, including rigging ballot boxes, intimidation or vote-buying (Cantú and García-Ponce 2015; Collier and Vicente 2014; Frye, Reuter and Szakonyi 2019). More than just winning elections, parties may also employ the tools of electoral manipulation to build big vote margins, to discourage rivals from competing in future elections, or dissuade their supporters from turning out to vote (Simpser 2012; 2013). But, as mentioned in previous chapters, more recently political actors have tended not to use these tools overtly but instead put a lot of work into builing electoral victories that reflect the actual preferences of voters. Real successes are better than bought ones, for many reasons: rigging elections is expensive, nationwide electoral malpractice has very high administrative costs and, most importantly, citizens, in general, disapprove of such tactics (Reuter and Szakonyi 2021). Research has also found that, on one hand, electoral manipulation makes a victory look suspicious and, on the other, can be used to give the impression of invincibility (Magaloni 2006).

Several studies have showed that the fairness of elections influences people's views about political authority and institutions (Birch 2008; Blader and Tyler 2003; Magalhães and Aguiar-Conraria 2018). Such studies argue that, normatively, fairness and integrity are required for every election, and voters' attitudes to malpractice may differ depending on whether they support the winners or the losers. For example, voters become more suspicious of elections won by parties they oppose (Beaulieu 2014), and seldom vote against 'their' party to punish political wrong-doing such as corruption and violations of democratic ideals (Graham and Svolik 2020; Svolik 2019; Klašnja 2017). Solaz, de Geus and De Vries (2018) even say that partisans may be more likely to be corrupt out of loyalty to their party. In a recent and detailed study Aarslew (2022), borrowing from Gaines et al. (2007), defines a sequence of behaviours by voters when they witness electoral fraud. According to this sequence, first voters decide whether the fraud has happened, then they think about its meaning (i.e. how important it is) and finally they decide whether to alter their opinions or not.

When people acquire information that runs counter to deeply held beliefs, they may deny it or say it does not matter (Taber and Lodge 2006). In that perspective, accurate information may even promote motivated thinking, as individuals may become very selective in how they assign blame and responsibility (Bisgaard 2019), finding ways to avoid blaming 'their' party. Partisans tend to neglect the electoral malpractices of their party and show more sensitivity to allegations about other parties (Claassen and Ensley 2016). More importantly, when partisans are subjected to accusations of electoral malpractice, they develop an unavoidable dissonance between their party choice and the actual malpractice. Because dissonance is uncomfortable, they tend to change one of their beliefs, and since it is hard for them to abandon their party, they may prefer to change how they regard wrongdoing or find ways to avoid blaming their party (Tomz and Weeks 2020).

Accordingly, one option for voters is to not change the vote they had already decided to cast. This choice is well documented since, for one thing, motivated reasoning theories suggest that partisanship provides lenses that make voters more likely to perceive onformation beneficial to their political orientation (Campbell et al. 1960, 130–35). In other words, it is likely that voters' previous beliefs and knowledge guide their actions upon receiving new information, and they are pretty selective about how they assign credit or blame (Doherty and Wolak 2012; Bisgaard 2019). From this perspective, partisans do not mind when their party resorts to electoral misconduct since they have different standards for evaluation. These standards also tend to exaggerate the outrage about out-group misconduct (Anderson and Tverdova 2003). In addition, partisans also tend to downplay wrong-doings of their own party, to show them as not serious and minimise the adverse effects.

It sometimes happens that voters change their perceptions but not their behaviour. That is to say, although voters may reconsider their party preferences, this may not be enough to alter their vote choice. Even though citizens demand elections with integrity, they also have distinct party preferences, and partisans may be ready to tolerate unfair methods if these produce favourable outcomes (Bøggild 2015; Brockner and Wiesenfeld 1996; Magalhães and Aguiar-Conraria 2018). In other words, voters may respond differently to unjust methods when they achieve the desired outcomes because structural constraints affect the moral anger resulting from unfair practices. This is a different stance to the motivated reasoning theories, explained in the previous paragraph, which argue that individuals see evidence of wrong-doing without prejudice and respond adversely to it. Providing evidence for this explanation, Graham and Svolik (2020) showed that American voters would prefer to vote for a candidate from their party who opposes democratic principles than to switch parties. Findings show that voters fail to prioritise democratic ideals when conflicts arise with their political identity, and hence fail to recognise misconduct within their own party. In sum, according to this perspective, voters may tend to tolerate electoral misconduct, depending on how much they desire a particular political result.

However, voters *may* change their vote after evaluating allegations of malpractice. As one of the groups most sensitive to electoral malpractice, regime supporters are more likely than opponents to think that elections are fair since they are more likely to believe regime propaganda. In consequence, partisanship biases may keep them from believing allegations of malpractice (Reuter and Szakonyi 2021). Accordingly, it is plausible to expect that regime supporters are most likely to punish incumbents when they find out about electoral dishonesty. That is to say, weakly aligned voters or 'swing voters' who already have doubts about how fair elections might be are less likely to change how they vote on learning of fraud (Reuter and Szakonyi 2021). Electoral manipulation can potentially decrease support for the incumbent, even among devoted supporters, since it is illegal and those responsible are breaking the law.

Additionally, each instance of election manipulation also has moral valance. Though moral assessments of electoral manipulation are complex and underinvestigated, the information at hand suggests that most voters consider it improper (Gonzalez Ocantos, de Jonge and Nickerson 2014). So, although there are good reasons to think incumbents may lose votes if voters find out they have rigged elections, few studies have looked at this idea. In an early example, Weitz-Shapiro (2014) showed that middle-class voters abandon politicians who participate in vote-buying. In a more recent example, Gutiérrez-Romero and LeBas found that voters are less inclined to support politicians rumoured to have participated in pre-election misconduct (Gutiérrez-Romero and LeBas 2020).

I argue that perceptions of the legitimacy of elections play a crucial role in voters' decisions under such circumstances. In their seminal study, Elklit and Reynolds (2002) argued that, with political efficacy, individual experiences of the conduct of elections constitute a significant factor in developing democratic legitimacy. At the same time, they also argued that the quality of election administration should be included among the factors that must be carefully studied and analysed before judging how legitimate an election was.

According to the relevant literature, citizens follow a source of authority for three reasons: first, they fear being penalised by enforcement agents; second, they see compliance as being in their self-interest; and third, they feel the authority merits obedience. Although studies of the first two processes of coercion and co-optation are common, it is relatively less likely to find academic work on the third mechanism, legitimacy (Gerschewski 2013). Stressing the importance of the first two motivations, research has shown that institutions operating in illiberal settings, electoral management bodies (EMBs) for instance, have the potential to help sustain that system (Gandhi and Lust-Okar 2009; Brancati 2014). At the same time, elections help governments in illiberal settings learn about the public's policy preferences, enabling them to react to dissatisfaction or reward their base while limiting the opposition by demonstrating the regime's strength and popularity (Magaloni 2010; Brownlee 2011). Although highly illuminating, this literature has generally ignored elections' capacity to legitimise governments. Voters have their own opinions on the legitimacy of the political system, i.e. the degree to which the ruler has the authority to make governance choices, regardless of the individual citizen's agreement with such decisions (Dukalskis and Gerschewski 2017). Although legitimacy views exist at the individual level, societal norms on what provides credibility to a political system will significantly impact the public's views, generating a need for all political systems to strive for legitimacy by persuading citizens that their government conforms to these norms (Tyler 2006).

Administrations in illiberal settings tend to use force and co-optation to reproduce their systems. They also have to establish a level of legitimacy, needing less pressure and co-optation to retain control while proving their right to govern (Dickson, Gordon and Huber 2015). Since using force can lead to crises that impair the regime's financial and repressive ability, relying on them to a lesser extent should result in higher resilience to adverse shocks. In such settings, elections carry out an unusual and multi-faceted function. Since democracy is now a virtually universal norm that shapes ideas of the right to rule, virtually all governments, even totalitarian ones, claim to be democratic. Free and fair elections, in that sense, are commonly acknowledged as the most important tool by which rulers show their commitment to democratic government. Accordingly, governments often utilise elections to legitimise themselves by persuading their constituents that they rule democratically (Yukawa, Kushima and Hidaka 2020; O'Donnell 2007). To achieve that aim, these regimes should also convince voters that elections conform to democratic norms and that they, as citizens, indeed have an authentic voice in who wins (Williamson 2021). Even where they succeed in doing so, citizens usually doubt the legitimacy of administrations (Rothstein 2009). Accordingly, it is highly probable that citizens may discount elections in such settings, regardless of their support for democracy or evaluations of electoral integrity. Similarly, other characteristics that affect perceptions of legitimacy, such as effective and honest governance, may be more relevant for those living under these regimes (Levi, Tyler and Sacks 2009).

In light of the above discussion, although the literature presents scientific evidence on the link between electoral integrity and legitimacy, we have only scant knowledge of how this link shapes voting behaviour. In consequence, this chapter argues that YSK's decision damaged the credibility of the 2019 İstanbul elections and created a legitimacy problem, resulting in significant numbers of voters changing their vote choice. Accordingly, the study tests the following hypothesis:

> H1: Although the YSK's repeat decision provided a second chance for the incumbent AKP to win, AKP supporters thought that YSK's decision had damaged the credibility of the elections.

Data and Methods

The study's sample was randomly selected among 959 electoral neighbourhoods of İstanbul. For that purpose, first, the research team compiled the electoral data published for the most recent seven elections, which is published at the ballot-box level, and aggregated it at district level. Then, six clusters were formed after a cluster analysis which considered how votes were split between the parties standing, differences and variances among the neighbourhoods during those seven elections. Third, these neighbourhood clusters were stratified, and sample sizes were determined proportionately to the current number of voters in each cluster. The design targeted a +/− 0.03 margin of error at the 95 per cent confidence interval and, accordingly, 8 participants were selected for interview from each of the 125 neighbourhoods that appeared in the final sample. During the design and implementation of the survey, the research team employed neither any type of quota nor household address substitutions; and after validation of the questionnaires returned, analysis is based on 1,019 households in 37 districts of Istanbul.

This survey included a list experiment designed to measure perceptions of the repeat election decision of the YSK. A list experiment is an analytical tool where respondents give the number of items on a list that correspond to their experience but refrain from identifying specific items. It is an unobtrusive method for measuring participation in or experience of sensitive topics, such as electoral studies (Blair and Imai 2010; Gilens, Sniderman and Kuklinski 1998; Imai et al. 2011; Imai and Tingley 2012; Toros and Birch 2019). This study followed a conventional design and randomly assigned respondents to control and treatment groups. The control group were shown a list of factors shaping an election's credibility and asked to indicate how many items had been influential in their evaluations of the credibility of the March 2019 elections. The treatment group were shown the same list with the addition of one extra item – the YSK's decision to repeat the election. Both groups were asked to indicate how many items had shaped their evaluations, but not which ones. Since respondents are instructed not to disclose the items that shape their perception, there is no way of knowing whether any individual in the treatment group assessed the YSK's decision as harmful to the election's credibility. However, by comparing the average number of items selected between the two groups, we can determine what proportion of respondents thought the YSK's decision had damaged the credibility of the election. Let us assume the mean for the control group was 1 and that for the treatment group 1.5, respectively. The mean in the treatment condition represents the proportion of respondents who thought the YSK's decision harmful, which would be 50 per cent in this example. Going one step further, to explore the relationships between respondents' characteristics and their answers to our sensitive item, we employed the technique suggested by Blair and Imai (2010). Their method moves beyond the difference-in-means mentioned above by developing new multi-variate regression estimators for various types of list experiment. Hence, their methodology provides researchers with essential tools to efficiently examine who is more likely to answer sensitive items in the affirmative, and which respondents are likely to answer sensitive questions differently, depending on whether asked directly or indirectly, through a list experiment.

The wording of the list experiment question was as follows:

Q: Recently, we have witnessed some problems related to the elections. Now I will present some examples of issues that were thought to harm the credibility of the last local election. We are curious about which of the following, in your opinion, has impacted the credibility of the previous election. Please do not tell me which ones, only tell me how many.

There were doubts about the last local election's credibility because . . .

Control Group
1. The media did not convey election news in a fair and equal manner
2. There was not enough information about this election
3. Votes were not counted fairly

Treatment Group
1. The media did not convey election news in a fair and equal manner
2. There was not enough information about this election
3. Votes were not counted fairly
4. YSK cancelled the elections in Istanbul (sensitive item)

Respondents also answered the following direct question: 'Do you think the YSK's decision to repeat the election in Istanbul damaged the credibility of this election?' Lastly, they answered questions on partisanship and demographic characteristics.

The results indicate that voters evaluated the YSK's decision as having negative impact on the credibility of the elections and that a list experiment proved a valuable way to measure this.

The first two rows of the second column of Table 6.1. display the mean values for the control and treatment groups, which were 2.1 and 2.7, respectively. As the third column of Table 1 suggests, when asked directly 54 per cent of respondents in the control group stated that the YSK's decision had damaged the credibility of the election. In the list experiment, on the other hand, 60 per cent of voters thought that the repeat election decision had discredited the elections (by selecting the additional item added to the list). The difference between the control and treatment groups is significant at the .01 level. Finally, the third column of Table 6.1 indicates a 6 per cent difference in perception between those in the first group who received the direct question and those in the second group who answered the list experiment. These results confirm the utility of list experiments in this context. Figure 6.1. presents this difference graphically.

The analysis also tried to establish whether AKP supporters backed the YSK's decision, using Blair and Imai's technique. The model used the perceptions of the credibility of elections as the dependent variable. The primary independent variable, AKP party identification, is a dummy, where '1' denotes support for the AKP and '0' all other positions. The models, coupled with demographics, were also controlled for political interest and turnout in the March elections.[1] To

Table 6.1 Descriptive results

	List experiment – # items identified	Estimated (%)
Control	2.10 (0.78)	54 (asked directly)
Treatment	2.70 (0.96)	60 (additional item on list)

*Means (standard errors)

[1] The analysis is carried out using the R package 'List: Multivariate Statistical Analysis for the Item Count Technique' (Blair and Imai 2010)

Mean Differences

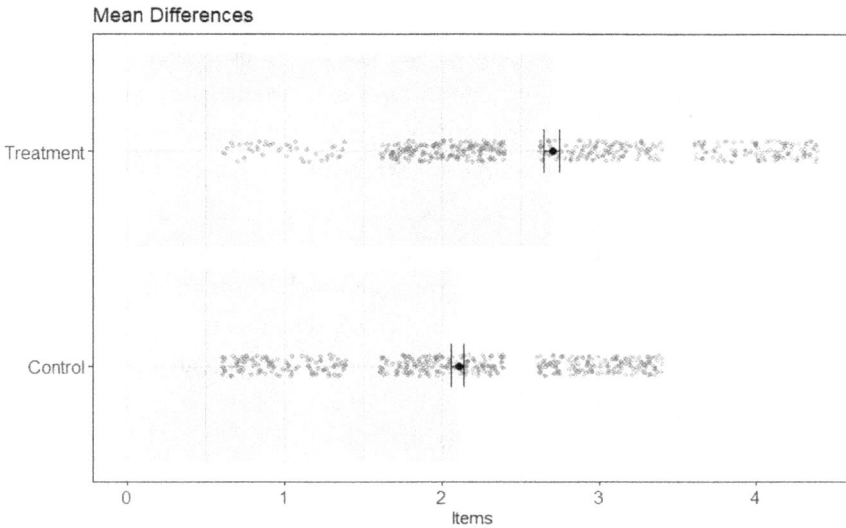

Figure 6.1 Difference between treatment and control groups

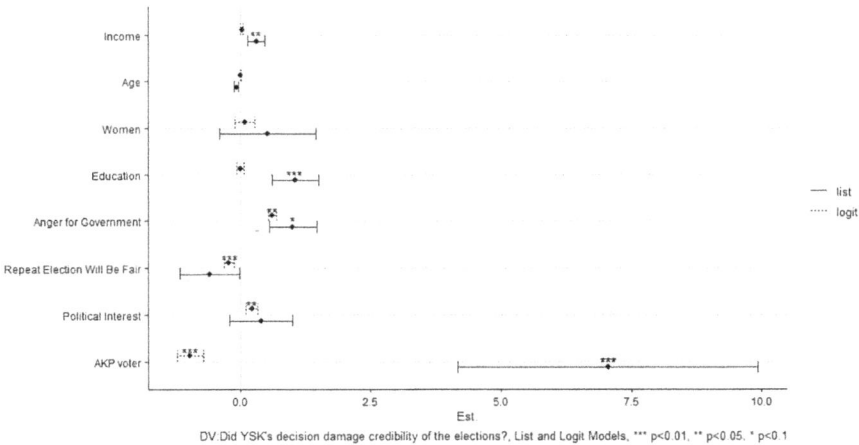

DV:Did YSK's decision damage credibility of the elections?, List and Logit Models, *** p<0.01, ** p<0.05, * p<0.1

Figure 6.2 Evaluations of the credibility of elections and AKP partisanship

recall, we hypothesise that, like other party voters, supporters of the incumbent AKP also thought YSK's decision had damaged the credibility of the elections. Figure 6.2 presents the coefficient plots of our model. The model designated by solid lines represents the list experiment results, and the one with dashed lines shows the coefficients of the logistic regression of the direct question.

Findings show that although the coefficient for the AKP voters was negative and significant in the logit model, it turned out to be positive and significant in the list model. This finding indicates that, when asked indirectly via the list experiment tool, AKP partisans displayed their discomfort at the YSK's decision. These results provide part-support for H1.

Conclusion

This chapter focused on the 2019 İstanbul rerun elections and described the repercussions and consequences of the YSK's decision for electoral integrity. The rerun election for mayor of İstanbul was a highly anticipated event that attracted significant attention in Turkey and internationally. The election was seen as a major test of the political strength of the ruling AKP and President Recep Tayyip Erdogan, who had dominated Turkish politics for over a decade. Ekrem İmamoğlu, the CHP candidate, campaigned on a platform of transparency, accountability and change and found a strong base among voters, and he secured a decisive victory, winning with a margin of nearly 800,000 votes. It was also seen as a sign that the AKP's grip on power was weakening and that the Turkish electorate was becoming increasingly dissatisfied with the party's performance. The election was also significant for Turkey's democracy, as it marked the first time in twenty-five years that the opposition had won control of İstanbul. This was seen as a positive sign for Turkish democracy and a step towards a more pluralistic and competitive political landscape.

Electoral manipulation can work in favour of the incumbent in certain conditions, although the effectiveness of such tactics can vary depending on the specific circumstances. Incumbent governments may use electoral manipulation to maintain their hold on power through overt efforts to interfere with the electoral process or through more subtle tactics such as gerrymandering or voter suppression.

Whether or not citizens perceive these tactics as manipulative can depend on several factors. For example, citizens may be more likely to perceive electoral manipulation as illegitimate if it involves overt interference with the electoral process, such as voter intimidation or ballot-stuffing. On the other hand, more subtle tactics, such as gerrymandering or voter suppression, may be less likely to be perceived as manipulative, especially if they are not widely understood or presented as being necessary for other reasons. Partisanship can also change how people see election fraud. For example, voters who strongly support the incumbent party or candidate may be less likely to see its tactics as manipulative. In contrast, voters who support the opposition party may be more critical of such tactics.

Perceptions of electoral manipulation can influence voting behaviour. If individuals believe the electoral process is being rigged in favour of the incumbent, they may be less likely to vote for the incumbent or even vote at all. This can erode the perceived legitimacy of the electoral process and lead to widespread distrust of the political system. Consequently, elections must be conducted with integrity to retain public trust in the democratic process and ensure its effectiveness.

In conclusion, the 2019 İstanbul rerun mayoral election was a major political event that had significant implications for Turkish politics and the country's future direction. It was a turning point for Turkish democracy and a sign of a more competitive and pluralistic political landscape.

References

Aarslew, Laurits F. 2022. 'Why Don't Partisans Sanction Electoral Malpractice?' *British Journal of Political Science*, 53 (2), 407–23. https://doi.org/10.1017/S0007123422000126.

Anderson, Christopher J. and Yuliya V. Tverdova. 2003. 'Corruption, Political Allegiances, and Attitudes Toward Government in Contemporary Democracies'. *American Journal of Political Science* 47 (1): 91–109. https://doi.org/10.1111/1540-5907.00007.

Beaulieu, Emily. 2014. 'From Voter ID to Party ID: How Political Parties Affect Perceptions of Election Fraud in the US'. *Electoral Studies* 35 (35): 24–32. https://doi.org/10.1016/j.electstud.2014.03.003.

Birch, Sarah. 2008. 'Electoral Institutions and Popular Confidence in Electoral Processes: A Cross-National Analysis'. *Electoral Studies* 27 (2): 305–20. https://doi.org/10.1016/j.electstud.2008.01.005.

Bisgaard, Martin. 2019. 'How Getting the Facts Right Can Fuel Partisan-Motivated Reasoning'. *American Journal of Political Science* 63 (4). https://doi.org/10.1111/ajps.12432.

Blader, Tom R. and Steven L. Tyler. 2003. 'A Four-Component Model of Procedural Justice: Defining the Meaning of a "Fair" Process'. *Personality & Social Psychology Bulletin* 29 (6): 747–58. https://doi.org/10.1177/0146167203029006007.

Blair, Graeme and Kosuke Imai. 2010. 'List: Statistical Methods for the Item Count Technique and List Experiment'. The Comprehensive R Archive Network (CRAN). https://cran.r-project.org/web/packages/list/list.pdf.

Bøggild, Troels. 2015. 'How Politicians' Reelection Efforts Can Reduce Public Trust, Electoral Support, and Policy Approval'. *Political Psychology* 37 (6): 901–19. https://doi.org/10.1111/pops.12303.

Brancati, Dawn. 2014. 'Democratic Authoritarianism: Origins and Effects'. *Annual Review of Political Science* 17 (1): 313–26. https://doi.org/10.1146/annurev-polisci-052013-115248.

Brockner, Batia M. and Joel Wiesenfeld. 1996. 'An Integrative Framework for Explaining Reactions to Decisions: Interactive Effects of Outcomes and Procedures'. *Psychological Bulletin* 120 (2): 189–208. https://doi.org/10.1037/0033-2909.120.2.189.

Brownlee, Jason. 2011. 'Executive Elections in the Arab World: When and How Do They Matter?' *Comparative Political Studies* 44 (7): 807–28. https://doi.org/10.1177/0010414011402034.

Campbell, Angus, Philip Converse, Warren Miller and Donald E. Stokes. 1960. *The American Voter*. Ann Arbor, MI: University of Michigan Press.

Cantú, Francisco and Omar García-Ponce. 2015. 'Partisan Losers' Effects: Perceptions of Electoral Integrity in Mexico'. *Electoral Studies* 39: 1–14. https://doi.org/10.1016/j.electstud.2015.03.004.

Claassen, Ryan L. and Michael J. Ensley. 2016. 'Motivated Reasoning and Yard-Sign-Stealing Partisans: Mine Is a Likable Rogue, Yours Is a Degenerate Criminal'. *Political Behavior* 38 (2). https://doi.org/10.1007/s11109-015-9313-9.

Collier, Paul and Pedro C. Vicente. 2014. 'Votes and Violence: Evidence from a Field Experiment in Nigeria'. *Economic Journal*. https://doi.org/10.1111/ecoj.12109.

Dickson, Eric S., Sanford C. Gordon and Gregory A. Huber. 2015. 'Institutional Sources of Legitimate Authority: An Experimental Investigation'. *American Journal of Political Science* 59 (1): 109–27. https://doi.org/10.1111/ajps.12139.

Doherty, David and Jennifer Wolak. 2012. 'When Do the Ends Justify the Means? Evaluating Procedural Fairness'. *Political Behavior* 34: 301–23. https://doi.org/10.1007/s11109-011-9166-9.

Dukalskis, Johannes and Alexander Gerschewski. 2017. 'What Autocracies Say (and What Citizens Hear): Proposing Four Mechanisms of Autocratic Legitimation'. *Contemporary Politics* 23 (3): 251–68. https://doi.org/10.1080/13569775.2017.1304320.

Elklit, Jørgen and Andrew Reynolds. 2002. 'The Impact of Election Administration on the Legitimacy of Emerging Democracies: A New Comparative Politics Research

Agenda'. *Commonwealth & Comparative Politics* 40 (2): 86–119. https://doi.org/10.1080/713999584.

Frye, Timothy, Ora John Reuter and David Szakonyi. 2019. 'Hitting Them With Carrots: Voter Intimidation and Vote Buying in Russia'. *British Journal of Political Science* 49 (3): 857–81. https://doi.org/10.1017/S0007123416000752.

Gaines, James H., Paul J. Quirk, Buddy Peyton, Jay Verkuilen and Brian J. Kuklinski. 2007. 'Same Facts, Different Interpretations: Partisan Motivation and Opinion on Iraq'. *The Journal of Politics* 69 (4): 957–74. https://doi.org/10.1111/j.1468-2508.2007.00601.x.

Gandhi, Ellen and Jennifer Lust-Okar. 2009. 'Elections under Authoritarianism'. *Annual Review of Political Science* 12 (1): 403–22. https://doi.org/10.1146/annurev.polisci.11.060106.095434.

Gerschewski, Johannes. 2013. 'The Three Pillars of Stability: Legitimation, Repression, and Co-Optation in Autocratic Regimes'. *Democratisation* 20 (1): 13–38. https://doi.org/10.1080/13510347.2013.738860.

Gilens, Martin, Paul M. Sniderman and James H. Kuklinski. 1998. 'Affirmative Action and the Politics of Realignment'. *British Journal of Political Science*. https://doi.org/10.1017/S0007123498000143.

Gonzalez Ocantos, Ezequiel, Chad Kiewiet de Jonge and David W. Nickerson. 2014. 'The Conditionality of Vote-Buying Norms: Experimental Evidence from Latin America'. *American Journal of Political Science*. https://doi.org/10.1111/ajps.12047.

Graham, Matthew H. and Milan W. Svolik. 2020. 'Democracy in America? Partisanship, Polarisation, and the Robustness of Support for Democracy in the United States'. *American Political Science Review* 114 (2): 392–409. https://doi.org/10.1017/S0003055420000052.

Gutiérrez-Romero, Roxana and Adrienne LeBas. 2020. 'Does Electoral Violence Affect Vote Choice and Willingness to Vote? Conjoint Analysis of a Vignette Experiment'. *Journal of Peace Research* 57 (1): 77–92. https://doi.org/10.1177/0022343319892677.

Imai, Kosuke, Luke Keele, Dustin Tingley and Teppei Yamamoto. 2011. 'Unpacking the Black Box of Causality: Learning about Causal Mechanisms from Experimental and Observational Studies'. *American Political Science Review* 105 (4): 765. https://doi.org/10.1017/s0003055411000414.

Imai, Kosuke and Dustin Tingley. 2012. 'A Statistical Method for Empirical Testing of Competing Theories'. *American Journal of Political Science* 56 (1): 218–36. https://doi.org/10.1111/j.1540-5907.2011.00555.x.

Klašnja, Marko. 2017. 'Uninformed Voters and Corrupt Politicians'. *American Politics Research* 45 (2): 256–79. https://doi.org/10.1177/1532673x16684574.

Levi, Audrey, Tom R. Tyler and Margaret Sacks. 2009. 'Conceptualizing Legitimacy, Measuring Legitimating Beliefs'. *American Behavioral Scientist* 53 (3): 354–75. https://doi.org/10.1177/0002764209338797.

Magalhães, Pedro C. and Luís C. Aguiar-Conraria. 2018. 'Procedural Fairness, the Economy, and Support for Political Authorities'. *Political Psychology* 40 (1): 165–81. https://doi.org/10.1111/pops.12500.

Magaloni, Beatriz. 2006. *Voting for Autocracy: Hegemonic Party Survival and Its Demise in Mexico*. Cambridge: Cambridge University Press.

———. 2010. 'The Game of Electoral Fraud and the Ousting of Authoritarian Rule'. *American Journal of Political Science* 54 (3). https://doi.org/10.1111/j.1540-5907.2010.00458.x.

O'Donnell, Guillermo. 2007. 'The Perpetual Crises of Democracy'. *Journal of Democracy* 18 (1): 5–11. https://doi.org/10.1353/jod.2007.0012.

Reuter, Ora John and David Szakonyi. 2021. 'Electoral Manipulation and Regime Support'. *World Politics* 73 (2): 275–314. https://doi.org/10.1017/S0043887120000234.

Rothstein, Bo. 2009. 'Creating Political Legitimacy: Electoral Democracy versus Quality of Government'. *American Behavioral Scientist* 53 (3): 311–30. https://doi.org/10.1177/0002764209338795.

Simpser, Alberto. 2012. 'Does Electoral Manipulation Discourage Voter Turnout? Evidence from Mexico'. *The Journal of Politics* 74 (3): 782–95. https://doi.org/10.1017/S0022381612000333.

———. 2013. *Why Governments and Parties Manipulate Elections: Theory, Practice, and Implications*. Cambridge: Cambridge University Press. https://doi.org/10.1017/CBO9781139343824.

Solaz, Catherine E., Roosmarijn de Geus and Hector De Vries. 2018. 'In-Group Loyalty and the Punishment of Corruption'. *Comparative Political Studies* 52 (6): 896–926. https://doi.org/10.1177/0010414018797951.

Svolik, Milan W. 2019. 'Polarisation versus Democracy'. *Journal of Democracy* 30 (3): 20–32. https://doi.org/10.1353/jod.2019.0039.

Taber, Charles S. and Milton Lodge. 2006. 'Motivated Skepticism in the Evaluation of Political Beliefs'. *American Journal of Political Science* 50 (3): 755–69. https://doi.org/10.1111/j.1540-5907.2006.00214.x.

Tomz, Michael and Jessica L. P. Weeks. 2020. 'Public Opinion and Foreign Electoral Intervention'. *American Political Science Review* 114 (3). https://doi.org/10.1017/S0003055420000064.

Toros, Emre and Sarah Birch. 2019. 'Who Are the Targets of Familial Electoral Coercion? Evidence from Turkey.' *Democratisation* 26 (8): 1342–61. https://doi.org/10.1080/13510347.2019.1639151.

Tyler, Tom R. 2006. 'Psychological Perspectives on Legitimacy and Legitimation'. *Annual Review of Psychology* 57 (1): 375–400. https://doi.org/10.1146/annurev. psych.57.102904.190038.

Weitz-Shapiro, Rebecca. 2014. *Curbing Clientelism in Argentina: Politics, Poverty, and Social Policy.* New York: Cambridge University Press.

Williamson, Scott. 2021. 'Elections, Legitimacy, and Compliance in Authoritarian Regimes: Evidence from the Arab World'. *Democratisation* 28 (8): 1483–1504. https://doi.org/10.1080/13510347.2021.1929180.

Yukawa, Taku, Kaoru Kushima and Kaori Hidaka. 2020. 'Coups and Framing: How Do Militaries Justify the Illegal Seizure of Power?' *Democratisation* 27 (5): 816–35. https://doi.org/10.1080/13510347.2020.1740207.

7

HOW DO PUBLIC PERCEPTIONS OF PROBLEMS WITH ELECTORAL INTEGRITY SHAPE TRUST IN GOVERNMENT?

Introduction

Do problems related to electoral integrity shape trust in institutions? If so, how? As the credibility of the elections worldwide appears, more and more, to be called into distrust owing to doubts about false news, widespread voter fraud, voter intimidation, cyber attacks and gerrymandering, the damaging impact of these events spills over and raises broader questions, especially on the cornerstones of democratic functioning. Accordingly, this chapter analyses the link between electoral integrity and trust in government.

In the mid-1970s Michel Crozier, Samuel Huntington and Joji Watanuki opened a discussion on what they termed 'the increasing delegitimation of authority', in which they argued that the operation of democracy itself is integral to a high degree of public trust in democratic government and its institutions. This argument resonates in many areas as leading policy leaders and elected officials remain convinced that a severe challenge faces representative democracy as trust levels fluctuate. In December 2014 the President of the European Commission regarded the 'public negativity about politics and politicians, the resentment' as the critical issue facing the European Union. The High Representative of the Union for Foreign Affairs and Security Policy indicated 'widespread democratic malaise' in January 2013, forty years after the Trilateral Commission was created (Zmerli and van der Meer 2017). Similarly, focusing on trust, prime ministers of Japan, the Netherlands and the United

Kingdom highlighted the collapse of political trust and pledged to reverse the process. Not surprisingly, the issue has also found a considerable place in scholarly debate (Thomassen 2015). The relevance of political trust was first raised by Almond and Verba (1963) in the context of the Second Wave of democratisation, and the issue elevated and regained prominence after the Third Wave of democratisation during the 1970s.

During the early years, these academic discussions on trust argued that representative democracy might not survive an ongoing trust crisis (A. H. Miller 1974). However, the analyses that followed during the 1990s showed that democratic systems could live with low levels of trust in institutions. According to this new view, far from causing a collapse in democratic systems as a whole, low levels of trust force states' institutions to alter from within, causing some major institutional reconfigurations (Klingemann and Fuchs 1995, 6–7). A third and (so far) final view claims that low and diminishing levels of trust in politics do not inherently cause a crisis or change in representative democracy and its institutions. However, they should be monitored with great care since low levels of trust may signal democratic *malaise* (Norris 2011a). Four different areas of subject matter can be attributed to these views (van der Meer 2017). The first deals with political trust's conceptual and philosophical essence. The second line is primarily descriptive and focuses empirically on longitudinal trends and cross-national differences in political trust. The third area revolves around the human and contextual causes of political trust. The fourth examines the micro-, meso-, and macro-level consequences of political trust, or the lack of it.

Although previous research has provided evidence of a link between trust in institutions and well-functioning electoral processes (Birch 2008; 2010; Norris 2014), careful operationalisation is still needed to understand the relationship between electoral integrity and institutional trust. As these studies aptly suggest, it is logical to expect elections with integrity to diffuse trust in institutions. In that sense, it becomes vital to understand how electoral procedures are perceived in order to gain a more comprehensive picture of trust in institutions, alongside trust in other institutions that operate within the domains of the economy, healthcare and education, which citizens traditionally use to build trust. This chapter utilises the input and output theories of democratic legitimacy (Norris 2019) to unpack the above claim.

Electoral Integrity and Trust

Since the early 1960s, academics and practitioners have tried to understand the sources of trust in institutions since support for democratic systems as a whole is believed to rest upon popular trust in government structures, which include political parties, political assemblies and the judiciary. The decreasing levels of trust in these institutions can trigger authoritarian backsliding (Norris 2019). In that sense, the levels of trust in electoral processes becomes especially crucial since more and more voters have become highly distrustful of politicians, suspicious of national and foreign government structures, and disillusioned with political values and mechanisms. Lack of trust in the capacity of democratic organisations contributes to a lack of political participation, a decline in voting and disengagement from traditional politics (Birch 2010). Moreover, the deterioration of trust in institutions is often thought to boost mass support for authoritarian-populist leaders who manipulate fear that votes are being stolen and that electoral mechanisms are being manipulated (Norris 2017b). This specific problem is amplified in hybrid regimes that are more vulnerable to democratic backsliding (Levitsky and Ziblatt 2018), making trust in elections even more critical, possibly providing the only mechanism for peaceful transition between governments.

The literature mentioned above generally referred to the idea that citizens' support for political institutions can be conceptualised under five major headings, ranging from diffused/general trust to specific trust, where the latter refers to trust in institutions, such as parties, parliaments and governments (Easton 1965). General/diffused support for a political system necessitates interaction among many aspects, including trust in the government. First, there are ideological motives for people to trust the government. Such trust in government is amplified when individuals believe in shared goals and priorities or mutual interests (March and Olsen 1989) and regularly participate in political-administrative processes. However, trust in the government can also depend on institutional credibility, which implies consistent long-term familiarity with the government's structured framework, laws, functions and functioning. Macroeconomic indicators, such as economic performance and unemployment levels, may also affect the trust in governments (Miller and Listhaug 1999).

Easton's definition, mentioned above, incorporates two other core elements related to trust: process and output. In this classification, 'process' refers to the organisation of decision-making processes (i.e. how competent government employees are, the participation of actors and parties affectedby the decision, etc.). The trust in governments that execute well-designed administrative procedures is expected to be high, even where their 'output' is unfavourable for the actors taking part, simply because the process is viewed as acceptable. Conversely, 'output' involves the conventional question 'who gets what'. The basic assumption behind this element is that the public's trust in government depends on what they gain, regardless of the mechanism leading to the outcome. According to that understanding, if they wish to increase support governments should 'do the right thing' instead of focusing on 'doing it in the right ways' (Christensen and Lagreid 2005).

Governments accumulate the highest levels of trust when they combine the general and specific components of trust. They may perform highly diffuse tasks poorly where these have low impact on specific types of trust since dissatisfaction with lousy performance in administrative tasks does not threaten their basis. On the contrary, when low, diffuse support is combined with high, specific support this may mean that citizens are suspicious of their government. Still, their evaluations of their government are not negative in general (Goodsell 1994). Low scores for both types of trust suggest that the government is facing a crisis of legitimacy, and research has shown that a general decline of trust in political institutions is more worrying than dissatisfaction with specific individuals (Miller and Listhaug 1999).

Moreover, trust in government has both structural and personal features. In that sense, citizens' trust is directed to the system, and politicians may earn distinct types. That is to say, citizens may trust the political system as a whole, including the politicians, or they might trust the system but have intense mistrust of politics or of individual actors. This mistrust may be a result of negative experiences with government representatives. Alternatively, citizens may develop trust in politicians rather than in the whole system, where these actors are successful in their policy areas or have considerable charisma. Lastly, citizens may develop cynicism about the system and government authorities. Based on these distinctions between diffuse and concrete support, it is possible to argue that trust in individual elements will relate more to specific support, while trust in institutional elements is linked to diffuse support (Christensen and Lagreid 2005).

Satisfaction with institutional services, which builds trust, may be understood in both general and specific terms. This chapter focuses on the latter, discussing the relationship between experience of a public service, e.g. electoral services, and trust in government. Satisfaction with a public service depends on a wide range of components related to the process and the output of the service, and if the perceptions of the citizens about the service are primarily pleasant, they continue to trust the state (Kumlin and Esaiasson 2012; Rothstein and Stolle 2008). Although in some cases the service's mere presence may be enough to satisfy the citizenry, in other cases citizens expect quality and friendliness in the service providers, integrity among the service staff and honesty, reliability and efficacy from the services. However, when it comes to building trust, the public service's output matters more than its process functionality since friendliness and competence mean very little if the service does not produce the expected output.

So, how can we link these theoretical arguments with electoral integrity? A good starting point could be the argument of procedural performance since, as described above, evaluations of performance, including expectations of electoral integrity, shape trust in governments (Norris 2019). In consequence, there are several reasons to expect electoral integrity to be closely related to trust in governments since electoral processes involve a range of procedures. These procedures are crucial in a democratic setting since the government's legitimacy is based on the elections, at which ideally citizens deliver their popular consent via trustworthy and transparent electoral procedures.

Elections that meet the standards of electoral integrity that will ensure the orderly and peaceful transition of governments are likely to improve public assessment of democratic success in general and, in particular, trust for governments (Linde and Ekman 2003). In the opposite case, however, where citizens think that an election has produced an unfair output owing to integrity problems, the effect will probably spill over and trust in the political system as a whole will probably be impaired. However, trust in governments is not shaped solely through elections. The other critical determinants of trust in government are perceived integrity, transparency, justice, responsiveness and satisfaction with some public services (Murtin et al. 2018). Accordingly, electoral integrity is likely to be a vital part of these determinants since most citizens consider free and equal elections and the rule of law to be the main foundations of democracy

(Ferrín and Kriesi 2016). Elections are the most popular avenue along which citizens will engage in representative democracies, and if they work effectively, this is likely to contribute to favourable views of governments in general. While other political structures such as the courts or the national parliament are also important for building trust in governments, their activities are usually more remote from ordinary people's experience, rendering it harder to assess their success (Andrain and Smith 2006; Norris 2019). Accordingly, the following analysis will check citizens' level of trust in their government by linking their perceptions of electoral integrity and electoral malpractice, hypothesising that if citizens believe elections are conducted honestly, their trust in the government will increase. In contrast, if they think there is malpractice behind the elections, their trust in the government will decrease.

There are several reasons that make such an analysis worthwhile. First, the available longitudinal analyses based on the World Values Survey's (WVS) waves show that we have enough evidence to reconsider procedural theories attributable to the high levels of trust in governments in countries, without requiring international integrity standards. At the same time, we have also observed low levels of trust in governments in consolidated democracies with high levels of electoral integrity.

A growing literature also measures trust and confidence in elections and electoral integrity and the implications for cultural attitudes and civic engagement (Norris 2017a; Norris, Frank and Martínez i Coma 2014). Finally, it is becoming crucial to understand the relationship between trust in the government and electoral integrity. Several integrity-related problems might affect the electoral procedures covering pre-, post- and election-day activities, such as gerrymandering, vote-buying, electoral intimidation, biased electoral management and violence. These problems may be so severe that they call the legitimacy of the elections into question, a situation where citizens might start to rethink their trust in the government.

Surely, electoral integrity cannot be the only source for understanding trust in governments. In that sense, the theories of output legitimacy are helpful since they argue that people think primarily about the effects of government policies, the 'pocketbook economy', rather than about procedures and processes. These theories emphasise that citizens assess the government's performance on problems they think are crucial, such as those that affect household expenditures and savings (Norris 2019). Several studies have tested this argument to examine its relationship with trust in the government, but they have not produced consistent results.

Lastly, this analysis argues that political parties' position often influences trust in government and partisanship is assumed to be a crucial feature that prompts popular assessments of the government. Accordingly, perceptions of electoral processes may also condition trust in governments. In the particular Turkish case, the analysis has showed that the governing party has chiefly accused opposition parties of violent practices, whereas the opposition parties have tended to allege electoral fraud and other forms of misconduct, coupled with violence, against the governing party (Toros and Birch 2019).

Following the logic described above, it becomes essential to review what citizens think about elections and whether evaluations of elections relate to trust in the government. As in previous analyses in this book, what follows uses the sixth wave of the WVS to probe the proposed hypotheses.

Figure 7.1. provides evidence of trust in governments from a comparative perspective. It shows an association between trust in government, electoral integrity and malpractice at the national level. In countries where citizens perceive more problems related to electoral integrity, they tend to trust governments less. Countries like Peru, Mexico, Romania and Brazil are examples. On the other hand, high levels of perceived electoral integrity are associated with high levels of trust in the government, and countries like New Zealand, Sweden and the Netherlands are good examples of this. This finding is as expected, since problem-free elections are among the primary responsibilities of a government. It is also interesting to see some outliers, mostly in illiberal contexts, such as Kazakhstan, Turkey and Ethiopia. Although electoral problems are relatively high in these countries, governmental trust is not as low as we might have predicted. Possible explanations for this phenomenon are the different understandings of trust among citizens. That is to say, citizens may employ different standards while evaluating their governments. Another explanation may be based on regime propaganda portraying a political system as functioning better than it really is, and citizens relying on incorrect information (Xiang and Hmielowski 2017). The last explanation is a technical one: it is well known that respondents tend to give incorrect answers to sensitive survey questions as a consequence of 'social desirability bias'. Citizens may practice 'preference falsification' in an illiberal context to match their responses with the regime's

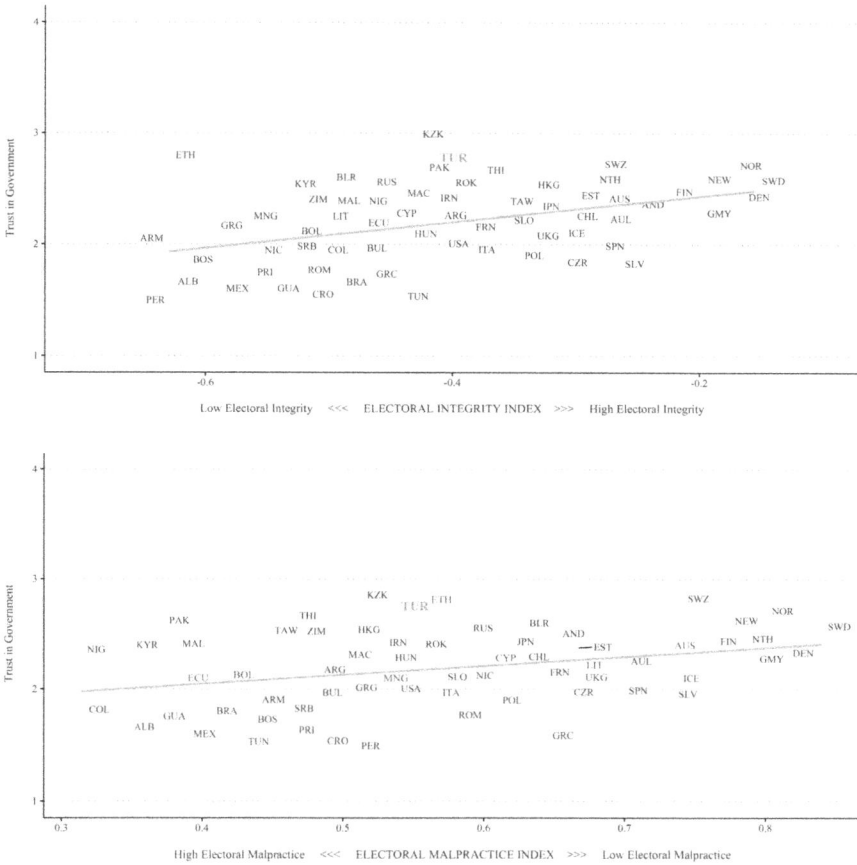

Figure 7.1 Trust in governments, electoral integrity and malpractice around the world

perceived desires (Kuran 1997). Given that oppressive governments frequently pay careful attention to what their citizens do and say and punish those who criticise official speech (Linz 2000), respondents will be quite likely to equate public opinion polls with government intelligence gathering. To the extent that people practise self-censorship to some degree and that the incidence of self-censorship depends on the perceived danger of repression or exclusion, reactions to critical issues are consistently skewed across countries and thus are not equivalent across countries where perceived risks vary.

Accordingly, several different factors could generate the picture in Figure 7.1 and, to understand these factors, Table 7.1 below shows a cross-national analysis in which trust in the government is the dependent variable. The first model,

Table 7.1 Cross-national analysis: trust in government

Predictors	Model 1	Model 2	Model 3
	World std beta	*World* std beta	*World* Disaggregated std beta
(Intercept)	0 (−0.01 to 0.01)	0 (−0.01 to 0.01)	0 (−0.01 to 0.01)
Integrity index	0.26 *** (0.25 to 0.26)	0.27 *** (0.26 to 0.28)	
Malpractice index	−0.15 *** (−0.15 to −0.14)	−0.16 *** (−0.17 to −0.16)	
Honest elections		0.03 *** (0.02 to 0.03)	0.01 ** (0.00 to 0.02)
Income		0.01 * (0.00 to 0.01)	0.01 ** (0.00 to 0.02)
Age		0.06 *** (0.06 to 0.07)	0.06 *** (0.05 to 0.07)
Gender (female)		0 (−0.00 to 0.01)	0 (−0.00 to 0.01)
Education		0.08 *** (0.08 to 0.09)	0.08 *** (0.07 to 0.09)
Votes are counted fairly			0.16 *** (0.15 to 0.17)
Journalists provide fair coverage of elections			0.06 *** (0.05 to 0.06)
Election officials are fair			0.12 *** (0.11 to 0.13)
Opposition candidates are prevented from running			0.07 *** (0.06 to 0.07)
TV news favours the governing party			−0.09 *** (−0.10 to −0.08)
Voters are bribed			−0.11 *** (−0.12 to −0.10)
Rich people buy elections			−0.11 *** (−0.12 to −0.10)
Voters are threatened with violence at the polls			0.06 *** (0.05 to 0.07)
Observations	78,613	78,613	78,613
R^2/R^2 adjusted	0.111/0.111	0.122/0.122	0.147/0.147

the base model, checks the relationship between the constructed indices and trust in the government. The second model incorporates additional, relevant, independent variables and controls. The third and final model uses the questions underlying the indices in a disaggregated form.

The base model's findings suggest that public perceptions of electoral integrity and malpractice strongly predict trust in the government. Both variables produced results in the expected directions: as electoral integrity increases, trust in governments increases, and as electoral malpractice increases, trust in governments decreases. The second model introduces two independent variables – honest elections and income – parallel to the theoretical discussion above, combined with three control variables. The independent variables are also significantly associated with trust in the government: a citizen who values honest elections and has a higher income level tends to trust the government more. Lastly, among the control variables, age and education were found to be related to trust in the government: older and better educated citizens tend to trust their government more. The third and final model, which checks the robustness of these findings using the disaggregated items that make up the indices, displays a similar picture to the previous models. The third model also shows that the best predictor for trust in the government is the fair counting of votes, followed by fair electoral officers.

Despite its own experience of multiple democratic breakdowns, since the 1950s Turkey has maintained the fundamental values of electoral democracy. While doing so, the country has struggled to consolidate its democratic system into a full liberal democracy owing to a highly divided political environment with problems such as repression of political opponents and media outlets and declining freedom of expression. In that sense, Turkey provides an exciting setting in which to check the link between electoral integrity and trust in government. Several studies have attempted to explain political trust in the Turkish setting. In a recent example, Aydın and Cenker (2012) explored the determinants of confidence in the Turkish government by utilising sociocultural, performance and party explanations. They found that performance and party affiliation provide the best explanations of trust in the government, and Turkish citizens place greater emphasis on 'government as the incumbent' than on 'government as a democratic institution'. Karakoç (2013) checked the linkage between ethnicity and political trust by focusing on an alternative dimension of the phenomenon and found that, though Kurds have low levels of trust in political institutions, they do not distrust all institutions equally. Karakoç (2013) also argued that, contrary to the studies on the winner/loser debate in long-standing democracies, winners in general and Kurdish winners in particular (those who voted for the Adalet ve Kalkınma Partisi, Justice and Development Party, AKP) are not distinguishable from the rest of society in their level of trust in political institutions. In a more recent study, Ertan, Aytaç and Çarkoğlu (2019) found a positive relationship between political trust and satisfaction of individuals with their lives in general and their economic circumstances, their level of interpersonal trust and perceptions of political efficacy. Moreover, contrary to Karakoç's arguments for Kurds, they provide evidence for high trust in the government among the supporters of the AKP. They also add that Kurdish and Alevi communities and those living in urban areas seem to have relatively lower political trust levels. These findings showed that institutional and cultural approaches to political trust have explanatory power in the Turkish context.

As discussed in Chapters Three and Four, by the end of 2019 Turkey had held three parliamentary, two presidential, and two local elections and a constitutional referendum that raised concerns with electoral integrity to the top of the political agenda. These concerns include allegations of multiple types of fraud and electoral violence, reaching a climax in 2018 during the combined presidential and parliamentary elections, which were held after a short but tense campaigning period, but more importantly, under a state of emergency. Although the government declared that the election was transparent, the atmosphere was hardly conducive to a level playing field for many reasons, including the opposition's limited access to the media and state resources (Kirişçi 2018). Figure 7.2. shows levels of trust in the government in Turkey throughout thirty years.

Figure 7.2. covers data on trust in the government collected from the second to the seventh waves of the WVS, dating back to 1991. Several governments were in office during this period: the Anavatan Partisi (Motherland Party, ANAP) in 1990; a Refah Partisi (Welfare Party, RP) and Doğru Yol Partisi (True Path Party, DYP) coalition took over in 1996; another coalition, between the Demokratik Sol Parti (Democratic Left Party, DSP), Milliyetçi Hareket Partisi (Nationalist Action Party, MHP) and ANAP coalition entered office in 2001; and the AKP has ruled the country since 2002. It is interesting to see that trust in the government significantly increased during the reign

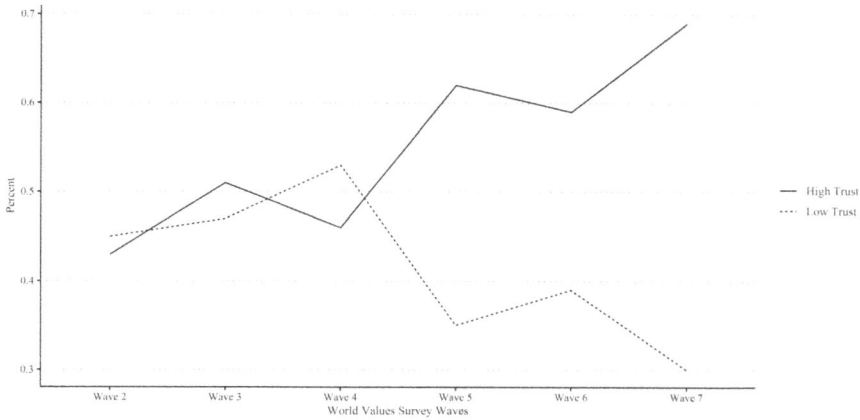

Figure 7.2 Trust in the government, Turkey

of the AKP (Waves 5, 6 and 7) when the country faced the electoral integrity problems mentioned in this book. Levels of trust in the government were high during the previous single-party government led by the ANAP (Wave 3) and decreased under the coalition governments during the 1990s. This finding shows that a majoritarian rather than a consensual conceptualisation of democracy is more salient in the Turkish public's eyes (Cinar and Kose 2020). Given the problems of electoral institutions during the second decade of this century, it can be argued that citizens prefer majoritarian political institutions, in light of the higher level of political trust they display, in unconsolidated democracies (Cinar 2016).

So how do electoral integrity problems relate to trust in the government in Turkey? Table 7.2, using indices identical to those in Table 7.1, provides empirical evidence for the country. Findings indicate that, although there are several similarities, there are also some crucial differences. As with the cross-national evidence, Model 4 confirms a significant link between electoral integrity and malpractice, on one hand, and trust in the government on the other. For both indices, the coefficient signs appeared as expected. In the results for Model 5, however, we observe a different picture. Although the cross-national evidence showed that trust in governments rose with belief in the importance of honest elections and high levels of income, in the Turkish case the honest elections variable proved insignificant, and the sign of the income variable is reversed. The first finding on honest elections can be related to Turkish

Table 7.2 Analysis of Turkey: trust in government

Predictors	Model 4 std beta	Model 5 std beta	Model 6 Disaggregated std beta	Model 7 std beta
(Intercept)	0.03 (−0.04 to 0.04)	0.02 (−0.04 to 0.04)	0.02 (−0.04 to 0.04)	−0.29*** (−0.35 to −0.23)
Integrity index	0.39*** (0.35 to 0.43)	0.39*** (0.35 to 0.43)		0.32 *** (0.28 to 0.36)
Malpractice index	−0.18*** (−0.22 to −0.14)	−0.17*** (−0.22 to −0.13)		−0.07*** (−0.12 to −0.03)
Honest elections		0.02 (−0.04 to 0.04)	−0.02 (−0.06 to 0.02)	−0.03 (−0.07 to 0.01)
Income		−0.06** (−0.11 to −0.02)	−0.05** (−0.10 to −0.01)	−0.05* (−0.09 to −0.01)
Age		0.04 (−0.01 to 0.08)	0.04* (0.00 to 0.09)	0.04 (−0.01 to 0.08)
Gender (female)		0.02 (−0.02 to 0.06)	0.01 (−0.03 to 0.05)	0.02 (−0.02 to 0.06)
Education		0.11*** (0.06 to 0.15)	0.11*** (0.06 to 0.15)	0.09*** (0.05 to 0.13)
Votes are counted fairly			0.34*** (0.29 to 0.39)	
Journalists provide fair coverage of elections			0.02 (−0.03 to 0.06)	
Election officials are fair			0.12*** (0.07 to 0.17)	
Opposition candidates are prevented from running			0.04 (−0.01 to 0.09)	
TV news favours the governing party			−0.06* (−0.11 to −0.01)	
Voters are bribed			−0.04 (−0.10 to 0.01)	
Rich people buy elections			−0.07* (−0.12 to −0.01)	
Voters are threatened with violence at the polls			0.01 (−0.06 to 0.05)	
CHP voter				0.61*** (0.50 to 0.71)
HDP voter				0.72*** (0.57 to 0.88)

	Model 4	Model 5	Model 6	Model 7
İyi voter				0.58*** (0.40 to 0.76)
MHP voter				0.38*** (0.26 to 0.51)
Observations	1,832	1,832	1,832	1,832
R²/R² adjusted	0.207/0.207	0.218/0.215	0.243/0.238	0.289/0.285

*p<0.05 **p<0.01 ***p<0.001

The comparison category for model 7 is AKP voter

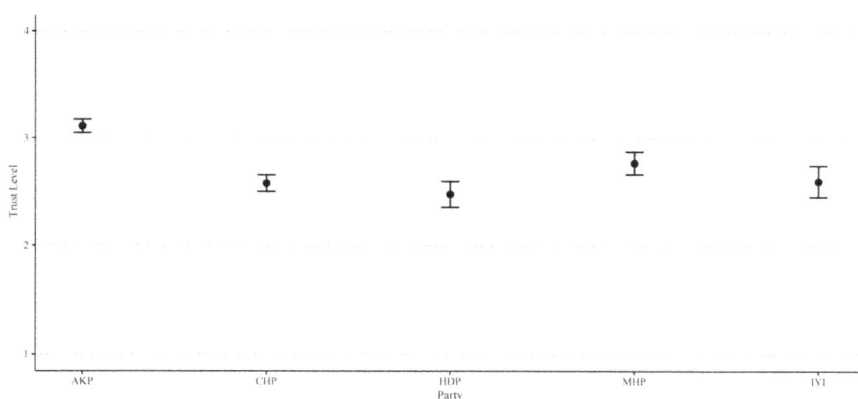

Figure 7.3 Predicted values of trust in government and partisanship

citizens' low levels of political efficacy. The finding on income levels can be related to two factors. The first is the belief in an omnipotent Turkish state, often equated with governments, which are expected to eliminate societal differences (Heper 1985). The second possible explanation relates to partisanship levels tested in Model 7.

As Model 7 shows, partisanship significantly shapes the perception of trust in government. AKP voters were chosen to be the comparison category since this is the party in government (with the support of its small partner MHP). Compared to AKP voters, other party voters trust the government significantly less. Interestingly, this finding is also valid for the MHP, the minor partner in the governing coalition. Figure 7.3 displays the predicted values of trust in government by partisanship.

Conclusion

Public perceptions of electoral integrity problems play a crucial role in shaping trust in government. When citizens believe that elections are free, fair and transparent, this strengthens their trust in the government and the institutions that support it. Conversely, when they believe that the election process has been compromised, this undermines trust in government and creates an environment of political uncertainty. In that sense, free and fair elections allow citizens to have a voice in choosing their leaders and making decisions about the future of their country. When citizens believe that the election process is not being conducted fairly, this raises questions about the legitimacy of the election results and the government that emerges from those elections.

Findings presented in this chapter show that if citizens believe that the election has been rigged, they start to question the very foundations of democratic governance. This lack of trust can lead to cynicism, apathy and disengagement from the political process, as citizens feel their voices and votes do not matter. Additionally, if problems with electoral integrity persist over time, they can further erode public trust in government. This can be particularly damaging in countries where the rule of law is weak, as it raises questions about the ability of the government to ensure that other aspects of governance are also conducted fairly and transparently.

Additionally, the impact on trust in the government of public perceptions of problems with electoral integrity can be far-reaching and long-lasting. When citizens distrust the election process, they may also begin to question the broader legitimacy of the government and the institutions that support it, such as the judiciary and the media. This lack of trust can lead to a loss of support for the government, making it harder for the government to implement policies and achieve its goals. It can also lead to social unrest and political polarisation, as citizens who feel their voices and votes are not being heard may resort to protests, demonstrations and other forms of activism to express their frustration and anger. In addition to these adverse effects, public perceptions of problems with electoral integrity can also undermine the stability of a country. When citizens do not believe that elections are free and fair, political uncertainty may follow, leading to instability and unrest.

Governments and electoral institutions must address public perceptions of problems of integrity and restore trust in the election process. This can be done through a range of measures, including conducting elections transparently and impartially, with clear rules and procedures in place to prevent fraud and other forms of electoral misconduct. Such measures can include practices like the use of independent election observers, transparent vote-counting processes and the publication of election results in a timely and accessible fashion. Additionally, it would be beneficial to provide citizens with accurate and timely information about the election process, so they can make informed decisions and hold the government accountable: this can be achieved with measures such as publicising the rules and procedures for conducting elections, providing information about candidate eligibility and making election-related data and information readily available to the public. Although far from complete, taking these steps will help governments and electoral institutions build trust in the election process and, in turn, trust in government.

References

Almond, G. and S. Verba. 1963. *The Civic Culture*. Princeton, NJ: Princeton University Press.

Andrain, Charles F. and James T. Smith. 2006. *Political Democracy, Trust and Social Justice: A Comparative Overview*. Boston, MA: Northeastern University Press.

Ariely, Gal. 2015. 'Trusting the Press and Political Trust: A Conditional Relationship'. *Journal of Elections, Public Opinion and Parties* 25 (3): 351–67. https://doi.org/1 0.1080/17457289.2014.997739.

Aydın, Aylin and Cerem I. Cenker. 2012. 'Public Confidence in Government: Empirical Implications from a Developing Democracy'. *International Political Science Review* 33 (2): 230–50. https://doi.org/10.1177/0192512111417027.

Bennett, Stephen Earl, Staci L. Rhine and Richard S. Flickinger. 2001. 'Assessing Americans' Opinions about the News Media's Fairness in 1996 and 1998'. *Political Communication* 18 (2). https://doi.org/10.1080/105846001750322961.

Birch, Sarah. 2008. 'Electoral Institutions and Popular Confidence in Electoral Processes: A Cross-National Analysis'. *Electoral Studies* 27 (2): 305–20. https://doi.org/10.1016/j.electstud.2008.01.005.

———. 2010. 'Perceptions of Electoral Fairness and Voter Turnout'. *Comparative Political Studies*. https://doi.org/10.1177/0010414010374021.

Christensen, Tom and Per Lagreid. 2005. 'Trust in Government: The Relative Importance of Service Satisfaction, Political Factors, and Demography'. *Public Performance & Management Review* 28 (4): 487–511. https://doi.org/10.1080/15309576.2005 .11051848.

Cinar, Kursat. 2016. 'Local Determinants of an Emerging Electoral Hegemony: The Case of Justice and Development Party (AKP) in Turkey'. *Democratisation* 23 (7): 1216–35. https://doi.org/10.1080/13510347.2015.1077228.

Cinar, Kursat and Tekin Kose. 2020. 'Political Trust in Nonconsolidated Democracies: The Turkish Case in Comparative Perspective'. *Political Science Quarterly* 135 (3): 467–97. https://doi.org/https://doi.org/10.1002/polq.13067.

Coffé, Hilde. 2017. 'Citizens' Media Use and the Accuracy of Their Perceptions of Electoral Integrity'. *International Political Science Review* 38 (3): 281–97. https://doi.org/10.1177/0192512116640984.

Curran, James, Shanto Iyengar, Anker Brink Lund and Inka Salovaara-Moring. 2009. 'Media System, Public Knowledge and Democracy: A Comparative Study'. *European Journal of Communication*. https://doi.org/10.1177/0267323108098943.

Easton, D. 1965. *A Systems Analysis of Political Life*. New York, London, Sydney: John Wiley & Sons.

Ertan, Güneş, Selim Erdem Aytaç and Ali Çarkoğlu. 2019. 'Türkiye'de Siyasi Kurumlara Güven: Kültürel Ve Kurumsal Açıklamalar Ile "Kazanan Takim" Etkisinin Rolü.' *Hacettepe Üniversitesi İktisadi ve İdari Bilimler Fakültesi Dergisi* 37 (1): 65–88. https://doi.org/10.17065/huniibf.363402.

Ferrín, Mónica and Hanspeter Kriesi. 2016. 'Introduction: Democracy – The European Verdict.' In *How Europeans View and Evaluate Democracy*, edited by Mónica Ferrín and Hanspeter Kriesi, 1–20. Oxford: Oxford University Press. https://doi.org/10.1093/acprof:oso/9780198766902.003.0001.

Goodsell, C. 1994. *The Case for Bureaucracy: A Public Administration Polemic*. Chatham, NJ: Chatham House.

Graber, Doris A. 1988. *Processing the News: How People Tame the Information Tide*. New York: Longman.

Heper, Metin. 1985. *The State Tradition in Turkey*. Walkington, UK: Eothen.

Inglehart, Ronald and Christian Welzel. 2003. 'Political Culture and Democracy: Analysing Cross-Level Linkages.' *Comparative Politics* 36 (1): 61–79.

Jamieson, Kathleen Hall and Joseph N. Cappella. 2008. *Echo Chamber: Rush Limbaugh and the Conservative Media Establishment*. New York: Oxford University Press.

Karakoç, Ekrem. 2013. 'Ethnicity and Trust in National and International Institutions: Kurdish Attitudes toward Political Institutions in Turkey'. *Turkish Studies* 14 (1): 92–114. https://doi.org/10.1080/14683849.2013.766986.

Kirişçi, Kemal. 2018. 'How to Read Turkey's Election Results.' Brookings Institution blog, https://www.brookings.edu/blog/order-from-chaos/2018/06/25/how-to-read-turkeys-election-results/.

Klingemann, Hans-Dieter and Dieter Fuchs. 1995. 'Citizens and the State: A Changing Relationship?' In *Citizens and the State*, edited by Hans-Dieter Klingemann and Dieter Fuchs. Oxford: Oxford University Press.

Kumlin, Staffan and Peter Esaiasson. 2012. 'Scandal Fatigue? Scandal Elections and Satisfaction with Democracy in Western Europe, 1977–2007.' *British Journal of Political Science* 42 (2): 263. https://doi.org/10.1017/s000712341100024x.

Kuran, Timur. 1997. *Private Truths, Public Lies: The Social Consequences of Preference Falsification*. Cambridge, MA: Harvard University Press.

Ladd, Jonathan M. 2012. 'When Politicians Attack: Party Cohesion in the Media'. *Public Opinion Quarterly* 76 (1): 182–86.

Levitsky, S. and D. Ziblatt. 2018. *How Democracies Die*. London: Penguin Random House UK.

Linde, Jonas and Joakim Ekman. 2003. 'Satisfaction with Democracy: A Note on a Frequently Used Indicator in Comparative Politics'. *European Journal of Political Research*. https://doi.org/10.1111/1475-6765.00089.

Linz, Juan. 2000. *Totalitarian and Authoritarian Regimes*. Boulder, CO: Lynne Rienner Publishers.

March, J. G. and J. P. Olsen. 1989. *Rediscovering Institutions: The Organizational Basis of Politics*. New York: Free Press.

Miller, A. and O. Listhaug. 1999. 'Political Performance and Institutional Trust'. In *Critical Citizens: Global Support for Democratic Governance*, edited by Pippa Norris, 204–16. Oxford: Oxford University Press.

Miller, Arthur H. 1974. 'Political Issues and Trust in Government: 1964–1970'. *American Political Science Review* 68 (3). https://doi.org/10.2307/1959140.

Murtin, Fabrice, Lara Fleischer, Vincent Siegerink, Arnstein Aassve, Yann Algan, Romina Boarini, Santiago Gonzalez et al. 2018. 'Trust and Its Determinants: Evidence from the Trustlab Experiment'. OECD Statistics Working Papers, No. 2018/02, Paris: OECD Publishing. https://doi.org/10.1787/869ef2ec-en.

Norris, Pippa. 2011a. *Democratic Deficit: Critical Citizens Revisited*. Cambridge: Cambridge University Press.

———. 2011b. 'Political Communication.' In *Comparative Politics*, edited by Daniele Caramani, 352–370. Oxford: Oxford University Press.

———. 2014. *Why Electoral Integrity Matters*. Cambridge: Cambridge University Press. https://doi.org/10.1017/CBO9781107280861.

———. 2017a. 'Electoral Systems and Electoral Integrity.' In *The Oxford Handbook of Electoral Systems*, edited by Erik S. Herron, Robert J. Pekkanen and Matthew S. Shugart. Oxford: Oxford University Press. https://doi.org/10.1093/oxfordhb/9780190258658.013.10.

——. 2017b. 'Why Populism Is a Threat to Electoral Integrity.' London School of Economics Europe Blog. https://blogs.lse.ac.uk/europpblog/2017/05/16/why-populism-is-a-threat-to-electoral-integrity/.

——. 2019. 'Do Perceptions of Electoral Malpractice Undermine Democratic Satisfaction? The US in Comparative Perspective.' *International Political Science Review* 40 (1): 5–22. https://doi.org/10.1177/0192512118806783.

Norris, Pippa, Richard W. Frank and Ferran Martínez i Coma. 2014. *Advancing Electoral Integrity*. Oxford: Oxford University Press.

Putnam, R. D. 2000. *Bowling Alone: The Collapse and Revival of American Community*. New York: Simon & Schuster.

Reporters without Borders. 2021. 'Media Ownership Monitor: Turkey'.

Rothstein, Bo and Dietlind Stolle. 2008. 'The State and Social Capital: An Institutional Theory of Generalized Trust'. *Comparative Politics*. https://doi.org/10.5129/001041508X12911362383354.

Scheufele, Dietram A. and Matthew C. Nisbet. 2002. 'Being a Citizen Online: New Opportunities and Dead Ends'. *Harvard International Journal of Press/Politics* 7 (3): 55–75. https://doi.org/10.1177/1081180x0200700304.

Schuck, Andreas R. T., Hajo G. Boomgaarden and Claes H. de Vreese. 2013. 'Cynics All Around? The Impact of Election News on Political Cynicism in Comparative Perspective.' *Journal of Communication* 63 (2). https://doi.org/10.1111/jcom.12023.

Tal-Or, Nurit, Jonathan Cohen, Yariv Tsfati and Albert C. Gunther. 2010. 'Testing Causal Direction in the Influence of Presumed Media Influence'. *Communication Research* 37 (6): 801–24. https://doi.org/10.1177/0093650210362684.

Thomassen, Jacques. 2015. 'What's Gone Wrong with Democracy, or with Theories Explaining Why It Has?' In *Citizenship and Democracy in an Era of Crisis: Essays in Honour of Jan W. van Deth*, edited by Thomas Poguntke, Sigrid Rossteutscher, Rudiger Schmitt-Beck and Sonja Zmerli, 34–53. Abingdon: Routledge. https://doi.org/10.4324/9781315750248.

Toros, Emre and Sarah Birch. 2019. 'Framing Electoral Impropriety: The Strategic Use of Allegations of Wrong-Doing in Election Campaigns'. *British Journal of Middle Eastern Studies*. https://doi.org/10.1080/13530194.2019.1566694.

Tsfati, Yariv and Gal Ariely. 2014. 'Individual and Contextual Correlates of Trust in Media Across 44 Countries'. *Communication Research* 41 (6). https://doi.org/10.1177/0093650213485972.

TÜİK. 2018. 'Yazılı Medya İstatistikleri.' Ankara. https://data.tuik.gov.tr/Bulten/Index?p=Yazili-Medya-ve-Uluslararasi-Standart-Kitap-Numarasi-Istatistikleri-2021-45833.

Tunç, Aslı. 2015. 'Media Ownership and Financing in Turkey.' https://turkey.mom-gmr.org/en/.

Van der Meer, Tom W. G. 2017. 'Political Trust and the "Crisis of Democracy"'. *Oxford Research Encyclopedias* (May 2018): 1–23. https://doi.org/10.1093/acrefore/9780190228637.013.77.

Weibel, David, Bartholomaus Wissmath and Rudolf Groner. 2008. 'How Gender and Age Affect Newscasters' Credibility – An Investigation in Switzerland'. *Journal of Broadcasting and Electronic Media* 52 (3). https://doi.org/10.1080/08838150802205801.

Xenos, Michael and Patricia Moy. 2007. 'Direct and Differential Effects of the Internet on Political and Civic Engagement'. *Journal of Communication* 57 (4): 704–18. https://doi.org/10.1111/j.1460-2466.2007.00364.x.

Xiang, Jun and Jay D. Hmielowski. 2017. 'Alternative Views and Eroding Support: The Conditional Indirect Effects of Foreign Media and Internet Use on Regime Support in China'. *International Journal of Public Opinion Research*. https://doi.org/10.1093/ijpor/edw006.

Zmerli, Sonja and Tom van der Meer. 2017. *Handbook on Political Trust*. Cheltenham: Edward Elgar Publishing. https://doi.org/10.4337/9781782545118.

8

HOW DO PERCEPTIONS OF ELECTORAL INTEGRITY RELATE TO ELECTORAL EXPECTATIONS?

Introduction

We are passing through an era in which voters view election results as 'surprising' more frequently than ever, whether they are on the winning or losing side. According to the Election Tracking Survey of the US midterms in 2022 carried out by FiveThirtyEight/Ipsos, for example, 44 per cent of all American voters and 57 per cent of Republicans said they were surprised by the results. Other global examples include the 2023 Nigerian presidential and general elections, the 2021 Iraqi general elections and the 2019 Australian general elections, to mention only a few. This feeling of surprise indeed refers to a gap between voters' perceptions about the elections and the actual outcomes. As discussed below, although the available literature has produced valuable insights about the consequences of this gap, we have scant knowledge about the causes of this phenomenon. To try to fill this niche, this chapter, using the term 'surprised voter', will focus on the underlying integrity and other individual-level factors that shape electoral expectations.

For several reasons, focusing on this gap is crucial for integrity studies. For one thing, citizens' electoral expectations relate conceptually to their trust in government and satisfaction with democracy (Anderson and LoTempio 2002). Solid empirical evidence shows that the supporters of politicians who have lost elections tend to hold more negative opinions about democracy and government than those on the winning side. Moreover, these surprised losers perceive less electoral responsiveness, think elections lack integrity and doubt the legitimacy of the electoral processes (Hollander 2014). Accordingly, understanding this phenomenon will provide essential insight and an alternative perspective on citizens' trust in the political system and their satisfaction with democracy. We also know that the peaceful acceptance of electoral results and establishing consent around these results, win or lose, is an essential component of a well-functioning democracy (Anderson et al. 2005, 1–13). In that perspective, ultimately, perhaps, elections are the only tool for legitimately determining who has won and establishing consent among the losers (Nadeau and Blais 1993). Accordingly, it becomes important to conduct further research into the circumstances that lead citizens to this disappointed and surprised stance.

In this context, 'surprised voter' describes voters who expected their rivals to be unsuccessful, and is contrasted with rival supporters who are not surprised by the election outcome. This chapter argues that there is a relationship between perceptions of electoral integrity and the shape of electoral expectations, based on news consumption patterns, combined with varying levels of trust in the media. This argument is based on the well-rooted literature investigating the relationship between media consumption and political behaviour (Putnam 2000; Nie et al. 2010; Ansolabehere, Behr and Iyengar 1991). Against this background, this chapter argues that, while positive perceptions of integrity combined with diversified news exposure should reduce surprise in an electoral outcome, concentration on limited outlets will increase it. Likewise, varying levels of trust in the media shape the perception of surprise.

In addition to these factors, this chapter also argues that electoral expectations and the feeling of surprise are shaped by partisanship. As mentioned in Chapters Four, Six and Seven, early studies on this link showed differences between the 'wishful thinking' indulged in by partisans of left and right parties (Babad and Yacobos 1993). More recent studies focused on the link between media use and partisanship and provide valuable evidence on how trust in partisan sources plays a significant role in forming misperceptions by avoiding alternative sources of information (Hutchens et al. 2021). This literature shows that citizens tend to trust media sources that provide content coherent with their ideological positions and at the same time find conflicting sources less credible. In other words, people tend to consult politically aligned media outlets and find them credible and trustworthy (Kuru, Pasek and Traugott 2017). Lastly, research has found that exposure to partisan media contributes to political misperception, encourages inaccurate beliefs regardless of substantiated evidence and that the development of misperception is related more to exposure to partisan news than to untrustworthy content (Garrett, Weeks and Neo 2016; Weeks et al. 2021).

These arguments are tested here using the face-to-face survey data collected by E-IT after the 2018 Turkish presidential and parliamentary elections. Findings show solid empirical evidence in favour of these hypotheses: positive perceptions of electoral integrity and exposure to diversified news lowers perceptions of surprise, high trust in media outlets boosts them and partisanship is a significant variable that shapes this relationship.

Theoretical Background

Electoral Expectations and Electoral Integrity

Perceptions about elections are crucial to comprehending how people create their political environments and, more generally, how they perceive the political *per se*. More importantly, these perceptions influence levels of support for the legitimacy of democratic institutions (Nadeau and Blais 1993). It is also argued that the operation and stability of democratic polities are integrally tied to what voters perceive democratic government to be and how they do so (Rose 2008). This viewpoint derives naturally from the classic work of Easton (1965), who posited that democratic legitimacy rests on the extent to which people trust their government to behave rightly in most situations.

Citizens' expectations of electoral outcomes are driven by several factors. For example, voters' pre-election predictions of anticipated results can significantly impact their voting behaviour and hence the outcome of the elections (Plutowski, Weitz-Shapiro and Winters 2021). That is to say, in close races expectations may influence the decision to turn out or stay at home, and also provide the basis for developing tactical considerations (Bargsted and Kedar 2009). These examples and several others utilise the rationalist perspective, which regards these expectations as most probable if they are reasonably accurate and based on the best available information, such as polls, journalistic commentary or partisan mobilisation (Baden et al. 2022). In any case, these factors conduce to a healthy representation, making the issue crucial to understand,

and in that sense, matters related to electoral integrity appear to be a new and critical factor for understanding the phenomenon more comprehensively.

The existing work identified several determinants of electoral expectations, among them voters' ideological positions and media exposure (Kuru, Pasek and Traugott 2020). These works underlined the vast differences in politicians' claims, especially to the partisan media (Lelkes 2016). Some other studies have focused on the attention dedicated to candidates in the news, measured in terms of content and time, and found that controversial stories such as scandals increase a candidate's perceived chances (R. K. Mayer 2001; Geiß and Schäfer 2017).

Accordingly, this chapter hypothesises, first, that, like the factors mentioned above, matters of electoral integrity relate to perceived electoral expectations. I argue that views of electoral integrity, including evaluations of whether elections are fair, whether votes are correctly tallied, and whether elections are effective in increasing government responsiveness to citizens and others, shape the expectations about elections. As discussed in Chapters Four, Six and Seven, perceptions of electoral integrity are of particular theoretical importance since elections are essential to both the ideals and the practice of democracy, as the principal chance for ordinary citizens to engage in democratic government actively. Evaluations of electoral integrity are unique in that sense since other characteristics of legitimacy, such as trust in government officials, are likely to have different meanings for citizens during an election campaign than in a period out of the electoral cycle. This argument is consistent with the theoretical discussions in Chapters Six and Seven emphasising the significance of public perceptions of the electoral process for the health of the democratic regime.

When people are caught off guard by the results of an election, they may be more prone to question whether the process was conducted fairly, or not. For example, in the months preceding an election, if the polls published in media outlets identify a particular candidate as a winner, those exposed to this information may anticipate that this particular candidate will win by a substantial margin. If the opposite happens, this may suggest to them that the election had been rigged somehow or, at the very least, that there had been errors in counting the votes. By creating inflated expectations for a favoured candidate, media outlets that share the same world view may increase the likelihood that unsuccessful candidates will challenge the integrity of the election if their inflated expectations are not satisfied.

Based on these arguments, I formulate this chapter's first hypothesis as follows:

H1: Positive perceptions of electoral integrity decrease the chances of being surprised by election results.

News Consumption and Information Diversity

Analysing how the media shapes political information and behaviour is essential to comprehend the link between media consumption patterns and electoral expectations. Accordingly, the following paragraphs first focus on news consumption theories to understand how political knowledge and related voter perceptions are formed. This effort is crucial since Hollander (2014) aptly argues that the strength of voters' cognitive and motivational belief in victory depends on their political knowledge.

The early examples analysing this link identified news media as the primary source of political information, accompanied by interpersonal communication (Cho et al. 2009; Mutz and Martin 2001; Berkowitz and Pritchard 1989). When people seek political information from media outlets, inevitably they have to make choices among the diverse and various ideological perspectives available. The ground theories about news consumption have primarily focused on selective exposure and suggest that voters prefer to consume like-minded messages rather than opposing ones (Iyengar et al. 2009; Festinger 1964). As one of the earliest examples in this research, Festinger's (1957) theory of 'cognitive dissonance' explains this outcome by arguing that when exposed information is inconsistent with one's beliefs, the resulting dissonance arouses psychological discomfort. To reduce this particular discomfort, people tend to select more desirable or supportive messages and reject less desirable or opposing ones, which can lead to misperception and misinterpretation of information.

Similarly, in another early example, Sears and Freedman (1967) showed that voters seem to be exposed disproportionately to communications that support their opinions. That is to say, while political belief motivates the decision what to read and watch, read and watched content shapes political belief; the more like-minded (reinforcing) messages are consumed; hence biased perception ensues. A few studies have also stopped to examine this link within the context of voting behaviour and found citizens tend to consume information that supports their expectations and ignore messages providing evidence to the contrary (Babad, Hills and O'Driscoll 1992).

Beyond these ground-setting works, the current line of research on selective exposure concentrates on the online dimension of the phenomenon since people have started to get more and more of their news online. This shift opened up new research opportunities with updated research questions, and several early examples argue that the internet increased the chances of being exposed to diverse perspectives (Wojcieszak and Mutz 2009; Lee et al. 2014). However, several others provided solid evidence for the opposite case and reported that internet users tend to choose like-minded media outlets and prefer to consume political news that aligns with their ideologies (Sunstein 2007; Garrett 2009; Iyengar et al. 2009). The latter line of findings resonates with the continuing research on social media. Evidence shows that individuals tend to communicate within very similar networks on social media, and dominantly conservative or ideologically extreme individuals do this to a greater extent (Boutyline and Willer 2017). Hence, the amplified interaction and attachment of similar citizens create partisan 'echo chambers' of reaffirmation (Cinelli et al. 2021; Hong and Kim 2016), in which users consume and produce information that suits the norms of their group and reinforces what has already been believed.

Moreover, any alternative standpoint is labelled as misinformation, and alternative propositions are ignored in these echo chambers, providing a suitable ground for the rapid spread of genuine misinformation (Dubois and Blank 2018; Vicario et al. 2016; Törnberg 2018). More recently, by employing algorithms based on machine learning, it is now possible to target users with highly personalised messages based on their digital footprints. As a result, any kind of information targeting these echo chambers has become more tailor-made and hence more granulated, mainly within the circles of behavioural advertising. By eliminating challenging information, 'filter bubbles' obstruct exposure to alternative information and trap users in echo chambers by providing them with compatible information that they are known to be likely to accept, resulting in the amplification of ideological segregation (Bozdag and van den Hoven 2015; Flaxman, Goel and Rao 2016). This automated mechanism can potentially hinder awareness of political events and views, including ones relating to elections.

One alternative line of research diverges from the above stance and claims that, although the internet facilitates the filtering of information and empowers the user to make selections, it is unlikely that everyone will encounter similar views all the time. This particular branch of literature underlines that users are frequently exposed to challenging information, especially in the digital environment where numerous and diverse news outlets exist. Considering political communication, online citizens are very likely to be exposed to opposing messages and aware of the possible electoral results. Against this background, several researchers have used the term 'selective reading' and argued that listening to or watching congenial news does not necessarily prevent exposure to uncongenial or conflicting messages (Garrett 2009; Valentino et al. 2009; Stroud 2014).

Based on the theoretical discussion detailed above, it becomes possible to argue that continuously consuming information that individuals already agree with will reinforce expectations and lead to disappointments when these expectations are not realised. In line with the presented background, I argue that undiversified media exposure will reinforce biased political beliefs, amplify wishful expectations and propagate misperceptions about political events, including election results. By the same token, the intention to seek diverse information from alternative sources, including the internet and social media, increases the chance of being exposed to content with alternative and opposing views, which may reduce the risk or consequences of entering an echo chamber (Dubois and Blank 2018). Accordingly, diverse media use may set the ground for a more realistic and unbiased set of expectations and enrich one's political knowledge, including knowledge of elections, which should diminish wishful thinking (Dolan and Holbrook 2001). Against this background, it becomes coherent to argue that the tendency to rely on one's own and similar-minded opinions, and purposefully reject others, will promote surprise. Based on this assumption, I offer a second hypothesis as follows:

H2: Exposure to diverse media content for news consumption decreases the chances of being surprised by election results.

Trust in Media

This chapter now goes on to argue that high trust in the media shapes electoral expectations. Although different scientific traditions define and apply the concept of trust differently, almost all definitions of trust refer to a connection between a trustor and a trustee; although the possibility of betrayal i spresent, the trustee is positively expected to work in the best interests of the trustor (R. C. Mayer, Davis and Schoorman 1995; Rousseau et al. 1998; McKnight, Cummings and Chervany 1998). Within the domain of political communication, media trust refers to a connection between people and media based on citizens' expectations that the media will function well and provide accurate, reliable and timely information (Strömbäck et al. 2020; Hutchens et al. 2021). Existing research richly describes the individual and contextual variables that predict media trust, including factors such as exposure to news media, education, partisanship, trust in political institutions, the emergence of new media sources and, finally, misinformation (Hopmann, Shehata and Strömbäck 2015; Ognyanova 2019; Tsfati and Ariely 2014; Van Duyn and Collier 2019; Jones-Jang, Kim and Kenski 2020). However, this analysis is more interested in a possible outcome of trust in media and argues that as citizens' trust in media sources increases, they tend to perceive what is served by these sources as the 'sole truth', and that this may conflict with reality.

First, following Tsfati (2003), it can be argued that it makes little sense to follow media sources that one does not trust. Citizens follow the news expecting to acquire accurate knowledge about the world. Since they have to maximise the utility in this process, owing to the impossibility of responding to all news all the time, they tend to disregard numerous alternative stimuli. Likewise, several studies on agenda-setting, framing and priming have demonstrated how media trust moderates its impacts (Druckman 2001a; 2001b; Xiao, Borah and Su 2021). From that perspective, these studies provide empirical evidence of the relevance of trust in media outlets for citizens during their perception-shaping, knowledge-building and participation-mobilisation practices (Kaufhold, Valenzuela and de Zúñiga 2010; Ardèvol-Abreu and de Zúñiga 2017). Findings show that if citizens perceive the content provider as 'objective, impartial, accurate, or unbiased', they are more likely to trust the material's validity, and if they are suspicious of such content, agenda-setting impacts of the media diminish (Xiao, Borah and Su 2021). Last, Ladd (2010) showed that decades of studies have repeatedly demonstrated that individuals who trust the media are more prone to accept its messages._

Researchers who approached the phenomenon using another but relevant perspective found that people consume factually questionable content because they lack trust in the media (Guess, Nyhan and Reifler 2020). Thus, it could be argued that people may prefer to engage with incorrect information instead of changing the source they trust, since the perceived values of a source are important (Schaffner and Luks 2018; Kuru, Pasek and Traugott 2017). Therefore, the source of information becomes more important than the information itself, and individuals' trust in the source becomes more significant, playing a more prominent role in the building of misperceptions (Hutchens et al. 2021). Reversing this logic, scepticism about public news can increase critical thinking, which could reduce misperception (Kyriakidou et al. 2022; Vraga, Kim and Cook 2019). The literature argues that when voters believe particular media are not providing accurate and unbiased coverage of political events, they are more likely to rely on other media sources. In other words, when citizens do not trust the information they are exposed to, they tend to find alternative information, and may check 'facts' to validate political news.

During election periods, when political misinformation dominates the political environment, voters frequently expose fabricated campaign news to manipulate public opinion (Weeks et al. 2021; Guess, Nyhan and Reifler 2020; Gottfried et al. 2013; Allcott and Gentzkow 2017). This type of content is purposefully designed to add 'noise' and create more sensational news (Guo and Vargo 2020), spilling over to social and mainstream media (Tsfati et al. 2020; Altay, Hacquin and Mercier 2022). Accordingly, during the electoral cycle, critical evaluation of such content becomes even more crucial since voters tend to assess information as accurate and true if it originates from the media outlets with which they are already aligned and that they trust (Garrett, Weeks and Neo 2016; Weeks and Garrett 2014). This task has recently become even more complicated since many of us are exposed to a colossal amount of online news daily. Without editorial filters that print and broadcast media have developed to help them disseminate reliable political news by investigating the topic and background of information, the news appearing online has worrying potential to be manipulative and wrong. Supporting this argument, scholars agree that the decentralised World Wide Web is a very fertile environment in which to disseminate misinformation (Vicario et al. 2016). Working on the causes and consequences of such exposure, some studies claim that exposure to untrustworthy news has been overstated (Guess, Nyhan and Reifler 2020). Others, however, show just the opposite and have provided solid evidence that misinformation, even after correction, continues to shape people's beliefs, especially when the audience finds the source credible (Walter and Tukachinsky 2020; Lazer et al., 2018). Moreover, research has also shown that the source of reported information plays an essential role in political trust, and voters have high confidence in partisan media (Ladd 2010).

Based on these discussions, it is plausible to argue that believing in fake news and misinformation relates to the individual's trust in particular media sources. Such biased belief may affect political perceptions, and consequently electoral results, since simply trusting what is read, heard and watched without criticism is associated with political misperception (Hutchens et al. 2021). In other words, citizens who trust media are more likely to fail to distinguish between facts and fiction. As Tsfati (2003) argues, media shifts the trustful audience and alters their perceptions according to the reported climate of the political environment, and when voters trust media, they tend to accept what is presented. Parallel to those arguments that underline the persuasive power of media, I suggest that trust in media will moderate the perception of surprise and propose a third hypothesis as follows:

> H3: High levels of trust in media increase the chances of being surprised by election results.

Partisanship

Lastly, this section argues that partisanship shapes electoral expectations. When conceptualised as an emotional link between the party and the voter, partisanship becomes a tool for positively distinguishing one party's supporters from another's (Huddy, Mason and Aarøe 2015). Such a link has been shown to be very solid and resistant to the effects of short-term economic and political fluctuations on non-issue-based voting. Accordingly, strong partisans tend to disregard changes in their party's policy positions and feel compelled to argue against political content that runs counter to the set of concepts and beliefs they regard as definitional (Kim, Taber and Lodge 2010).

Against this background, it is not surprising that electoral cycles become crucial when partisanship is in question since levels of partisanship tend to rise during elections. Several works show that since strong partisans will be most affected by the outcome of an election, it is natural for them to increase the amount of political activity they engage in during election times (Huddy, Mason and Aarøe 2015).

At this particular point, the concept of partisan-motivated reasoning also becomes helpful in explaining how people's political views, values and emotions at that time may impact their perceptions of electoral outcomes. Considering that individuals' political views are influenced by their motivations, effort and knowledge of the political environment, identification with a political party is a pervasive and vital aspect of an individual's identity that influences perceptions. Supporting that argument, several works have demonstrated the significance of partisan-motivated reasoning in perceptions and interpretations of political events. These works refer to a wide range of events, including warfare, exposure to information and the need for ideologically compatible media content (Bolsen, Druckman and Cook 2014; Druckman, Fein and Leeper 2012). These studies also help to support the notion that political parties can influence public views, primarily by highlighting individuals' unwillingness to reflect on communications they receive and the prevalence of the partisan lens. Thus, partisans react to political events impulsively and without much thought, and a strong party supporter will adopt an explanation that minimises the negative consequences of the facts.

I also argue that, in the Turkish case, there is a regional dimension to partisan reasoning and hence electoral expectations. In Turkey, the eastern and south-eastern Anatolian region, where the Kurdish ethnic minority is highly concentrated, has experienced extreme ideological and political polarisation since the 1970s. In addition, this is an undeveloped region with a substantial Kurdish minority that has traditionally promoted separatist aspirations and has more recently prioritised the establishment of ethnic rights within the confines of Turkish governmental institutions. Accordingly, research focusing on the regional aspects of Turkish politics has to come to terms with what is often referred to in Turkish political discourse as the 'Kurdish question', which has always been a central issue for Turkish politics (Toros 2012; Kirişçi and Winrow 1997; Gunter 2004; Kirişçi 2004; Yavuz and Özcan 2006). The issue's significance elevated recently, since it does not sit comfortably with the country's drive towards democratisation, and manifested itself in political terms, which has consequences for electoral politics. Since historic conflicts heighten ethnic tensions, we expect these tensions to accentuate the effect of partisanship on electoral perceptions. In other words, historical and ethnic tensions in the region should condition electoral perceptions.

Currently, the primary political vehicle for the ethnic Kurdish population is the Halkların Demokratik Partisi (People's Democratic Party, HDP), which is not only closely aligned with the Kurdish ethnic group living in the region but also with Kurds living in other parts of the country. As Sarigil (2018b) aptly argues, a significant area of conflict in the Turkish context falls in the domain of electoral politics. Beginning in the early 2000s, the electoral popularity of pro-Islamic and conservative parties such as the AKP rose in the region, polarising the voting base among the Kurdish community (Sarigil 2018a, 105). Since, in multi-ethnic countries, prejudice against out-groups is a principal component in political rivalry and a common determinant of party identification, bias against such groups is a common factor in political competition and a frequent determinant of electoral expectations.

Hence I argue that partisanship shapes citizens' interpretation of electoral expectations during an electoral cycle; partisans are more likely to judge events in favour of their parties. Parallel to the arguments that show the power of partisan-motivated reasoning in evaluating political developments, I suggest that partisanship will shape the perception of surprise and propose a fourth hypothesis, as follows:

H4: High levels of partisanship increase the chances of being surprised by election results.

Data, Method and Findings

The data used to examine these hypotheses are drawn from the Electoral Integrity in Turkey (EI-T) survey. The survey fields a range of questions on electoral behaviour, including a battery of questions asking respondents to assess electoral outcomes compared to their pre-electoral expectations. In the most recent survey, the battery included eight questions about expectations using a five-point Likert scale ranging from 1, 'I was not expecting that result at all', to 5, 'I was definitely expecting that result'. Among these questions, we used the question on expectations that the HDP would pass the 10 per cent threshold for representation, as the dependent variable of our study. This choice was based on the assessment that, looking at the facts behind the eight questions in the battery, the vote share achieved by the HDP coincided least with respondents' expectations and with reality, making it the most surprising result. The dependent variable was recoded in binary form, and the first two categories were grouped as low expectation – the 'surprised' category (scored as 1) – and others – 'not surprised' (scored as 0).

To test the first hypothesis, a factor analysis was applied to the battery of seven electoral integrity questions. This analysis provided two dimensions, which were labelled 'integrity' and 'malpractice', for consistency with earlier analysis in this book. Then the factor scores were extracted to provide the necessary weights for each observation. Finally, two indices with the same names were created as independent variables, to test the relationship of these variables with electoral expectations.

To test the second hypothesis, the analysis used two questions that tap into trust in TV and broader press reporting, measured by a four-point Likert scale. Like the dependent variable, these variables were converted into binary by combining the appropriate levels under 'High trust' and 'Low trust'.

The battery within the questionnaire that measured frequency of studying the news and consumption was used to test the third hypothesis. This battery lists seven sources of political news: print magazines, TV, daily newspapers, radio news, email, friends and the internet. The battery also requested information on frequency of consuming news from these sources, ranging from 'daily' to 'not at all'. To create an independent variable to fit the third hypothesis, first frequency of usage of these individual sources was reduced to a binary ('1' denoting frequent use, '0' otherwise). Then, scores were compiled for each respondent to determine a 'diversity score', ranging between 0 and 7, with higher scores indicating a broader range of media used. Finally, three diversity levels were constructed by combining the first two, middle three and last two levels of the diversity scores, indicating 'Low-level', 'Medium-level' and 'High-level' diversity in news consumption. For hypothesis four, the analysis used the vote choice of respondents. Table 8.1 shows descriptive statistics for these variables.

Table 8.1 provides supportive insights for all four hypotheses we set ourselves. First and foremost, analysis shows that more than 60 per cent of the voters were surprised by the election results. Second, the analyses of the integrity index show that as we move from low to high levels of perceived integrity,

Table 8.1 Descriptive statistics of variables

Integrity variables

	Integrity			Malpractice		
	Low	Medium	High	Low	Medium	High
Not surprised	113	222	21	117	217	22
	29%	41.3%	44.7%	57.9%	31.7%	25.3%
Surprised	276	315	26	85	467	65
	71%	58.7%	55.3%	42.1%	68.3%	74.7%
Total	389	537	47	202	684	87
	100%	100%	100%	100%	100%	100%

Media variables

	Trust in TV		Trust in other press		Information diversity		
	Low	High	Low	High	Low	Medium	High
Not surprised	368	108	363	109	149	247	84
	43.1%	29.3%	42.2%	31.1%	40.2%	35.6%	50.3%
Surprised	486	261	498	242	222	447	83
	56.9%	70.7%	57.8%	68.9%	59.8%	64.4%	49.7%
Total	854	369	861	351	371	694	167
	100%	100%	100%	100%	100%	100%	100%

the percentage surprised by the result reduces from 71 per cent to 55 per cent. This finding supports hypothesis one, that citizens perceiving high levels of integrity also have accurate perceptions about electoral outcomes and are not surprised by election results. We observe a similar pattern for the malpractice index. As we move from low to high levels of perceived malpractice, we observe a 30 per cent increase in the percentage of voters surprised by the outcome, meaning that citizens perceiving high levels of malpractice tend to be more surprised by election results.

Third, these statistics also show that the share of surprised voters is high among those with high levels of trust in both classes of media outlet. In Table 8.1, nearly 14 per cent more of the respondents who tend to trust TV news were surprised by the election results than of those who do not. Although slightly less than the finding on trust in TV, this gap was still 11 percentage points wide for the independent variable that captures trust in other press outlets. Lastly, the findings related to the information diversity variable also support our hypothesis. The surprise level is high among respondents with low or medium diversity in news consumption patterns, compared to those getting their news from a wide range of sources.

The analysis continues with a multi-variate analysis of the determinants of surprise, hypothesising that the variables listed in Table 8.2 are predictors in a series of logistic regression models combined with the partisanship variable.

Table 8.2 Logistic regression models applied to electoral perceptions

Predictors	Model 1	Model 2	Model 3
Integrity – Medium	−0.18 (−0.17)	0.11 (−0.2)	0.12 (−0.2)
Integrity – High	−1.26*** (−0.38)	−0.77* (−0.43)	−0.78* (−0.43)
Malpractice – Medium	0.90*** (−0.2)	0.50** (−0.24)	0.49** (−0.25)
Malpractice – High	1.96*** (−0.35)	1.37*** (−0.42)	1.37*** (−0.42)
High trust – TV	0.44** (−0.18)	0.27 (−0.19)	0.28 (−0.19)
High trust – Other press	0.17 (−0.18)	0.09 (−0.19)	0.08 (−0.19)
Information diversity – Medium	0.08 (−0.17)	−0.07 (−0.19)	−0.03 (−0.2)
Information diversity – High	−0.58** (−0.23)	−0.79*** (−0.24)	−0.75*** (−0.26)
AKP partisan		3.47*** (−0.5)	3.49*** (−0.5)
CHP partisan		3.01*** (−0.5)	3.03*** (−0.5)

Predictors	Model 1	Model 2	Model 3
İyi partisan		1.98***	2.03***
		(−0.62)	(−0.63)
MHP partisan		3.37***	3.39***
		(−0.56)	(−0.56)
Other partisans		3.02***	3.06***
		(−0.52)	(−0.53)
Income			0
			(−0.04)
Female			−0.06
			(−0.16)
Age			0.01
			(−0.01)
(Intercept)	−0.19	−2.90***	−3.13***
	(−0.27)	(−0.54)	(−0.71)
Observations	909	909	909
R² Tjur	0.088	0.187	0.189
Deviance	1106.937	1009.27	1007.362
AIC	1124.937	1037.27	1041.362
AICc	1125.137	1037.739	1042.049
log-likelihood	−553.469	−504.635	−503.681

*p<0.1 **p<0.05 ***p<0.01

Reference categories for the independent variables of integrity, malpractice, trust, diversity and partisanship are 'Low integrity', 'Low malpractice', 'Low trust', 'Low diversity' and 'HDP', respectively; reported coefficients are logged odds and standard errors are shown in parenthesis

Although I have shown selected results, the models presented in Table 2 provide evidence to support the set of hypotheses. The analyses fitted logistic models (estimated using ML) to predict whether the respondent was surprised by the election results, with the independent variables described above. The overall model's explanatory power is moderate, with a Tjur's R^2 = 0.19.

The first model covers only the core electoral integrity and media variables. The results for the integrity variables do not show a statistically significant relationship between the low and middle levels of integrity, but we observe a statistically significant relationship between the low and high levels of the electoral integrity index. That is to say, the odds of being surprised are 72 per cent lower among respondents perceiving high levels of electoral integrity than among those perceiving low levels of integrity. We observe a similar but statistically stronger significant relationship among all categories of the malpractice index. While the odds of being surprised are twice as high in the middle category, compared to those perceiving low levels of malpractice, the odds increase to seven times when the low malpractice category is compared to the high malpractice category. Both integrity indices provided statistically significant relationships with the expected signs, aligning with the proposed hypotheses.

The media variables in Model 1 provided only partial support for our hypotheses. While the model does not find a statistically significant relationship for the 'trust in other press' variable, the relationship between electoral expectations and trust in TV is significant with the expected sign. More specifically, the odds of being surprised are 50 per cent more among the respondents with high trust in TV than those with low trust. Lastly, we observe a statistically significant relationship between levels of information diversity and surprise at the election results: being in the high category of informational diversity reduces the odds of being surprised by electoral outcomes by 44 per cent. This finding is also parallel to hypothesis two.

Model 2 adds the partisanship variables to the first model. The comparison category was set to compare the other partisans with HDP partisans, in line with the theoretical arguments outlined above. The first point to mention about Model 2 is the continuing statistically significant relationships of the core independent variables introduced in Model 1. Regarding the partisanship variable, we see significant relationships for all of the parties under investigation. That is to say, being a follower of any party other than the HDP increased the chances of having misplaced electoral expectations. Figure 8.1 below displays the predicted probabilities of this relationship.

Model 3 adds the control variables to Model 2. All the coefficients that were statistically significant in previous models are also found significant when controlled for age, gender and income. However, none of the control variables produced statistically significant results.

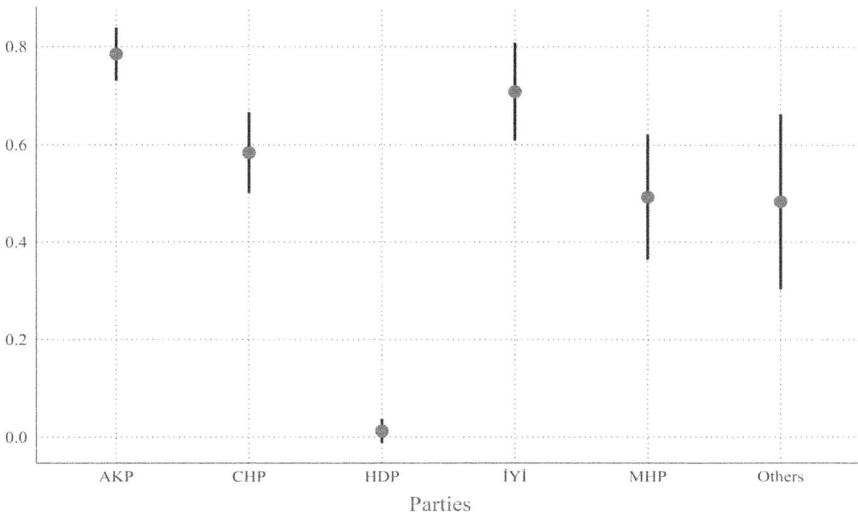

Figure 8.1 Partisanship and electoral expectations

Discussion

In this chapter I have provided empirical evidence on the relationship between electoral integrity and expected results, and the analysis shows that perceived high levels of integrity tend to co-exist with accurate electoral expectations. This significant result may be attributable to several reasons. First, it can be argued that when an election is conducted with high levels of integrity, it inspires trust and confidence in the electorate. When voters have confidence that their opinions will be heard and that the political process will be fair and open, their belief in the validity of the election results lays the groundwork for reasonable anticipations. Second, it is logical to expect that integrity in election administration encourages openness, which guarantees voters access to accurate and trustworthy information. This ought to contain details about the candidates, their stances on various issues and the voting process itself. Voters with access to complete and objective information are better able to make informed judgements and build more correct expectations for the forthcoming election. Third, since high levels of electoral integrity guarantee that the voting process will be objective and open to all registered voters, it ensures that every voter qualified to cast a ballot can do so and that each of their ballots is given the same weight in the final tally. Accordingly, voters can build expectations based on the electorate's collective will when they perceive that the process is fair and that all views will be acknowledged. As a result, voters ought to develop expectations that more accurately predict the outcome of the election. By the same token, the absence of manipulation and fraud may help voters feel confident that the election process is free from undue influence. In that case, citizens can form accurate expectations based on their genuine preferences. To summarise, it can be argued that high electoral integrity fosters an environment of trust, transparency, fairness and accountability, which are essential for accurate electoral expectations. When the electoral process is perceived as credible and legitimate, voters can form expectations based on reliable information and a belief in the integrity of the process itself.

This chapter also aimed to understand the link between perceptions of electoral problems and trust in the media. The information provided by conventional media such as print press and TV is unquestionably likely to be the main source of information from which people derive insight into public events, including elections, and shape their opinions. Accordingly, it is suggested that this information ought to have crucial impact on political consciousness (Curran et al. 2009; Graber 1988). Well-informed citizens with high levels of political knowledge are commonly seen as a significant feature of democratic societies. Understanding the democratic actors' proposals helps voters to take reasoned decisions and engage effectively in the electoral process (Coffé 2017). Furthermore, evaluations of the quality of the elections relate to the assessments of political legitimacy and can be expected to influence how citizens engage in the political system (Birch 2010). Given the consequences of perceptions of electoral integrity, understanding the impact on the media of such perceptions is vital since an unbiased, vivid and free media is an integral part of a well-functioning democracy. Having said that, however, there is no consensus regarding the influence of the media on political processes. While some scholars evaluate the media as a highly entertainment-oriented environment, negatively impacting social capital (Putnam 2000; Scheufele and Nisbet 2002), other empirical evidence shows that more frequent use of media sources increases political knowledge (Xenos and Moy 2007).

On the other hand, trust in the media is shaped by several factors. Carried out mainly by scholars in communication sciences, the available research has predominantly used experimental research designs to understand how different types of news outlet affect trust in and credibility of the media (Weibel, Wissmath and Groner 2008; Ariely 2015). The existing literature suggests that, unlike political institutions, the media cannot impose authoritative rules and formal control on citizens. Accordingly, these studies measured intangible factors such as media distrust and media credibility (Bennett, Rhine and Flickinger 2001; Jamieson and Cappella 2008). Studies also have shown that trust in the media moderates media impact on viewers (J. M. Ladd 2012) and influences their choice of news media (Jamieson and Cappella 2008). In consequence, citizens' trust in the media significantly shapes audiences' choices for understanding politics.

The existing research also underlined the differences between dissimilar media environments. It has been argued that the general autonomy of media environments affects trust in the government (Tal-Or et al. 2010; Tsfati and Ariely 2014; Schuck, Boomgaarden and de Vreese 2013; Norris 2011). That is to say, when the media enjoys high levels of autonomy from governments, trust in government tends to deteriorate since the media may have a fairly free hand in assessing government business, including elections. For many, this is an ideal condition for democratic functioning: the more democratic a polity, the less its citizens trust politics; and thus, it is argued, greater media independence is required if people are to become critical of and properly scrutinise the political sphere (Inglehart and Welzel 2003). Simply put, trust in governments will decline when the media are more autonomous. Figure 8.2, using World Values Survey data, portrays the empirical evidence for this argument.

However, in regimes with low levels of autonomy, it has been argued that those who trust the government trust the media more, especially if it conveys good things about the government (Ariely 2015).

Lastly, I would comment on the findings related to the connection between electoral integrity, partisanship and expectations that, in summary, electoral integrity entails the conduct of elections fairly and transparently, emphasising impartiality and equality for all candidates and parties. However, partisanship fuelled by strong political allegiances can occasionally undermine the sense of electoral integrity. When decisions or actions favour opposing parties, partisan bias may cause citizens to question the fairness of election processes. This demonstrates the need to protect the perception of impartiality in order to

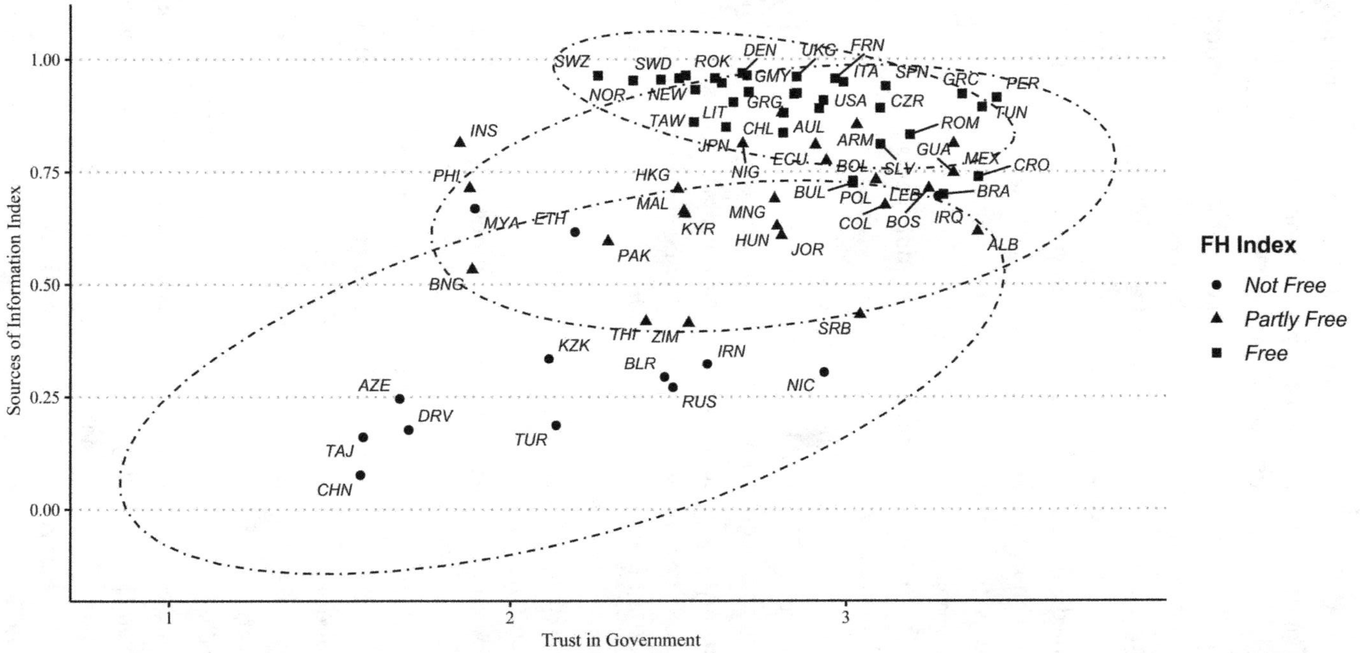

Figure 8.2 Trust in government and alternative sources of information

preserve the perception of election integrity. As this chapter demonstrated, partisanship substantially impacts on election expectations, and individuals tend to connect their expectations with their party preferences. Owing to their faith and belief in their party's philosophy, partisans may anticipate that their favoured party or candidate will perform well in elections. In contrast, adherents of competing parties may have diverse expectations, resulting in a range of forecast electoral outcomes.

Conclusion

This chapter focused on the underlying integrity and individual-level variables that affect electoral expectations. Empirical research suggests that supporters of political actors who have lost elections hold more unfavourable views of democracy and governance than supporters of the winners. Furthermore, these 'surprised losers' see reduced electoral responsiveness, believe elections lack integrity and question the validity of political processes. So, understanding this phenomenon provides insight into and a different viewpoint on citizens' faith in the political system and contentment with democracy.

The basic premise of this chapter is its argument that expectations about elections are shaped by opinions of electoral integrity, including assessments of whether elections are fair, whether votes are accurately counted and whether elections successfully boost government responsiveness to citizens. This is of special theoretical significance since elections are vital to both democratic ideals and democratic practice, as the principal opportunity for ordinary individuals to participate actively in a democratic administration. Evaluations of electoral integrity play a distinct part, in that other aspects of legitimacy, such as trust in government officials, are likely to have different connotations for citizens during an election campaign from those at other times. This argument is also consistent with the theoretical arguments in Chapters Four, Six and Seven emphasising the importance of public perceptions of the electoral process for the health of the democratic system.

In addition to perceptions of electoral integrity, this chapter also argued that, combined with partisanship, patterns of news consumption and varying levels of trust in the media shape electoral expectations. Although early studies showed the differences between the 'wishful thinking' of partisans of left and right parties, recent studies have focused on the link between media use and partisanship and provided valuable evidence on how trust in partisan sources plays a significant role in forming misperceptions. Additionally, research has showed that exposure to partisan media contributes to political misperception, encouraging inaccurate electoral expectations that take little account of substantiated evidence.

The analysis showed that perceived high levels of integrity are indeed associated with correct expectations for election results. This finding can be interpreted as confirming that the electorate's trust and confidence, access to accurate and trustworthy information, and the lack of manipulation and fraud all contribute to appropriate electoral expectations. In other words, high levels of electoral integrity establish a climate of trust, openness, fairness and accountability, all of which are required for correct electoral predictions. Voters can build expectations based on trustworthy information and confidence in the process's integrity when the election process is seen as credible and genuine.

References

Allcott, Hunt and Matthew Gentzkow. 2017. 'Social Media and Fake News in the 2016 Election'. *Journal of Economic Perspectives*. https://doi.org/10.1257/jep.31.2.211.

Altay, Sacha, Anne Sophie Hacquin and Hugo Mercier. 2022. 'Why Do so Few People Share Fake News? It Hurts Their Reputation.' *New Media and Society* 24 (6). https://doi.org/10.1177/1461444820969893.

Anderson, Christopher J., André Blais, Shaun Bowler, Todd Donovan and Ola Listhaug. 2005. *Losers' Consent: Elections and Democratic Legitimacy*. Oxford: Oxford University Press. https://doi.org/10.1093/0199276382.001.0001.

Anderson, Christopher J. and Andrew J. LoTempio. 2002. 'Winning, Losing and Political Trust in America'. *British Journal of Political Science* 32 (2). https://doi.org/10.1017/S0007123402000133.

Ansolabehere, Stephen, Roy Behr and Shanto Iyengar. 1991. 'Mass Media and Elections'. *American Politics Quarterly* 19 (1): 109–39. https://doi.org/10.1177/1532673X9101900107.

Ardèvol-Abreu, Alberto and Homero Gil de Zúñiga. 2017. 'Effects of Editorial Media Bias Perception and Media Trust on the Use of Traditional, Citizen, and Social Media News'. *Journalism & Mass Communication Quarterly* 94 (3): 703–24. https://doi.org/10.1177/1077699016654684.

Ariely, Gal. 2015. 'Trusting the Press and Political Trust: A Conditional Relationship'. *Journal of Elections, Public Opinion and Parties* 25 (3): 351–67. https://doi.org/10.1080/17457289.2014.997739.

Babad, Elisha, Michael Hills and Michael O'Driscoll. 1992. 'Factors Influencing Wishful Thinking and Predictions of Election Outcomes'. *Basic and Applied Social Psychology* 13 (4): 461–76. https://doi.org/10.1207/s15324834basp1304_6.

Babad, Elisha and Eitan Yacobos. 1993. 'Wish and Reality in Voters' Predictions of Election Outcomes'. *Political Psychology* 14 (1). https://doi.org/10.2307/3791392.

Baden, Christian, Maximilian Overbeck, Eedan Amit-Danhi, Tali Aharoni and Keren Tenenboim Weinblatt. 2022. 'What Are the Chances? How Media Coverage and Intrinsic Tendencies Shape Voters' Probabilistic Estimates about Candidates' Electoral Prospects in the Two-Round 2022 French Presidential Elections'. In ECREA European Communication Conference. Aarhus, Denmark. https://scholars.huji.ac.il/christianbaden/publications/what-are-chances-how-media-coverage-and-intrinsic-tendencies-shape.

Bargsted, Matias A. and Orit Kedar. 2009. 'Coalition-Targeted Duvergerian Voting: How Expectations Affect Voter Choice under Proportional Representation'. *American Journal of Political Science* 53 (2): 307–23. http://www.jstor.org/stable/25548120.

Bennett, Stephen Earl, Staci L. Rhine and Richard S. Flickinger. 2001. 'Assessing Americans' Opinions about the News Media's Fairness in 1996 and 1998'. *Political Communication* 18 (2). https://doi.org/10.1080/105846001750322961.

Berkowitz, Dan and David Pritchard. 1989. 'Political Knowledge and Communication Resources'. *Journalism Quarterly* 66 (3). https://doi.org/10.1177/107769908906600324.

Birch, Sarah. 2010. 'Perceptions of Electoral Fairness and Voter Turnout'. *Comparative Political Studies*. https://doi.org/10.1177/0010414010374021.

Bolsen, Toby, James N. Druckman and Fay Lomax Cook. 2014. 'The Influence of Partisan Motivated Reasoning on Public Opinion'. *Political Behavior* 36 (2): 235–62. https://doi.org/10.1007/s11109-013-9238-0.

Boutyline, Andrei and Robb Willer. 2017. 'The Social Structure of Political Echo Chambers: Variation in Ideological Homophily in Online Networks'. *Political Psychology* 38 (3). https://doi.org/10.1111/pops.12337.

Bozdag, Engin and Jeroen van den Hoven. 2015. 'Breaking the Filter Bubble: Democracy and Design'. *Ethics and Information Technology* 17 (4). https://doi.org/10.1007/s10676-015-9380-y.

Cho, Jaeho, Dhavan V. Shah, Jack M. McLeod, Douglas M. McLeod, Rosanne M. Scholl and Melissa R. Gotlieb. 2009. 'Campaigns, Reflection, and Deliberation: Advancing an O-S-R-O-R Model of Communication Effects'. *Communication Theory* 19 (1). https://doi.org/10.1111/j.1468-2885.2008.01333.x.

Cinelli, Matteo, Gianmarco de Francisci Morales, Alessandro Galeazzi, Walter Quattrociocchi and Michele Starnini. 2021. 'The Echo Chamber Effect on Social Media'. *Proceedings of the National Academy of Sciences of the United States of America* 118 (9). https://doi.org/10.1073/pnas.2023301118.

Coffé, Hilde. 2017. 'Citizens' Media Use and the Accuracy of Their Perceptions of Electoral Integrity'. *International Political Science Review* 38 (3): 281–97. https://doi.org/10.1177/0192512116640984.

Curran, James, Shanto Iyengar, Anker Brink Lund and Inka Salovaara-Moring. 2009. 'Media System, Public Knowledge and Democracy: A Comparative Study'. *European Journal of Communication*. https://doi.org/10.1177/0267323108098943.

Dolan, Kathleen A. and Thomas M. Holbrook. 2001. 'Knowing versus Caring: The Role of Affect and Cognition in Political Perceptions'. *Political Psychology* 22 (1). https://doi.org/10.1111/0162-895X.00224.

Druckman, James N. 2001a. 'On the Limits of Framing Effects: Who Can Frame?' *Journal of Politics* 63: 1041–66.

———. 2001b. 'The Implications of Framing Effects for Citizen Competence'. *Political Behavior* 23: 225–56.

Druckman, James N., Jordan Fein and Thomas J. Leeper. 2012. 'A Source of Bias in Public Opinion Stability'. *American Political Science Review* 106 (2): 430. https://doi.org/10.1017/s0003055412000123.

Dubois, Elizabeth and Grant Blank. 2018. 'The Echo Chamber Is Overstated: The Moderating Effect of Political Interest and Diverse Media'. *Information Communication and Society* 21 (5). https://doi.org/10.1080/1369118X.2018.1428656.

Easton, D. 1965. *A Systems Analysis of Political Life*. New York: John Wiley and Sons Inc.

Festinger, L. 1964. *Conflict, Decision, and Dissonance*. Palo Alto, CA: Stanford University Press.

Festinger, Leon. 1957. *A Theory of Cognitive Dissonance*. Palo Alto, CA: Stanford University Press.

Flaxman, Seth, Sharad Goel and Justin M. Rao. 2016. 'Filter Bubbles, Echo Chambers, and Online News Consumption'. *Public Opinion Quarterly* 80 (S1). https://doi.org/10.1093/poq/nfw006.

Garrett, R. Kelly. 2009. 'Echo Chambers Online?: Politically Motivated Selective Exposure among Internet News Users'. *Journal of Computer-Mediated Communication* 14 (2). https://doi.org/10.1111/j.1083-6101.2009.01440.x.

Garrett, R. Kelly, Brian E. Weeks and Rachel L. Neo. 2016. 'Driving a Wedge Between Evidence and Beliefs: How Online Ideological News Exposure Promotes Political

Misperceptions'. *Journal of Computer-Mediated Communication* 21 (5): 331–48. https://doi.org/10.1111/jcc4.12164.

Geiß, Stefan and Svenja Schäfer. 2017. 'Any Publicity or Good Publicity? A Competitive Test of Visibility- and Tonality-Based Media Effects on Voting Behavior'. *Political Communication* 34 (3): 444–67. https://doi.org/10.1080/10584609.20 16.1271068.

Gottfried, Jeffrey A., Bruce W. Hardy, Kenneth M. Winneg and Kathleen Hall Jamieson. 2013. 'Did Fact Checking Matter in the 2012 Presidential Campaign?' *American Behavioral Scientist* 57 (11). https://doi.org/10.1177/0002764213489012.

Graber, Doris A. 1988. *Processing the News: How People Tame the Information Tide.* New York: Longman.

Guess, Andrew M., Brendan Nyhan and Jason Reifler. 2020. 'Exposure to Untrustworthy Websites in the 2016 US Election'. *Nature Human Behaviour* 4 (5): 472–80. https://doi.org/10.1038/s41562-020-0833-x.

Gunter, Michael M. 2004. 'The Kurdish Question in Perspective'. *World Affairs,* 199–200.

Guo, Lei and Chris Vargo. 2020. '"Fake News" and Emerging Online Media Ecosystem: An Integrated Intermedia Agenda-Setting Analysis of the 2016 US Presidential Election'. *Communication Research* 47 (2). https://doi.org/10.1177/0093650218777177.

Hollander, Barry A. 2014. 'The Surprised Loser: The Role of Electoral Expectations and News Media Exposure in Satisfaction with Democracy'. *Journalism and Mass Communication Quarterly* 91 (4). https://doi.org/10.1177/1077699014543380.

Hong, Sounman and Sun Hyoung Kim. 2016. 'Political Polarisation on Twitter: Implications for the Use of Social Media in Digital Governments'. *Government Information Quarterly* 33 (4). https://doi.org/10.1016/j.giq.2016.04.007.

Hopmann, David Nicolas, Adam Shehata and Jesper Strömbäck. 2015. 'Contagious Media Effects: How Media Use and Exposure to Game-Framed News Influence Media Trust'. *Mass Communication and Society* 18 (6): 776–98. https://doi.org/ 10.1080/15205436.2015.1022190.

Huddy, L., L. Mason and Lene Aarøe. 2015. 'Expressive Partisanship: Campaign Involvement, Political Emotion, and Partisan Identity'. *American Political Science Review* 109: 1–17. https://doi.org/10.1017/S0003055414000604.

Hutchens, Myiah J., Jay D. Hmielowski, Michael A. Beam and Ekaterina Romanova. 2021. 'Trust Over Use: Examining the Roles of Media Use and Media Trust on Misperceptions in the 2016 US Presidential Election'. *Mass Communication and Society* 24 (5): 701–24. https://doi.org/10.1080/15205436.2021.1904262.

Inglehart, Ronald and Christian Welzel. 2003. 'Political Culture and Democracy: Analysing Cross-Level Linkages'. *Comparative Politics* 36 (1): 61–79.

Iyengar, Shanto, Kyu S. Hahn, Heinz Bonfadelli and Mirko Marr. 2009. '"Dark Areas of Ignorance" Revisited: Comparing International Affairs Knowledge in Switzerland and the United States'. *Communication Research* 36 (3): 341–58. http://crx. sagepub.com/cgi/content/abstract/36/3/341.

Jamieson, Kathleen Hall and Joseph N. Cappella. 2008. *Echo Chamber: Rush Limbaugh and the Conservative Media Establishment*. New York: Oxford University Press.

Jones-Jang, S. Mo, Dam Hee Kim and Kate Kenski. 2020. 'Perceptions of Mis- or Disinformation Exposure Predict Political Cynicism: Evidence from a Two-Wave Survey during the 2018 US Midterm Elections'. *New Media & Society* 23 (10): 3105–25. https://doi.org/10.1177/1461444820943878.

Kaufhold, Kelly, Sebastian Valenzuela and Homero Gil de Zúñiga. 2010. 'Citizen Journalism and Democracy: How User-Generated News Use Relates to Political Knowledge and Participation'. *Journalism & Mass Communication Quarterly* 87 (3–4): 515–29. https://doi.org/10.1177/107769901008700305.

Kim, Sung-youn, Charles Taber and Milton Lodge. 2010. 'A Computational Model of the Citizen as Motivated Reasoner: Modeling the Dynamics of the 2000 Presidential Election'. *Political Behavior* 32 (1): 1–28. https://doi.org/10.1007/s11109-009-9099-8.

Kirişçi, Kemal. 2004. 'The Kurdish Question and Turkish Foreign Policy'. In *The Future of Turkish Foreign Policy*, edited by Lenore G. Martin and Dimitris Keridis, 277–315. Cambridge, MA: The MIT Press.

Kirişçi, Kemal and Gareth M. Winrow. 1997. *The Kurdish Question and Turkey*. London: Frank Cass.

Kuru, Ozan, Josh Pasek and Michael W. Traugott. 2017. 'Motivated Reasoning in the Perceived Credibility of Public Opinion Polls'. *Public Opinion Quarterly* 81 (2): 422–46. https://doi.org/10.1093/poq/nfx018.

Kuru, Ozan, Josh Pasek and Michael W. Traugott. 2020. 'When Polls Disagree: How Competitive Results and Methodological Quality Shape Partisan Perceptions of Polls and Electoral Predictions'. *International Journal of Public Opinion Research* 32 (3): 586–603. https://doi.org/10.1093/ijpor/edz035.

Kyriakidou, Maria, Marina Morani, Stephen Cushion and Ceri Hughes. 2022. 'Audience Understandings of Disinformation: Navigating News Media through a Prism of Pragmatic Scepticism'. *Journalism*, July, 146488492211142. https://doi.org/10.1177/14648849221114244.

Ladd, Jonathan. 2010. 'The Role of Media Distrust in Partisan Voting'. *Political Behavior* 32 (4): 567–85. https://doi.org/10.1007/s11109-010-9123-z.

Ladd, Jonathan M. 2012. 'When Politicians Attack: Party Cohesion in the Media'. *Public Opinion Quarterly* 76 (1): 182–86.

Lazer, David M. J. et al. 2018. 'The Science of Fake News'. *Science* 359: 1094–6. https://doi.org/10.1126/science.aao2998

Lee, Jae Kook, Jihyang Choi, Cheonsoo Kim and Yonghwan Kim. 2014. 'Social Media, Network Heterogeneity, and Opinion Polarization'. *Journal of Communication* 64 (4). https://doi.org/10.1111/jcom.12077.

Lelkes, Yphtach. 2016. 'Mass Polarisation: Manifestations and Measurements'. *Public Opinion Quarterly* 80: 392–410. https://doi.org/10.1093/POQ/NFW005.

Mayer, Roger C., James H. Davis and F. David Schoorman. 1995. 'An Integrative Model Of Organizational Trust'. *Academy of Management Review* 20 (3). https://doi.org/10.5465/amr.1995.9508080335.

Mayer, Russell K. 2001. 'What to Expect from Electoral Expectations'. *Harvard International Journal of Press/Politics* 6 (3): 71–89. https://doi.org/10.1177/108118001129172233.

McKnight, D. Harrison, Larry L. Cummings and Norman L. Chervany. 1998. 'Initial Trust Formation in New Organizational Relationships'. *The Academy of Management Review* 23 (3): 473–90. https://doi.org/10.2307/259290.

Mutz, Diana C. and Paul S. Martin. 2001. 'Facilitating Communication across Lines of Political Difference: The Role of Mass Media'. *American Political Science Review* 95 (1). https://doi.org/10.1017/s0003055401000223.

Nadeau, Richard and André Blais. 1993. 'Accepting the Election Outcome: The Effect of Participation on Losers' Consent'. *British Journal of Political Science* 23 (4). https://doi.org/10.1017/S0007123400006736.

Nie, Norman H., Darwin W. Miller, Saar Golde, Daniel M. Butler and Kenneth Winneg. 2010. 'The World Wide Web and the US Political News Market'. *American Journal of Political Science* 54 (2). https://doi.org/10.1111/j.1540-5907.2010.00439.x.

Norris, Pippa. 2011. 'Political Communication'. In *Comparative Politics*, edited by Daniele Caramani, 352–370. Oxford: Oxford University Press.

Ognyanova, Katherine. 2019. 'The Social Context of Media Trust: A Network Influence Model'. *Journal of Communication* 69 (5): 539–62. https://doi.org/10.1093/joc/jqz031.

Plutowski, Luke, Rebecca Weitz-Shapiro and Matthew S. Winters. 2021. 'Voter Beliefs and Strategic Voting in Two-Round Elections'. *Political Research Quarterly* 74 (4): 852–65. https://doi.org/10.1177/1065912920940791.

Putnam, R. D. 2000. *Bowling Alone: The Collapse and Revival of American Community*. New York: Simon & Schuster.

Rose, Richard. 2008. 'Turkish Voters and Losers' Consent'. *Turkish Studies* 9: 363–78. https://doi.org/10.1080/14683840802012116.

Rousseau, Denise M., Sim B. Sitkin, Ronald S. Burt and Colin Camerer. 1998. 'Introduction to Special Topic Forum: Not so Different after All: A Cross-Discipline View of Trust'. *The Academy of Management Review* 23 (3): 393–404. http://www.jstor.org/stable/259285.

Sarigil, Zeki. 2018a. *Ethnic Boundaries in Turkish Politics: The Secular Kurdish Movement and Islam*. New York: New York University Press.

———. 2018b. 'Ethnic and Religious Prejudices in the Turkish Social Landscape'. *European Sociological Review* 34 (6): 711–27. https://doi.org/10.1093/esr/jcy036.

Schaffner, Brian F. and Samantha Luks. 2018. 'Misinformation or Expressive Responding?' *Public Opinion Quarterly* 82 (1): 135–47. https://doi.org/10.1093/poq/nfx042.

Scheufele, Dietram A. and Matthew C. Nisbet. 2002. 'Being a Citizen Online: New Opportunities and Dead Ends'. *The Harvard International Journal of Press/Politics* 7 (3): 55–75. https://doi.org/10.1177/1081180x0200700304.

Schuck, Andreas R. T., Hajo G. Boomgaarden and Claes H. de Vreese. 2013. 'Cynics All around? The Impact of Election News on Political Cynicism in Comparative Perspective'. *Journal of Communication* 63 (2). https://doi.org/10.1111/jcom.12023.

Sears, David O. and Jonathan L. Freedman. 1967. 'Selective Exposure to Information: A Critical Review'. *Public Opinion Quarterly* 31 (2). https://doi.org/10.1086/267513.

Strömbäck, Jesper, Yariv Tsfati, Hajo Boomgaarden, Alyt Damstra, Elina Lindgren, Rens Vliegenthart and Torun Lindholm. 2020. 'News Media Trust and Its Impact on Media Use: Toward a Framework for Future Research'. *Annals of the International Communication Association* 44 (2): 139–56. https://doi.org/10.1080/23808985.2020.1755338.

Stroud, Natalie Jomini. 2014. *Selective Exposure Theories*, edited by Kate Kenski and Kathleen Hall Jamieson, Vol. 1. Oxford: Oxford University Press. https://doi.org/10.1093/oxfordhb/9780199793471.013.009_update_001.

Sunstein, Cass R. 2007. *Republic 2.0*. Princeton, NJ: Princeton University Press.

Tal-Or, Nurit, Jonathan Cohen, Yariv Tsfati and Albert C. Gunther. 2010. 'Testing Causal Direction in the Influence of Presumed Media Influence'. *Communication Research* 37 (6): 801–24. https://doi.org/10.1177/0093650210362684.

Törnberg, Petter. 2018. 'Echo Chambers and Viral Misinformation: Modeling Fake News as Complex Contagion'. *PLoS ONE* 13 (9). https://doi.org/10.1371/journal.pone.0203958.

Toros, Emre. 2012. 'The Kurdish Problem, Print Media, and Democratic Consolidation in Turkey'. *Asia Europe Journal* 10 (4): 317–33. https://doi.org/10.1007/s10308-012-0336-0.

Tsfati, Yariv. 2003. 'Media Skepticism and Climate of Opinion Perception'. *International Journal of Public Opinion Research* 15 (1). https://doi.org/10.1093/ijpor/15.1.65.

Tsfati, Yariv and Gal Ariely. 2014. 'Individual and Contextual Correlates of Trust in Media Across 44 Countries'. *Communication Research* 41 (6). https://doi.org/10.1177/0093650213485972.

Tsfati, Yariv, H. G. Boomgaarden, J. Strömbäck, R. Vliegenthart, A. Damstra and E. Lindgren. 2020. 'Causes and Consequences of Mainstream Media Dissemination of Fake News: Literature Review and Synthesis'. *Annals of the International Communication Association* 44 (2). https://doi.org/10.1080/23808985.2020.1759443.

Valentino, Nicholas A., Antoine J. Banks, Vincent L. Hutchings and Anne K. Davis. 2009. 'Selective Exposure in the Internet Age: The Interaction between Anxiety and Information Utility'. *Political Psychology* 30 (4). https://doi.org/10.1111/j.1467-9221.2009.00716.x.

Van Duyn, Emily and Jessica Collier. 2019. 'Priming and Fake News: The Effects of Elite Discourse on Evaluations of News Media'. *Mass Communication and Society* 22 (1): 29–48. https://doi.org/10.1080/15205436.2018.1511807.

Vicario, Michela Del, Alessandro Bessi, Fabiana Zollo, Fabio Petroni, Antonio Scala, Guido Caldarelli, H. Eugene Stanley and Walter Quattrociocchi. 2016. 'The Spreading of Misinformation Online'. *Proceedings of the National Academy of Sciences of the United States of America* 113 (3). https://doi.org/10.1073/pnas.1517441113.

Vraga, Emily K., Sojung Claire Kim and John Cook. 2019. 'Testing Logic-Based and Humor-Based Corrections for Science, Health, and Political Misinformation on Social Media'. *Journal of Broadcasting & Electronic Media* 63 (3): 393–414. https://doi.org/10.1080/08838151.2019.1653102.

Walter, Nathan and Riva Tukachinsky. 2020. 'A Meta-Analytic Examination of the Continued Influence of Misinformation in the Face of Correction: How Powerful Is It, Why Does It Happen, and How to Stop It?' *Communication Research* 47 (2). https://doi.org/10.1177/0093650219854600.

Weeks, Brian E. and R. Kelly Garrett. 2014. 'Electoral Consequences of Political Rumors: Motivated Reasoning, Candidate Rumors, and Vote Choice during the 2008 US Presidential Election'. *International Journal of Public Opinion Research* 26 (4). https://doi.org/10.1093/ijpor/edu005.

Weeks, Brian E., Ericka Menchen-Trevino, Christopher Calabrese, Andreu Casas and Magdalena Wojcieszak. 2021. 'Partisan Media, Untrustworthy News Sites, and Political Misperceptions'. *New Media & Society*, July, 146144482110333. https://doi.org/10.1177/14614448211033300.

Weibel, David, Bartholomaus Wissmath and Rudolf Groner. 2008. 'How Gender and Age Affect Newscasters' Credibility – An Investigation in Switzerland'. *Journal of Broadcasting and Electronic Media* 52 (3). https://doi.org/10.1080/08838150802205801.

Wojcieszak, Magdalena E. and Diana C. Mutz. 2009. 'Online Groups and Political Discourse: Do Online Discussion Spaces Facilitate Exposure to Political Disagreement?' *Journal of Communication* 59 (1): 40–56. https://doi.org/10.1111/j.1460-2466.2008.01403.x.

Xenos, Michael and Patricia Moy. 2007. 'Direct and Differential Effects of the Internet on Political and Civic Engagement'. *Journal of Communication* 57 (4): 704–18. https://doi.org/10.1111/j.1460-2466.2007.00364.x.

Xiao, Xizhu, Porismita Borah and Yan Su. 2021. 'The Dangers of Blind Trust: Examining the Interplay among Social Media News Use, Misinformation Identification, and News Trust on Conspiracy Beliefs'. *Public Understanding of Science* 30 (8): 977–92. https://doi.org/10.1177/0963662521998025.

Yavuz, M. Hakan and Nihat Ali Özcan. 2006. 'The Kurdish Question and Turkey's Justice and Development Party'. *Middle East Policy* 13: 102–19.

9

POLICY PREFERENCES ON POSTPONEMENT OF ELECTIONS OWING TO COVID-19 – EVIDENCE FROM A CONJOINT EXPERIMENT

Introduction

Owing to the fast spread of COVID-19, elections were suspended or postponed in several countries including Canada, Mexico, Brazil, Argentina, the UK, Italy, Switzerland, France, Russia, South Africa, Iran, India and Australia between 2020 and 2022. Serious concerns have been raised about these delays, referring to the danger that such moves might compromise electoral integrity, fundamental freedoms and the rule of law by hiding behind the veil of 'the battle against the virus'. These critics have been justified since some governments have adopted further measures and suspended liberties, including freedom of movement and assembly, which are essential to any credible election process. Even after the pandemic waned, citizens all over the globe still worry about losing such liberties for good in 'return' for increased security.

Decisions how to conduct, and whether to postpone, elections are highly complex for several reasons. For one thing, decision makers must navigate constitutional and legal limitations with extreme caution and consider whether regulations might extend the mandates of incumbents 'undemocratically'. Second, conducting elections under extraordinary conditions like the COVID-19 pandemic may significantly restrict campaigning, lower voter participation and compromise the legitimacy of the elected institutions. Accordingly, both holding elections and delaying them under extraordinary conditions may threaten democratic functioning. During the pandemic, although clear paths were required to describe how current institutions might continue to operate after their mandates had expired, it is still unclear how democratic life will be sustained and how countries will return to 'normal'.

Although political science has examined elections extensively, we have only limited knowledge of delayed or postponed elections. One of the rare clauses related to the issue within the domain of international law, Article 4 of the International Covenant on Civil and Political Rights, states that the political actors responsible may refrain from fulfilling their duties in the event of a national emergency that threatens the survival of the nation and the existence of which has been formally announced. Even where that has occurred, any emergency provisions must be proportional, non-discriminatory, transitory and restricted in scope (Ellena and Shein 2020).

It is also much more common than is often thought to see elections delayed. According to Hyde and Marinov (2014), 144 states saw a 'suspended election' between 1945 and 2015. Rather than examining those cases, the literature primarily focuses on the timing of elections (James and Alihodžić 2020), mainly analysing snap elections, which are usually elections held earlier than planned within the provisions of existing constitutional regulations (Smith 2004; Alihodžić et al. 2019). Another line of research focused on natural disasters and their impact on elections related to vote share and turnout (Stein 2015; Bodet, Thomas and Tessier 2016; Stout 2018). Similarly, Morley (2018) considered how voters responded to unexpected events such as the 11 September 2001 attacks on New York city and Hurricane Katrina's destruction of New Orleans.

The COVID-19 pandemic constitutes a unique example, though. Spreading out from the Chinese city of Wuhan from 30 January 2020 (as of the time of writing, the date is still a matter of controversy), the pandemic was declared a Public Health Emergency of International Concern, and at least seventy nations and territories around the globe chose to delay upcoming elections for that reason (IDEA 2020). Obviously, there are significant risks in running an election during or shortly after a natural catastrophe because participants will need to move quickly and concentrate on, for example, control of the electoral registers by voters and parties and door-to-door verification of these records. Additionally, during election campaigns, candidates and parties usually organise large rallies and canvass voters' homes. Millions of individuals are on the move to vote on election day; vote counts are frequently conducted in crowded places, such as halls or voting centres, where social distancing is difficult owing to the large number of individuals present.

One line of literature argues that two long-term effects of the pandemic directly related to elections are already evident. First, it is argued that the 'common enemy' situation guarantees a ceasefire within societies where high levels of partisanship and polarisation are observed (Council of Europe 2020). The second effect is the reliance on experts, so governments can base their judgements on expert knowledge; since they serve the public, some institutions, especially health and scientific institutions, are admired and treasured (Fast and Waugaman 2016). These effects are called 'rally' or 'rally-round-the-flag' effects because they strengthen support for people or institutions affiliated with the country (Esaiasson et al. 2021; Dinesen and Jæger 2013). Focusing public attention directly on danger, rally effects are regarded as a means of enhancing security in a climate of instability (Doty, Peterson and Winter 1991). Under such conditions, political elites are also expected to play a significant part, and it is anticipated that continuous elite messaging will influence public opinion in the direction of the message. However, an alternative branch of the literature argues that the 'rally-round-the-flag' effect should not be taken for granted (Amat et al. 2020). Research has demonstrated that citizens typically find reasons to criticise their government for inefficiency during and after natural disasters like the pandemic. Such criticisms can reduce institutional trust at the height of the crisis (van der Weerd et al. 2011; Healy and Malhotra 2009).

In any case, many other factors may affect perceptions relating to the postponement of elections. That is to say, even during extraordinary times like pandemics, some deeply rooted political considerations, such as partisanship, can still shape how a postponement is perceived.

During the first two decades of this century, a significant amount of political science research consistently analysed problems associated with the phenomenon of partisanship and polarisation. Several studies claimed that partisanship has recently changed and developed into a specific type that shapes social identity, especially a particular kind known as affective polarisation. Although we know that affective polarisation – the tendency to disapprove of, distrust and even hate those from another party (Iyengar, Sood and

Lelkes 2012) – is on the rise, surprisingly we have only scant knowledge about how it affects our policy choices. Motivated by this gap in our knowledge, the present chapter investigates a single dimension of this puzzle: how partisanship and affective polarisation shaped policy choices that were proposed in response to the COVID-19 pandemic.

Such an effort is essential, for at least two reasons. First, by providing evidence about the power of partisanship and polarisation over policy choices, it will be possible to comment on whether these concepts matter for politics, and if so, how. Second, it would be of great benefit to understand whether political dispositions or practical considerations influence policy preferences. If the former is true, it is evident that policymakers should formulate approaches that exceed practical expectations, to make these policies function as planned. Although a research attempt as such is appealing, the scarcity of studies documenting the effect we are discussing shows the difficulties of carrying out such a study. According to Druckman et al. (2020), this difficulty stems from the fact that issue positions that shape policy preferences are endogenous to partisan dispositions, making it nearly impossible to find an issue that has not been shaped by partisanship. However, the COVID-19 pandemic provides us with a rare opportunity to carry out fairly pure research, since the scale of the pandemic rendered most partisans' starting assumptions inadequate.

Based on the arguments above, this chapter analyses whether partisanship and affective polarisation shaped the approval of policies related to COVID-19, and if so, how, by using a conjoint experiment fielded in a country-representative face-to-face survey. The analysis separates two policy areas – elections and media freedom – referring to newly developed policy responses to the COVID-19 pandemic. The findings show clear evidence that participants are more likely to approve policy proposals if their political party offers them. Moreover, this impact is more robust for affectively polarised citizens.

Partisanship and Affective Polarisation: A Theoretical Backdrop

The literature on partisanship has produced two opposed conceptions of the phenomenon: the 'expressive' and the 'instrumental' conceptions (Arceneaux and van der Wielen 2013; Lupu 2013). The first stance describes partisanship as a feeling of 'psychological connection' resulting from identifying with a party and the partisan category (Greene 1999; Campbell et al. 1980). The more recent works that followed this stance brought social identity theory into the picture and argued that belonging to a specific community is an essential aspect of an individual's sense of self. From that perspective, group identities assist individuals to positively distinguish themselves from others (Huddy, Mason and Aarøe 2015). Since it is a psychological state, partisanship can extend beyond the scope of politics and shape other dimensions of daily life. A second category of researchers, known generally as instrumentalists, argued that, on the contrary, partisan identities are products of rational assessments by individuals, and these assessments develop over the individuals' lifespan (Fiorina 1981; Johnston 2006, 333). From this viewpoint, party preferences have only a degree of consistency since they represent a 'rolling count' of assessments accruing throughout the individual's life, and validating previous evaluations involves a considerable amount of new knowledge (Laebens and Öztürk 2020).

From the instrumental standpoint, partisanship is an amalgamation of party performance, ideological convictions and policy alignment with the party by an individual who is influenced by current aspects of the political environment (Downs 1957; Achen 2002). This conceptualisation relates to the rational choice paradigm, which prioritises utility maximisation for political decision-making. In this framework, factors including economic evaluations (MacKuen, Erikson and Stimson 1989), policy preferences (Fiorina 1981) and evaluations of candidates (Garzia 2013) are taken into account by citizens who then abandon or sustain their party preferences. According to the competing expressive approach, on the other hand, partisanship is a long-lasting identity shaped by identification with a particular group, and gender, religion, ethnicity or race may all be factors in it (Green, Palmquist and Schickler 2002). Such an identification, in return, fosters an emotional commitment to the party, provides stability (voting is no longer really a choice) and loyalty can mitigate the impact of short-term events. Both approaches have attracted a considerable amount of support after producing solid empirical proofs, and there is growing evidence that both accounts of partisanship enlighten vote choice and public opinion at different times, in differing contexts and among different segments of the electorate (Arceneaux and van der Wielen 2013; Bullock 2011; Lavine, Johnston and Steenbergen 2013).

Although researchers have utilised both stances in their works, the expressive approach has recently gained popularity. The research that applies this stance has accurately accounted for the stability of partisan attachments, explained relative immunity to short-term economic and political fluctuations quite well, underlined the strong influence of partisanship on vote choice regardless of issue preferences, and showed the ability of partisan elites to influence rank-and-file partisans (Fowler and Kam 2007; Gerber, Huber and Washington 2010; Green, Palmquist and Schickler 2002; Greene 2002; Nicholson 2012; Cohen 2003; Dancey and Goren 2010). Moreover, research has also showed that partisans ignore alterations in their party's agendas and are driven to contend against political material that contradicts their partisan ideas and convictions (Taber and Lodge 2006; Lodge and Taber 2010; Lebo and Cassino 2007). In a recent study, Huddy, Mason and Aarøe (2015) combined the two approaches and showed that the level of competition during elections relates to the varying levels of partisanship. They argued that since, especially, strong partisans will suffer or benefit from the election results, they tend to boost their political activity during elections. However, this competitive spirit decreases between elections, allowing other identities or political reasons to take precedence in determining political activity. Thus, partisanship is undoubtedly a combination of instrumental and expressive elements, and the situations in which one or the other model prevails warrant more exploration (Bankert, Huddy and Rosema 2017).

Although such examples are pretty convincing, there are still many reasons to believe that the distinction between expressive and instrumental partisanship is still critical. To begin with, the two models have entirely different conceptions of the democratic citizenry. According to the instrumental model, voters resemble the ideal citizen, capable of skilfully navigating the political environment and making political judgements based on a thorough assessment of available political options, and presumably willing to do this. In the expressive model, by contrast, voters are compelled to protect the party to preserve its reputation, highlighting politics' tribal element. In that sense, the expressive approach provides a base for understanding biased and motivated reasoning. Partisans tend to demote ideas that contradict their views, focus on supportive rather than contrary explanations and continuously pursue information that supports their political position (Kunda 1990). This stance contradicts the instrumental view that theorises voters as impartial and capable of rationally processing political information. Secondly, both models also differ in their conceptualisation of democratic accountability. In the instrumental view, it is assumed that when voters engage more with the candidates during and after an election period, they will convey the electorate's issue preferences and, in return, expect legislation or other action consistent with those preferences (Bankert, Huddy and Rosema 2017). In the expressive view, however, since policy implications will be vague, they do not guarantee normative democratic ideals.

At this very point, social identity theory seems likely to help us understand partisanship more comprehensively. Tajfel (1981) defines social identity as a subjective experience of belonging to a group that has varying degrees, usually accompanied by a desire to favour the group, resulting in an in-group bias. This last point is quite crucial since, once identified with a party, voters are compelled to defend and reinforce the party's viewpoints, in order to preserve the uniqueness of their party (Turner et al. 1987). Hence, safeguarding and promoting group status is the central tenet of the social identity approach, combined with the formation of in-group bias. From this, it is logical to expect individuals who identify themselves closer to the party to have the highest in-group bias and work most actively to maximise their party's chances of electoral success and status (Andreychik and Gill 2009; Fowler and Kam 2007; Ethier and Deaux 1994). In that mindset, the group's achievements and misfortunes become personal, forcing the individual to maintain the group's uniqueness, particularly when the group's position or status is threatened (Mackie, Devos and Smith 2000). For these reasons, social identity theory gives a more comprehensive and dynamic account of expressive partisanship than earlier studies.

As a final point, it is crucial to focus on the literature on the origins of partisanship. To that end, it is worth mentioning social categorisation theory, which provides the cognitive underpinnings for social identity (Turner et al. 1987), where prototypes define the groups. These prototypes characterise the group and communicate information about its essential qualities. People judge how well they fit the party profile based on their perceived closeness to these prototypes or group stereotypes. Partisan prototypes or preconceptions are persistent, explaining why partisanship mainly remains steady, despite changes in a party's programme and economic performance. Partisanship, from this view, is the consequence of a cognitive matching process in which individuals compare their self-image to social groupings connected with a political party

(Bankert, Huddy and Rosema 2017). This matching process may also correspond with demographic identities such as ethnicity, gender, class, etc. To shed light on such combinations, Roccas and Brewer (2002) used the term 'identity complexity'. They assessed how different social groups are perceived to share similar characteristics and discovered that individuals who belong to highly overlapping groups are more reactive to group-based threats than members of groups that do not overlap so often or so greatly. Research that utilises this theoretical viewpoint has showed that Republican partisans in the USA share evangelical and conservative values to a high degree, while liberal and secular values are more common among the Democrat partisans. In other countries, parties founded on religious, regional or ethnic identities, such as the Scottish National Party in the United Kingdom or the Sweden Democrats, combine social conservatism with a solid nationalistic identity (Bankert, Huddy and Rosema 2017).

Affective polarisation draws on literature that depicts partisanship as a group identity (Greene 2004; Huddy, Mason and Aarøe 2015; Iyengar et al. 2019). This literature argues that party identities are often established during early adulthood and remain mostly fixed, resulting in significant continuities in electoral decisions (Niemi and Jennings 1991; Dinas 2014a; 2014b). Such a robust individual feature spills over and establishes views and patterns of interaction with the other dimension of politics (Campbell et al. 1960; Johnston 2006; Carsey and Layman 2006). The two components of affective polarisation develop in that process: positive feelings towards one's preferred group and negative feelings towards non-preferred groups. It is also possible that individuals may simultaneously have positive or negative feelings towards in- and out-groups (Richardson 1991). The literature also provides evidence that negative feelings towards out-groups do not stem from positive feelings towards one's own group (Greene 2004; Brewer 1999).

Affective polarisation, in that sense, becomes a natural product of partisanship from a social identity perspective. That is to say, partisanship provides a base for identifying in- and out-groups and helps to pinpoint opposing partisans negatively and co-partisans positively (Iyengar and Westwood 2015, 691). This stance coincides with the understanding of polarisation as a function of emotions and identity, in contrast to the view that explains the phenomenon as a function of a gap between policy perspectives (Fiorina, Abrams and

Pope 2005). For example, studies in the USA show that the general public has become increasingly polarised on issues over the last twenty years (Abramowitz and Saunders 2008). According to Levendusky (2009), it started even earlier: the number of partisans identifying with the party that most closely matches their lifestyle has increased significantly since the 1980s. This increase has been accompanied by amplified misperceptions attached to out-groups (Levendusky and Malhotra 2016).

Additionally, as partisan and ideological identities merged, other social identities, such as race and religion, have also become moulded by partisanship. According to Mason (2015), cross-cutting identities shape affective polarisation. Mason's research has demonstrated that citizens with consistent partisan and ideological identities become more hostile towards the out-party without necessarily changing their ideological positions. Still, those whose religious, racial and partisan identities align react more emotionally to information that threatens their partisan or issue stances. Other research has also highlighted the importance of ideological polarisation for affective polarisation (Rogowski and Sutherland 2016). For example, Bougher (2017) showed that increased ideological extremism is associated with increased partisanship. Similarly, in their experimental work, Webster and Abramowitz (2017) showed the impact of perceptions of a candidate's liberal or conservative status on levels of affective polarisation.

Scholars frequently refer to the changing media environment to explain these high levels of partisanship and affective polarisation (Lelkes, Sood and Iyengar 2017). According to this argument, partisan media outlets awaken partisan identities and provide a base for political parties by portraying the prototypes of in-group partisans (Hogg 2001). Many studies provide examples to support this argument by referring to the partisan media outlets that portray opposing parties negatively, going as further as equating out-partisans to Nazis or Communists (Berry and Sobieraj 2014) and focusing excessively on out-party scandals that fuel hate for the out-group (Puglisi and Snyder 2011). In addition, the absence of impartial and objective content in other media outlets worsens this condition (Rogowski and Sutherland 2016; Levendusky 2013).

Another line of research on the link between media and partisanship tries to unveil the news preferences of partisans. While some studies have discovered evidence of selective news content paralleling ideological position

(Stroud 2011), others have found that partisans are inclined to choose politically neutral materials (Gentzkow and Shapiro 2011; Bakshy, Messing and Adamic 2015). In a similar manner, some studies have focused on the impact of access to the internet as a tool for information. While Lelkes, Sood and Iyengar (2017) discovered a slight positive connection between internet access and affective polarisation, Boxell, Gentzkow and Shapiro (2017) found affective polarisation high among people who rarely use social media and the internet. Research also shows that people who spend more time on social networking sites are more likely to be exposed to controversial information by network members (Bakshy, Messing and Adamic 2015). These conflicting findings imply that partisan content conveyed in media outlets may play a significant role in polarisation since users can amplify such content through social networks and two-step communication processes. However, it is still premature to draw definitive conclusions concerning the significance of 'echo chambers', whether in person or online, as sources of affective polarisation.

Lastly, research has also underlined that political campaigns have the potential to intensify partisan hostilities affecting voters, in different ways. Sood and Iyengar (2017) showed that people become more divided on election day than in periods out of the election cycle. Toros (2016) showed that campaigns that include negative advertisements cause varying levels of political efficacy among different partisans. Similarly, Michelitch and Utych (2018) argued that electoral campaigns portraying the opposing party as an existential danger cause high levels of polarisation. Lastly, research has also showed that the homogenisation of online and offline networks contributes to high levels of polarisation. For example, Gimpel and Hui (2015) demonstrated that increasing isolation among partisans amplifies polarisation.

Given the power of partisanship in profiling beliefs and world views, we may expect to see it having an impact on events in daily life, such as setting up business partnerships, choosing neighbourhoods to live in or even selecting partners to marry. On the last, several studies have made some interesting findings. Nicholson et al. (2016) found that people see co-partisans as more physically beautiful, and Iyengar, Sood and Lelkes (2012) showed that the percentage of Americans who would be somewhat or extremely unhappy if their child married someone from the opposing party has increased by approximately

35 percentage points over the last fifty years. In a more recent study, Huber and Malhotra (2017) checked the importance of political homophily in relationships and discovered that partisan similarity enhances the chances of exchanging messages, displaying levels similar to those found for matching education levels. Several other research projects produced similar findings on the effect of partisanship in different walks of life, including choosing friends (Pew Research Center 2017), neighbourhoods (Chopik and Motyl 2016) and online network interactions (Bakshy, Messing and Adamic 2015).

As well as personal and social relationships, partisanship also shapes economic behaviour. Michelitch's (2015) study found that Ghanaian taxi drivers accept reduced fares from co-partisans but demand higher fares from counter-partisans. In the US context, McConnell et al. (2018) showed that discovering the seller was a co-partisan nearly doubled the amount spent on a product, a gift card in this case, and Panagopoulos et al. (2016) discovered that one-fifth of participants in their study were less ready to accept a gift card from a firm that donates to the opposition party's political action committee. Partisanship also has a significant impact on how individuals view the condition of the economy. Bartels (2002) showed that citizens perceive macroeconomic indicators more positively if their party is in power.

Parallel to the global boom in the literature on partisanship and polarisation, studies focusing on the Turkish case have also increased. Writing on partisanship in an early and pioneering example, Kalaycıoğlu and Sarıbay (2007) displayed empirical evidence on the link between parental socialisation and partisanship in Turkey and showed that party identifications develop at very early stages in childhood. Kalaycıoğlu (2008), testing the relationship between partisanship and economic perceptions, also found that expectations of economic utility play a part in developing party identifications in Turkey. More recently, researchers have shed light on other dimensions of partisanship using several methodological tools. For example, through a series of experiments, Erişen (2013) and Aytaç and Çarkoğlu (2018) found that solid partisanship alters how political candidates are perceived. Similarly, in their recent studies, Kalaycıoğlu (2014; 2013), Aytaç, Çarkoğlu and Yıldırım (2017), Erdoğan and Uyan-Semerci (2018), and Çakır (2020) showed the importance of partisanship for vote choice, proving evidence for the sustaining significance of strong identification in the Turkish context.

Another recent study found that Turkey displayed the highest levels of affective polarisation and the third-highest levels of partisan polarisation and party system polarisation (Lauka, McCoy and Firat 2018). Erdoğan and Uyan-Semerci carried out an exceptional research series in 2015, 2017 (reported in 2018) and 2020 and provided similar evidence about the rising levels of polarisation in Turkey. In their most recent study, the authors surveyed the Turkish population to understand the levels of affective polarisation by utilising three dimensions of the subject mentioned in the literature: the social distance between political party supporters, the moral superiority felt by political party supporters and political intolerance directed towards the supporters of other political parties (Erdoğan and Uyan-Semerci 2021). Findings on social distance, meaning the desire of one group to be distant from another group, showed a worrying level. Approximately three out of four respondents stated they did not want to be a business partner or to see their child marry a partisan of the political party from which they feel most distant.

Similarly, findings on in-group/out-group perceptions of moral status showed that while respondents portrayed fellow partisans as patriotic (87 per cent), working for the benefit of the country (86 per cent), honourable (85 per cent), open-minded (84 per cent), intelligent (83 per cent) and generous (80 per cent), they tended to perceive most supporters of the party from which they wanted the greatest distance as hypocrites (86 per cent), selfish (85 per cent), arrogant (82 per cent), cruel (79 per cent), a threat to the country (78 per cent) and bigoted (77 per cent). Lastly, the picture for the dimension of tolerance does not change. Of respondents, 41 per cent thought that the political party from which they felt most distant should be banned from organising a rally in their city, and 48 per cent agreed with tapping the phones of supporters of the political party from which they felt most distant.

One line of research argues that these worrying levels of affective polarisation are an end product of the divisive populist rhetoric of the government party Adalet ve Kalkınma Partisi (the Justice and Development Party, AKP) and its leader Recep Tayyip Erdoğan. A defining feature of this rhetoric has been its use of an 'us' versus 'them' dichotomy. It contrasts 'the people', who are said to represent the public will and are represented politically by Erdoğan through his leadership of the AKP, with a 'Republican elite', who represent the 'establishment' and are embodied in the main opposition party, the Republican People's Party (Aydın-Düzgit and Balta 2019). Moreover, institutional factors such as the alteration of the regime to a 'Turkish style of presidency' based on majoritarianism and the militant media landscape have accelerated this worrying process (Özbudun 2014). Aydın-Düzgit and Balta (2019) aptly argue that this worrying level of polarisation is also linked with current indicators showing democratic backsliding in the country. Examples are several: Turkey's Freedom House rating fell from 'partly free' to 'not free' in 2018 (Freedom House 2018); the country slipped to 163rd place on the press freedom index in 2017 as a country with an 'unfree press' (Reporters Without Borders 2017); Turkey's rule of law has deteriorated significantly since 2014 according to World Bank governance indicators (World Bank 2014). Parallel to the global examples mentioned above, owing to the high levels of polarisation Turkish citizens have started to view non-political problems, alongside political issues, primarily through the lens of their own party connections, resulting in significant policy disparities.

Based on this theoretical discussion, it is sensible to argue that partisanship and affective polarisation have a solid potential to politicise seemingly neutral issues, causing individuals to view such matters through partisan lenses, including policy proposals. A coordinated and collective response to the pandemic is critical, and if factors such as affective polarisation have hindered such efforts, it becomes nearly impossible to fight the pandemic effectively. Several previous works have provided empirical evidence on how citizens evaluate government actors through partisan lenses. For example, Malhotra and Kuo (2008) and Healy, Kuo and Malhotra (2014) showed that individuals exhibit higher confidence in their co-partisans, and favourable assessments of them. In line with these studies, one might expect a similar perception of the policy proposals related to COVID-19. Accordingly, this study compares perceptions about responses to policies proposed by 'government', 'opposition' and 'experts'. The first two are highly political and hence polarised entities. The latter is a neutral entity, and by producing scientific responses to the pandemic, it is expected to mitigate impacts of partisanship during the experiments (Levendusky 2018).

In that framework, although partisan reactions to the government's and the opposition's policy proposals are expected to be widely separated during the experiments, asking about experts ought not to produce such a partisan reaction. In other words, it is sensible to expect that responses will follow partisan lines when the approval is asked for government, or opposition, policy proposals, but there is no reason for partisan identities to affect citizens' responses to policy proposals from an expert. Accordingly, the first two hypotheses of this study are:

H1a: When evaluating policy proposals related to electoral postponement because of COVID-19 citizens will prefer experts' proposals to other proposals.

H1b: When evaluating policy proposals related to electoral postponement because of COVID-19 citizens will prefer their parties' proposals to other parties' proposals.

Using the same logic, it is reasonable to expect that affectively polarised citizens will interpret nearly everything through partisan lenses. In such a condition, those individuals will also politicise the COVID-19 pandemic and tend to wish to convey their partisan affiliation, so as to distinguish themselves from 'the other side', including non-political actors such as experts. In line with this framework, the second hypothesis of this study is:

H2: As affective polarisation increases, partisans will be more critical when other parties propose electoral postponement because of COVID-19.

Data, Methods and Analysis

The data for testing the hypotheses are drawn from a conjoint experiment embedded in a face-to-face survey carried out on a nationally representative random sample of 1,629 Turkish citizens in 2020, stratified by region. The fieldwork was carried out by a professional public opinion company and involved face-to-face interviews in 12 NUTS-1 statistical areas, 29 provinces and 98 districts; respondents were selected using a multi-stage, stratified, clustered, random sampling procedure without replacement.

Conjoint analysis, which is a high-dimensional factorial experiment, is tool becoming widely used by political scientists because of its ability to examine the effects of multiple features on social phenomena with ease. Examples include the preferences of politicians (Campbell, Vivyan and Wagner 2019) and criteria for approval of immigrants (Bansak, Hainmueller and Hangartner 2016;

Leeper, Hobolt and Tilley 2020) and of public policies (Gallego and Marx 2017; Hankinson 2018). In conjoint experiments, respondents are expected to evaluate a sequence of different vignettes that illustrate a determined set of features, with combinations of randomly varied features.

In the conjoint experiment designed for this study, respondents were asked to evaluate a table containing two hypothetical COVID-19 policy proposals formulated by the government, the opposition and experts, each containing of a set of attributes related to elections. The attributes are randomly varied to form a series of pairwise comparisons. The resulting choice and rating of policies are then aggregated to estimate respondents' preferences for particular attributes. Following the framework described above, the respondents in the study evaluated three sets of pairwise hypothetical policy proposals with randomised attributes and were asked to state which policy proposal they preferred. In each set, the attributes were assigned randomly to allow the analysts to estimate the causal impact on policies of varying the attributes. The attributes, levels and example rounds used in the study were as follows:

Table 9.1 Attributes, levels and example rounds used in the study

Attribute	Level
Type of proposer	1. The government proposes the following policy 2. The opposition proposes the following policy 3. Experts propose the following policy
Elections	1. The government can postpone the scheduled elections indefinitely during the COVID-19 pandemic 2. The government should carry out the scheduled elections, even during the COVID-19 pandemic
Example Round	
The government proposes the following policy	The experts propose the following policy
The government can postpone the scheduled elections indefinitely during the COVID-19 pandemic	The government can postpone the scheduled elections indefinitely during the COVID-19 pandemic

Participants received the following introduction before evaluating the policy dyads:

> Discussions about the news have appeared in the media related to the COVID-19 pandemic. This news includes opinions about whether elections should be held during COVID-19. The table below shows some of the policy measures suggested by politicians or experts regarding these issues. Although not all of the measures you see below have been implemented, we ask you to consider for a moment that these measures are real. Please review these suggestions now.

The study's dependent variable was the policy choice, coded as '1' if the respondent supported the policy and '0' if not. Category variables were created to capture the attributes associated with a policy in a particular round, with reference categories as the first option. The moderator variables were set as partisanship and affective polarisation. To measure the levels of these two variables, the respondents were asked 'Is there a party that you feel close to?' and 'How close do you feel to the party you mentioned?' respectively. They were also asked what they felt about three government institutions (the Ministry of Health, the Turkish Medical Association and the presidency), with four answers offered ('no trust at all', 'some trust', 'trust' and 'full trust'), and some demographic information was collected. The statistical power for the design of this study was assessed as 0.93 (Lukac and Stefanelli 2020).

Since respondents made their choices in three rounds, the data set contains three times the number of choices as we have respondents. For the analysis, the responses were pooled at the individual level and estimations were carried out using ordinary least squares regression by clustering the standard errors at the respondent level. The inferential analysis started by calculating the main effects of dimensions on policy preference using the following formula (Leeper 2020b):

Policy Preference = $\beta 0 + \beta 1$Policy Proposer + $\beta 2$ Election Postponement + ϵi

Accompanying this equation, the following analysis calculates marginal means for testing hypotheses 1a and 1b. By averaging across all other features, marginal means display the means across all appearances of a particular conjoint feature level. Since respondents have two options in this study, marginal mean values above 0.5 designate high favourability, and values below 0.5 low favourability (Leeper 2020a). Figure 8.1. shows the marginal means of levels belonging to features of this study.

Figure 9.1 shows that the source of a policy matters significantly in evaluating policies. To be more precise, the policies coming from the experts received considerably more support than those coming from either the government or the opposition, and in this study opposition policies received minor support. Our findings also show that respondents supported proposals to hold elections on the due date marginally higher than proposals to postpone them. Figure 9.2 provides a more detailed picture of this finding by focusing on various sub-groups.

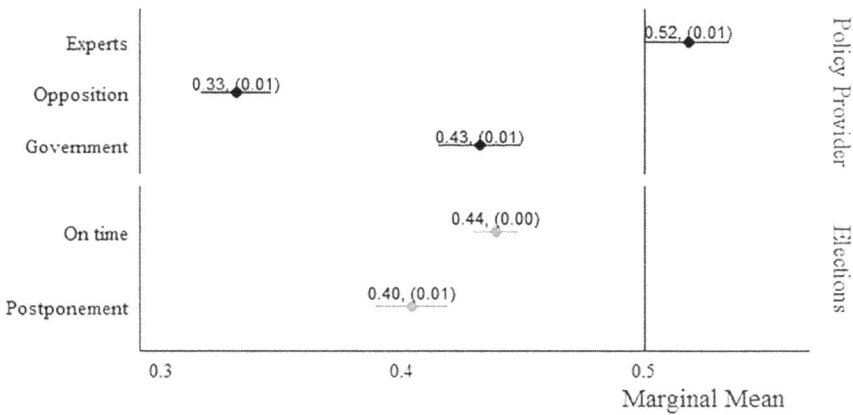

Figure 9.1 Marginal means

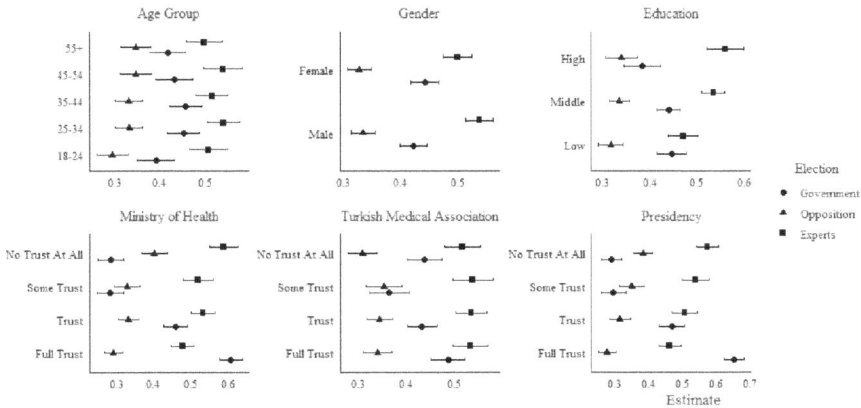

Figure 9.2 Marginal means of features analysed by sub-groups[1]

---

[1] Marginal means, 95 percent CIs; p <0.01 for all coefficients

The preference for particular proposals reveals a mixed picture across the sub-groups. As seen in Figure 9.2, analysed by age, gender or education experts' policy proposals received high approval levels, compared to other groups' proposals. However, we start to see signs of partisanship when we check the relationship between levels of trust in institutions. The respondents who expressed complete trust in the presidency and the Ministry of Health preferred proposals from the government more than proposals from the opposition, or from experts. Similarly, the respondents who expressed low trust in these government institutions preferred proposals from the opposition, or from experts.

Figure 9.3 below analyses these findings at the sub-group levels of party identification, which helps to elaborate hypotheses 1b and H2 further.

On the left side of the figure, we see the analysis conducted by party identification. Our findings indicate that partisans of the AKP and Milliyetçi Hareket Partisi (the Nationalist Action Party, MHP) differ from other parties in supporting policies supposedly coming from the government, and this difference is statistically different for AKP voters. Conversely, partisans of the Cumhuriyet Halk Partisi (the Republican People's Party, CHP), İyi Parti (the Good Party, İyi), and Halkların Demokratik Partisi (the People's Democratic Party, HDP) prefer experts' policy proposals over proposals from other sources.

Figure 9.3 partly supports all three hypotheses since the expected amplified result is only visible for the AKP and MHP voters. The bands show that partisans of the incumbent AKP who feel very close to the party tended to approve

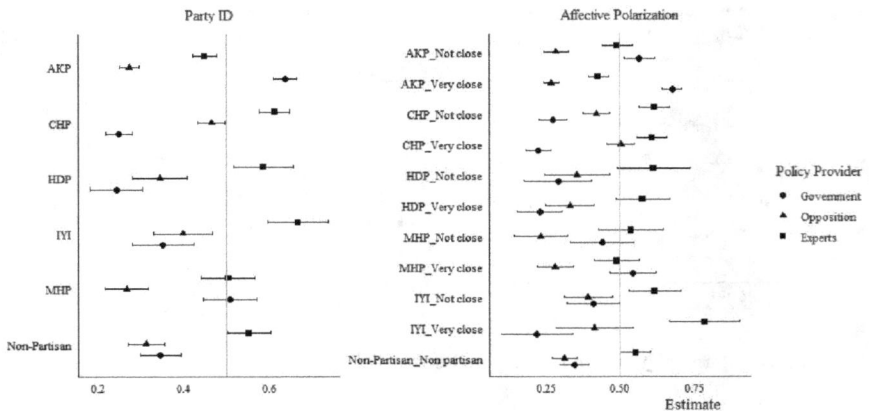

Figure 9.3 Approval of policies analysed by closeness to parties

policy proposals supposedly coming from the government more highly than party supporters who did not feel very close to the party. We see a similar but slightly different picture for MHP partisans: those who feel very close to the party tended to approve policy proposals supposedly coming from the government more highly than those supposedly from experts, while supporters who are not very close to the party approved the policy proposals supposedly coming from experts more highly than the supposed government proposals. For the other parties (CHP, İyi and HDP), there is no difference between close and distant partisans regarding preference for the supposed source of a policy.

Conclusion

This chapter, which aims to measure the factors determining citizens' reactions to policy announcements over the COVID-19 pandemic, produces at least two significant results. First of all, the findings show that policy recommendations from experts on COVID-19 were generally preferred to policy recommendations from the government or opposition, even if only slightly. Although this sounds like good news, there are some critical nuances. First, we see that levels of trust in various institutions mediate preferences for policy source: the findings showed that those with high trust in the Presidency and the Ministry of Health preferred policies supposedly from the government over those supposedly from experts (the choices shown participants were randomised). Furthermore, we see a totally different picture when we match policy evaluations with partisanship. The partisans of the ruling party AKP preferred policies supposedly coming from the government to those supposedly coming from the experts. Although the finding for the MHP, the other government bloc partner, is not as straightforward as that for AKP partisans it repeats itself for the People's Alliance. To put this differently, this finding indicates that almost half of the voters use some partisan criteria even when evaluating policies produced on a technical issue such as COVID-19.

The second important finding of the study is about the relationship between partisanship and polarisation. The results, in this survey based on policy issues related to COVID-19, showed polarisation only matters for partisans of the incumbent AKP. This sub-group tended to approve government policies more strongly than non-polarised AKP partisans. Based on this finding, I think it would not be wrong to argue that the determining factor regarding policy choices in Turkey's context is partisanship, not polarisation.

Before concluding, it would be appropriate to mention some limitations of the study and further research questions. The first technical limitation of the study relates to how polarisation is measured. The questionnaire asked how close the respondent felt to a party, not how distant they felt from another party, which is a common way of measuring polarisation. Another technical limitation is that only three sets of questions were asked, while conjoint experiments commonly ask five sets. The content of the study can also be criticised, because it only asked about policy proposals in one area: timing of elections. Undoubtedly, testing alternative policy proposals in similar studies will provide more holistic information on the subject. However, beyond the specific issues mentioned, this study still has some power in revealing partisanship's potential to politicise ongoing political conflicts.

References

Abramowitz, A. and K. Saunders. 2008. 'Is Polarisation a Myth?' *The Journal of Politics* 70: 542–55. https://doi.org/10.1017/S0022381608080493.

Achen, Christopher H. 2002. 'Parental Socialisation and Rational Party Identification'. *Political Behavior*. https://doi.org/10.1023/A:1021278208671.

Alihodžić, Sead, Nicholas Matatu, Oliver Joseph and Katrin Lewis. 2019. 'Timing and Sequencing of Transitional Elections'. International IDEA Policy Paper No. 18. https://doi.org/10.31752/idea.2019.13.

Amat, Francesc, Andreu Arenas, Albert Falcó-Gimeno and Jordi Muñoz. 2020. 'Pandemics Meet Democracy. Experimental Evidence from the COVID-19 Crisis in Spain.' *SocArXiv*.

Andreychik, Michael R. and Michael J. Gill. 2009. 'Ingroup Identity Moderates the Impact of Social Explanations on Intergroup Attitudes: External Explanations Are Not Inherently Prosocial'. *Personality and Social Psychology Bulletin* 35 (12): 1632–45. https://doi.org/10.1177/0146167209345285.

Arceneaux, Kevin and Ryan J. van der Wielen. 2013. 'The Effects of Need for Cognition and Need for Affect on Partisan Evaluations'. *Political Psychology* 34 (1): 23–42. https://doi.org/10.1111/j.1467-9221.2012.00925.x.

Aydın-Düzgit, Senem and Evren Balta. 2019. 'When Elites Polarize over Polarization: Framing the Polarization Debate in Turkey'. *New Perspectives on Turkey* 60: 153–76. https://doi.org/DOI: 10.1017/npt.2018.15.

Aytaç, S. Erdem and Ali Çarkoğlu. 2018. 'Presidents Shaping Public Opinion in Parliamentary Democracies: A Survey Experiment in Turkey'. *Political Behavior* 40 (2): 371–93. https://doi.org/10.1007/s11109-017-9404-x.

Aytaç, S. Erdem, Ali Çarkoğlu and Kerem Yıldırım. 2017. 'Taking Sides: Determinants of Support for a Presidential System in Turkey'. *South European Society and Politics* 22 (1): 1–20. https://doi.org/10.1080/13608746.2017.1280879.

Bakshy, Eytan, Solomon Messing and Lada A. Adamic. 2015. 'Exposure to Ideologically Diverse News and Opinion on Facebook'. *Science* 348 (6239). https://doi.org/10.1126/science.aaa1160.

Bankert, Alexa, Leonie Huddy and Martin Rosema. 2017. 'Measuring Partisanship as a Social Identity in Multi-Party Systems'. *Political Behavior* 39 (1): 103–32. https://doi.org/10.1007/s11109-016-9349-5.

Bansak, Kirk, Jens Hainmueller and Dominik Hangartner. 2016. 'How Economic, Humanitarian, and Religious Concerns Shape European Attitudes toward Asylum Seekers'. *Science* 354 (6309): 217 LP – 222. https://doi.org/10.1126/science.aag2147.

Bartels, M. 2002. 'The Beyond: Partisan Bias in Political Perceptions'. *Political Behavior* 24 (2).

Berry, Jeffrey M. and Sarah Sobieraj. 2014. *The Outrage Industry: Political Opinion Media and the New Incivility*. Oxford: Oxford University Press.

Bodet, Marc André, Melanee Thomas and Charles Tessier. 2016. 'Come Hell or High Water: An Investigation of the Effects of a Natural Disaster on a Local Election'. *Electoral Studies* 43. https://doi.org/10.1016/j.electstud.2016.06.003.

Bougher, Lori D. 2017. 'The Correlates of Discord: Identity, Issue Alignment, and Political Hostility in Polarized America'. *Political Behavior* 39: 731–62. https://doi.org/10.1007/S11109-016-9377-1.

Boxell, Levi, Matthew Gentzkow and Jesse M. Shapiro. 2017. 'Greater Internet Use Is Not Associated with Faster Growth in Political Polarization among US Demographic Groups'. *Proceedings of the National Academy of Sciences*. https://doi.org/10.1073/pnas.1706588114.

Brewer, Marilynn B. 1999. 'The Psychology of Prejudice: Ingroup Love or Outgroup Hate?' *Journal of Social Issues* 55 (3). https://doi.org/10.1111/0022-4537.00126.

Bullock, John G. 2011. 'Elite Influence on Public Opinion in an Informed Electorate'. *American Political Science Review* 105 (3): 496–515. https://doi.org/doi:10.1017/S0003055411000165.

Çakır, Semih. 2020. 'Polarised Partisanship, Over-Stability and Partisan Bias in Turkey'. *Turkish Studies* 21 (4): 497–523. https://doi.org/10.1080/14683849.2019.1678030.

Campbell, Angus, Philip E. Converse, Warren E. Miller and Donald E. Stokes. 1980. *The American Voter*. Chicago: University of Chicago Press.

———. 1960. *The American Voter*. Ann Arbor, MI: University of Michigan Press.

Campbell, Philip Cowley, Nick Vivyan and Markus Wagner. 2019. 'Legislator Dissent as a Valence Signal'. *British Journal of Political Science* 49 (1): 105–28. https://doi. org/10.1017/S0007123416000223.

Carsey, Thomas M. and Geoffrey C. Layman. 2006. 'Changing Sides or Changing Minds? Party Identification and Policy Preferences in the American Electorate.' *American Journal of Political Science* 50 (2): 464–77. https://doi.org/https://doi. org/10.1111/j.1540-5907.2006.00196.x.

Chopik, William J. and Matt Motyl. 2016. 'Ideological Fit Enhances Interpersonal Orientations'. *Social Psychological and Personality Science* 7 (8): 759–68. https:// doi.org/10.1177/1948550616658096.

Cohen, Geoffrey L. 2003. 'Party over Policy: The Dominating Impact of Group Influence on Political Beliefs'. *Journal of Personality and Social Psychology* 85 (5): 808–22. https://doi.org/10.1037/0022-3514.85.5.808.

Council of Europe. 2020. 'Elections and COVID 19.' https://rm.coe.int/election-and-covid-19/16809e20fe.

Dancey, Logan and Paul Goren. 2010. 'Party Identification, Issue Attitudes, and the Dynamics of Political Debate'. *American Journal of Political Science* 54 (3): 686–99. https://doi.org/10.1111/j.1540-5907.2010.00454.x.

Dinas, Elias. 2014a. 'Why Does the Apple Fall far from the Tree? How Early Political Socialisation Prompts Parent–Child Dissimilarity.' *British Journal of Political Science* 44 (4): 827–52. https://doi.org/DOI: 10.1017/S0007123413000033.

———. 2014b. 'Does Choice Bring Loyalty? Electoral Participation and the Development of Party Identification.' *American Journal of Political Science* 58 (2): 449–65. https://doi.org/https://doi.org/10.1111/ajps.12044.

Dinesen, Peter Thisted and Mads Meier Jæger. 2013. 'The Effect of Terror on Institutional Trust: New Evidence from the 3/11 Madrid Terrorist Attack'. *Political Psychology* 34 (6). https://doi.org/10.1111/pops.12025.

Doty, Richard M., Bill E. Peterson and David G. Winter. 1991. 'Threat and Authoritarianism in the United States, 1978–1987'. *Journal of Personality and Social Psychology* 61 (4). https://doi.org/10.1037/0022-3514.61.4.629.

Downs, Anthony. 1957. *An Economic Theory of Democracy*. New York: Harper and Row.

Druckman, James N., Samara Klar, Yanna Krupnikov, Matthew Levendusky and John Barry Ryan. 2020. 'How Affective Polarisation Shapes Americans' Political Beliefs: A Study of Response to the COVID-19 Pandemic'. *Journal of Experimental Political Science* 8 (3), 223–34. https://doi.org/10.1017/XPS.2020.28.

Ellena, Katherine and Erica Shein. 2020. 'Emergency Powers and the COVID-19 Pandemic: Protecting Democratic Guardrails'. International Foundation for

Electoral Systems, Stockholm. https://www.ifes.org/news/emergency-powers-and-covid-19-pandemic-protecting-democratic-guardrails.

Erdoğan, Emre and Pınar Uyan-Semerci. 2018. *Fanusta Diyaloglar*. 1st edn. İstanbul: İstanbul Bilgi Üniversitesi Yayınları.

———. 2021. 'Dimensions of Polarisation in Turkey 2020'. Turkuazlab, İstanbul. https://www.turkuazlab.org/en/dimensions-of-polarization-in-turkey-2020/.

Erişen, Elif. 2013. 'The Impact of Party Identification and Socially Supplied Disagreement on Electoral Choices in Turkey'. *Turkish Studies* 14 (1): 53–73. https://doi.org/10.1080/14683849.2013.766982.

Esaiasson, Peter, Jacob Sohlberg, Marina Ghersetti and Bengt Johansson. 2021. 'How the Coronavirus Crisis Affects Citizen Trust in Institutions and in Unknown Others: Evidence from "the Swedish Experiment"'. *European Journal of Political Research* 60 (3): 748–60. https://doi.org/10.1111/1475-6765.12419.

Ethier, Kathleen A. and Kay Deaux. 1994. 'Negotiating Social Identity When Contexts Change: Maintaining Identification and Responding to Threat'. *Journal of Personality and Social Psychology* 67 (2). https://doi.org/10.1037/0022-3514.67.2.243.

Fast, Larissa and Adele Waugaman. 2016. 'Fighting Ebola with Information: Learning From Data and Information Flows in the West Africa Ebola Response'. United Nations Office for the Coordination of Humanitarian Affairs. Washington, DC: OCHA Services. https://reliefweb.int/report/liberia/fighting-ebola-information-learning-use-data-information-and-digital-technologies.

Fiorina, Morris. 1981. *Retrospective Voting in American National Elections*. New Haven, CT: Yale University Press.

Fiorina, Morris P., S. J. Abrams and J. C. Pope. 2005. *Culture War? The Myth of a Polarised America*. New York: Pearson-Longman.

Fowler, James H. and Cindy D. Kam. 2007. 'Beyond the Self: Social Identity, Altruism, and Political Participation'. *The Journal of Politics* 69 (3): 813–27. https://doi.org/10.1111/j.1468-2508.2007.00577.x.

Freedom House. 2018. 'Freedom in the World 2018 scores'. https://freedomhouse.org/report/freedom-world/2018/scores

Gallego, Aina and Paul Marx. 2017. 'Multi-Dimensional Preferences for Labour Market Reforms: A Conjoint Experiment'. *Journal of European Public Policy* 24 (7): 1027–47. https://doi.org/10.1080/13501763.2016.1170191.

Garzia, Diego. 2013. 'Changing Parties, Changing Partisans: The Personalization of Partisan Attachments in Western Europe'. *Political Psychology* 34 (1): 67–89. https://doi.org/10.1111/j.1467-9221.2012.00918.x.

Gentzkow, Matthew and Jesse M. Shapiro. 2011. 'Ideological Segregation Online and Offline'. *The Quarterly Journal of Economics* 126 (4): 1799–1839. https://doi.org/10.1093/qje/qjr044.

Gerber, Alan S., Gregory A. Huber and Ebonya Washington. 2010. 'Party Affiliation, Partisanship, and Political Beliefs: A Field Experiment'. *American Political Science Review* 104 (4): 720–44. https://doi.org/doi:10.1017/S0003055410000407.

Gimpel, James G. and Iris S. Hui. 2015. 'Seeking Politically Compatible Neighbors? The Role of Neighborhood Partisan Composition in Residential Sorting.' *Political Geography* 48. https://doi.org/10.1016/j.polgeo.2014.11.003.

Green, Donald, Bradley Palmquist and Eric Schickler. 2002. *Partisan Hearts and Minds: Political Parties and the Social Identities of Voters*. New Haven, CT: Yale University Press.

Greene, Steven. 1999. 'Understanding Party Identification: A Social Identity Approach'. *Political Psychology* 20 (2): 393–403. https://doi.org/10.1111/0162-895X.00150.

———. 2002. 'The Social-Psychological Measurement of Partisanship'. *Political Behavior*. https://doi.org/10.1023/A:1021859907145.

———. 2004. 'Social Identity Theory and Party Identification'. *Social Science Quarterly* 85 (1): 136–53. https://doi.org/10.1111/j.0038-4941.2004.08501010.x.

Hankinson, Michael. 2018. 'When Do Renters Behave Like Homeowners? High Rent, Price Anxiety, and NIMBYism.' *American Political Science Review* 112 (3): 473–93. https://doi.org/DOI: 10.1017/S0003055418000035.

Healy, Andrew and Neil Malhotra. 2009. 'Myopic Voters and Natural Disaster Policy'. *American Political Science Review* 103 (3): 387–406. http://journals.cambridge.org/action/displayAbstract?fromPage=online&aid=6101720&fulltextType=RA&fileId=S0003055409990104.

Healy, Andrew, Alexander G. Kuo and Neil Malhotra. 2014. 'Partisan Bias in Blame Attribution: When Does It Occur?' *Journal of Experimental Political Science* 1 (2): 144–58. https://doi.org/DOI: 10.1017/xps.2014.8.

Hogg, Michael A. 2001. 'A Social Identity Theory of Leadership'. *Personality and Social Psychology Review* 5 (3): 184–200. https://doi.org/10.1207/S15327957PSPR0503_1.

Huber, G. and N. Malhotra. 2017. 'Political Homophily in Social Relationships: Evidence from Online Dating Behavior'. *The Journal of Politics* 79: 269–83. https://doi.org/10.1086/687533.

Huddy, L., L. Mason and Lene Aarøe. 2015. 'Expressive Partisanship: Campaign Involvement, Political Emotion, and Partisan Identity'. *American Political Science Review* 109: 1–17. https://doi.org/10.1017/S0003055414000604.

Hyde, Susan D. and Nikolay Marinov. 2014. 'Information and Self-Enforcing Democracy: The Role of International Election Observation'. *International Organization*. https://doi.org/10.1017/S0020818313000465.

IDEA. 2020. 'Global Overview of COVID-19: Impact on Elections.' https://www. idea.int/data-tools/tools/global-overview-covid-19-impact-elections.

Iyengar, Shanto and Sean J. Westwood. 2015. 'Fear and Loathing across Party Lines: New Evidence on Group Polarization'. *American Journal of Political Science* 59: 690–707. https://doi.org/10.1111/AJPS.12152.

Iyengar, S., G. Sood and Y. Lelkes. 2012. 'Affect, Not Ideology: A Social Identity Perspective on Polarization'. *Public Opinion Quarterly* 76 (4): 819.

Iyengar, Shanto, Yphtach Lelkes, Matthew Levendusky, Neil Malhotra and Sean J. Westwood. 2019. 'The Origins and Consequences of Affective Polarization in the United States'. *Annual Review of Political Science* 22: 129–46. https://doi. org/10.1146/ANNUREV-POLISCI-051117-073034.

James, Toby S. and Sead Alihodžić. 2020. 'When Is It Democratic to Postpone an Election? Elections During Natural Disasters, COVID-19, and Emergency Situations.' *Election Law Journal: Rules, Politics, and Policy* 19 (3): 344–62. https://doi.org/10.1089/elj.2020.0642.

Johnston, Richard. 2006. 'Party Identification: Unmoved Mover or Sum of Preferences?' *Annual Review of Political Science* 9 (1): 329–51. https://doi.org/10.1146/annurev.polisci.9.062404.170523.

Kalaycıoğlu, Ersin. 2014. 'Local Elections and the Turkish Voter: Looking for the Determinants of Party Choice'. *South European Society and Politics* 19 (4): 583–600. https://doi.org/10.1080/13608746.2014.993511.

———. 2013. 'Turkish Party System: Leaders, Vote and Institutionalisation'. *Southeast European and Black Sea Studies* 13 (4): 483–502. https://doi.org/10.1080/14683857.2013.859815.

———. 2008. 'Attitudinal Orientation to Party Organizations in Turkey in the 2000s'. *Turkish Studies* 9: 297–316. https://doi.org/10.1080/14683840802012058.

Kalaycıoğlu, Ersın and Ali Yaşar Sarıbay. 2007. 'İlkokul Çocuklarının Parti Tutmasını Belirleyen Etkenler.' In *Türkiye'de Politik Değişim ve Modernleşme*, edited by Ersın Kalaycıoğlu and Ali Yaşar Sarıbay, 501–15. İstanbul: Alfa Yayınları.

Kunda, Ziva. 1990. 'The Case for Motivated Reasoning'. *Psychological Bulletin* 108 (3): 480–98. https://doi.org/10.1037/0033-2909.108.3.480.

Laebens, Melis G. and Aykut Öztürk. 2020. 'Partisanship and Autocratization: Polarisation, Power Asymmetry, and Partisan Social Identities in Turkey'. *Comparative Political Studies* 54 (2): 245–79. https://doi.org/10.1177/0010414020926199.

Lauka, Alban, Jennifer McCoy and Rengin B. Firat. 2018. 'Mass Partisan Polarization: Measuring a Relational Concept'. *American Behavioral Scientist* 62 (1): 107–26. https://doi.org/10.1177/0002764218759581.

Lavine, Howard G., Christopher D. Johnston and Marco R. Steenbergen. 2013. *The Ambivalent Partisan: How Critical Loyalty Promotes Democracy*. New York: Oxford University Press. https://doi.org/10.1093/acprof:oso/9780199772759.001.0001.

Lebo, Matthew J. and Daniel Cassino. 2007. 'The Aggregated Consequences of Motivated Reasoning and the Dynamics of Partisan Presidential Approval'. *Political Psychology* 28 (6): 719–46. https://doi.org/10.1111/j.1467-9221.2007.00601.x.

Leeper, Thomas J. 2020a. 'Cregg: Simple Conjoint Analyses and Visualization'. https://cran.r-project.org/web/packages/cregg/readme/README.html.

———. 2020b. 'Introduction to Cregg'. 2020. https://cran.r-project.org/web/packages/cregg/vignettes/Introduction.html.

Leeper, Thomas J., Sara B. Hobolt and James Tilley. 2020. 'Measuring Subgroup Preferences in Conjoint Experiments'. *Political Analysis* 28 (2): 207–21. https://doi.org/DOI: 10.1017/pan.2019.30.

Lelkes, Yphtach, G. Sood and S. Iyengar. 2017. 'The Hostile Audience: The Effect of Access to Broadband Internet on Partisan Affect'. *American Journal of Political Science* 61: 5–20. https://doi.org/10.1111/AJPS.12237.

Levendusky, Matthew S. 2018. 'Americans, Not Partisans: Can Priming American National Identity Reduce Affective Polarisation?' *The Journal of Politics* 80 (1): 59–70. https://doi.org/10.1086/693987.

———. 2013. 'Partisan Media Exposure and Attitudes Toward the Opposition'. *Political Communication* 30 (4): 565–81. https://doi.org/10.1080/10584609.2012.737435.

———. 2009. *The Partisan Sort: How Liberals Became Democrats and Conservatives Became Republicans*. Chicago: University of Chicago Press.

Levendusky, Matthew S. and Neil Malhotra. 2016. '(Mis)Perceptions of Partisan Polarization in the American Public'. *Public Opinion Quarterly* 80 (S1): 378–91. https://doi.org/10.1093/poq/nfv045.

Lodge, Milton and Charles S. Taber. 2010. *The Rationalizing Voter*. New York: Cambridge University Press. https://doi.org/10.1017/CBO9781139032490.

Lukac, M. and A. Stefanelli. 2020. 'Conjoint Experiments: Power Analysis Tool.' https://mblukac.github.io/posts/2020/08/cj_poweranalysis/.

Lupu, Noam. 2013. 'Party Brands and Partisanship: Theory with Evidence from a Survey Experiment in Argentina'. *American Journal of Political Science* 57 (1): 49–64. https://doi.org/10.1111/j.1540-5907.2012.00615.x.

Mackie, Diane M., Thierry Devos and Eliot R. Smith. 2000. 'Intergroup Emotions: Explaining Offensive Action Tendencies in an Intergroup Context'. *Journal of Personality and Social Psychology* 79 (4): 602–16. https://doi.org/10.1037/0022-3514.79.4.602.

MacKuen, Michael B., Robert S. Erikson and James A. Stimson. 1989. 'Macropartisanship'. *American Political Science Review* 83 (4): 1125–42. https://doi.org/10.2307/1961661.

Malhotra, Neil and Alexander G. Kuo. 2008. 'Attributing Blame: The Public's Response to Hurricane Katrina'. *The Journal of Politics* 70 (1): 120–35. https://doi.org/10.1017/s0022381607080097.

Mason, L. 2015. '"I Disrespectfully Agree": The Differential Effects of Partisan Sorting on Social and Issue Polarization'. *American Journal of Political Science* 59: 128–45. https://doi.org/10.1111/AJPS.12089.

McConnell, C., Yotam Margalit, N. Malhotra and Matthew Levendusky. 2018. 'The Economic Consequences of Partisanship in a Polarised Era'. *American Journal of Political Science* 62: 5–18. https://doi.org/10.1111/AJPS.12330.

Michelitch, Kristin. 2015. 'Does Electoral Competition Exacerbate Interethnic or Interpartisan Economic Discrimination? Evidence from a Field Experiment in Market Price Bargaining.' *American Political Science Review* 109 (1): 43–61. https://doi.org/10.1017/S0003055414000628.

Michelitch, Kristin and Stephen Utych. 2018. 'Electoral Cycle Fluctuations in Partisanship: Global Evidence from Eighty-Six Countries'. *The Journal of Politics* 80 (2): 412–27. https://doi.org/10.1086/694783.

Morley, Michael T. 2018. 'Election Emergencies: Voting in the Wake of Natural Disasters and Terrorist Attacks'. *Emory Law Journal* 67 (3).

Nicholson, Stephen P. 2012. 'Polarising Cues'. *American Journal of Political Science* 56 (1): 52–66. https://doi.org/10.1111/j.1540-5907.2011.00541.x.

Nicholson, Stephen P., Chelsea M. Coe, Jason Emory and Anna V. Song. 2016. 'The Politics of Beauty: The Effects of Partisan Bias on Physical Attractiveness'. *Political Behavior* 38 (4): 883–98. https://doi.org/10.1007/s11109-016-9339-7.

Niemi, Richard G. and M. Kent Jennings. 1991. 'Issues and Inheritance in the Formation of Party Identification'. *American Journal of Political Science* 35 (4): 970–88. https://doi.org/10.2307/2111502.

Özbudun, Ergun. 2014. 'AKP at the Crossroads: Erdoğan's Majoritarian Drift'. *South European Society and Politics* 19 (2): 155–67. https://doi.org/10.1080/13608746.2014.920571.

Panagopoulos, Costas, Donald P. Green, Michael Schwam-Baird, Eric Moore and Kyle Endres. 2016. 'Risky Business: Does Corporate Political Giving Affect Consumer Behavior?' *Annual Meeting of the American Political Science Association, Philadelphia* 53 (9).

Pew Research Center. 2017. 'The Partisan Divide on Political Values Grows Even Wider'. *Universitas Nusantara PGRI Kediri*.

Puglisi, Riccardo and James M. Snyder. 2011. 'Newspaper Coverage of Political Scandals'. *The Journal of Politics* 73 (3): 931–50. https://doi.org/10.1017/S0022381611000569.

Reporters Without Borders. 2017. '2017 Press Freedom Index – ever darker world map'. https://rsf.org/en/2017-press-freedom-index-ever-darker-world-map.

Richardson, Bradley M. 1991. 'European Party Loyalties Revisited'. *American Political Science Review* 85 (3): 751–75. https://doi.org/DOI: 10.2307/1963849.

Roccas, Sonia and Marilynn B. Brewer. 2002. 'Social Identity Complexity'. *Personality and Social Psychology Review* 6 (2): 88–106. https://doi.org/10.1207/S15327957PSPR0602_01.

Rogowski, J. and Joseph L. Sutherland. 2016. 'How Ideology Fuels Affective Polarisation'. *Political Behavior* 38: 485–508. https://doi.org/10.1007/S11109-015-9323-7.

Smith, Alastair. 2004. *Election Timing*. Cambridge: Cambridge University Press.

Sood, Gaurav and Shanto Iyengar. 2017. 'Coming to Dislike Your Opponents: The Polarizing Impact of Political Campaigns'. *SSRN Electronic Journal*. https://doi.org/10.2139/ssrn.2840225.

Stein, Robert M. 2015. 'Election Administration during Natural Disasters and Emergencies: Hurricane Sandy and the 2012 Election'. *Election Law Journal: Rules, Politics, and Policy* 14 (1). https://doi.org/10.1089/elj.2014.0271.

Stout, Kevin R. 2018. 'Weathering the Storm: Conditional Effects of Natural Disasters on Retrospective Voting in Gubernatorial Elections – A Replication and Extension'. *Research and Politics* 5 (4). https://doi.org/10.1177/2053168018813766.

Stroud, Natalie Jomini. 2011. *Niche News: The Politics of News Choice*. Oxford: Oxford University Press. https://doi.org/10.1093/acprof:oso/9780199755509.001.0001.

Taber, Charles S. and Milton Lodge. 2006. 'Motivated Skepticism in the Evaluation of Political Beliefs'. *American Journal of Political Science* 50 (3): 755–69. https://doi.org/10.1111/j.1540-5907.2006.00214.x.

Tajfel, Henri. 1981. *Human Groups and Social Categories*. Cambridge: Cambridge University Press.

Toros, Emre. 2016. 'How to Run the Show? The Differential Effects of Negative Campaigning'. *Turkish Studies* 18 (2): 297–312. https://doi.org/10.1080/14683849.2016.1259575.

Turner, John, Michael Hogg, Penelope Oakes, Stephen Reicher and Margeret Wetherell. 1987. 'Rediscovering the Social Groups: A Self-Categorization Perspective'. *British Journal of Social Psychology* 94.

Van der Weerd, Willemien, Daniëlle R. M. Timmermans, Desirée J. M. A. Beaujean, Jurriaan Oudhoff and Jim E. van Steenbergen. 2011. 'Monitoring the Level of

Government Trust, Risk Perception and Intention of the General Public to Adopt Protective Measures during the Influenza A (H1N1) Pandemic in the Netherlands'. *BMC Public Health* 11. https://doi.org/10.1186/1471-2458-11-575.

Webster, Steven W. and A. Abramowitz. 2017. 'The Ideological Foundations of Affective Polarization in the US Electorate'. *American Politics Research* 45: 621–47. https://doi.org/10.1177/1532673X17703132.World Bank. 2014. 'Worldwide Governance Indicators'. https://databank.worldbank.org/source/worldwide-governance-indicators.

Part 4

CONCLUSION

CONCLUSION

This book attempts to constitute a unique and thorough approach to examining the causes and effects of compromised electoral integrity in Turkey. By integrating existing research with a particular case study, this volume contributes to the existing literature on electoral studies, voting and democratisation. Additionally, it links matters related to electoral integrity to an example of how such issues are relevant to an illiberal setting that operates on the margins of democracy. Indeed, the controversial elections in Turkey since 2010 mirror global trends related to electoral integrity worldwide. Several nations have suffered a range of problems related to election integrity, such as vote manipulation, ballot-box stuffing, abuse of state resources by political personnel, exclusion of opposition candidates, judges' failures to be impartial and violence, to name a few. Despite the ample research on these topics, a complete contextual perspective employing a case study to test the theoretical and empirical knowledge of global and context-based driving factors and the repercussions of damage to election integrity has been lacking. This volume attempts to fill this gap by focusing on the causes and effects of compromised electoral integrity, which has received less attention in the literature.

Electoral integrity is an idea that defines an ideal practical and normative framework for elections. Enjoying this broadly defined base for the term, our research on the subject examined the phenomena widely by evaluating the competence of polities to live up to this ideal in a variety of topic areas.

Of these topic areas, election fraud appears to be the most widely followed avenue of inquiry. Early works on electoral fraud argued that it could take several forms, including unjust legal arrangements and violence, referring to its indecisiveness and divergent tactics. Subsequent research developed terms like 'electoral malpractice' and 'electoral manipulation', significantly expanding the literature available. These works first point out the normative standards necessary for democratic elections and then provide empirical evidence of how many elections fall short of these standards owing to manipulations of electoral legislation and of vote choice, and poor or corrupt electoral administration. These works also underlined the importance of the existence of a robust civil society and free media for combating electoral fraud.

Similarly, finding a bridge between the integrity problem and violence, the term 'electoral violence' focused on the origins of violent behaviour around elections and its influence on democratic functioning. The literature highlighted the growing number of controversial elections worldwide and provided examples that ended with civil wars in multi-ethnic and economically underdeveloped societies. Other disciplines, such as international relations and gender and family studies, also attempted to understand the multi-faceted structure of the phenomenon.

Lately, scholarly attention to the subject has shifted towards analysing electoral institutions and their competence in administering elections. In this area, scholars have frequently tried to understand the tools and strategies employed by these institutions to harm electoral administration procedures and to unravel the repercussions of such tactics. This literature revealed that if elections are not conducted properly, there is a high likelihood of demonstrations, violence and even system collapses. It also analysed how electoral management bodies (EMBs) respond to claims of fraud and abuse, strengthen polling-day operations and control financing concerns.

This volume investigates election integrity through the lenses of several theoretical theories that it explores, combined with a fresh approach. As previously said, while research on electoral integrity is growing some areas remain underexamined, and this need is especially evident in describing the phenomena in different contexts to overcome the primary shortcoming of the current literature: that it mainly focuses on electoral procedures, international conventions and global norms related to elections.

Against this backdrop, Turkey seems to a perfect subject for such contextual analysis since problems of electoral integrity rose to the top of the country's political agenda after 2010. This was a period when many allegations of electoral fraud were raised against the ruling Adalet ve Kalkınma Partisi (the Justice and Development Party, AKP). The accusations included unlawful use of overprinted ballot papers, misappropriation of state finances, media censorship, tampering with the computer-aided voter index system and arranging power cuts during the vote count. Hence, while Turkey has a history of elections that have returned legitimate administrations reflecting the public will, recent events have raised concerns about the integrity of democratic procedures and called into question Turkey's claim to be an established democracy.

In keeping with the framework outlined in the introduction, the first substantial chapter of this volume offered a view of Turkey's political trends and election history up to 2010. Focusing on the concept of electoral integrity, the chapter investigated the electoral difficulties that the country has faced ever since the 1940s, finding that electoral violence was the most prevalent electoral problem between 1940 and 2010. Assessments based on data from the DIEV-T (database) show that further difficulties with election integrity manifested themselves after changes were made to electoral rules and regulations. In addition, the chapter details the growth of problems connected to the integrity of elections in Turkey. The information presented in this chapter gives insight into election problems that the country has been going through more recently.

Chapter Two continues the study that was started in the first chapter, with a particular emphasis on the first two decades of the twenty-first century, when election integrity issues rose to the top of the political agenda. It establishes a functional classification of challenges to electoral integrity and operationalises this classification, with the primary emphasis being placed on formal and nonformal institutions such as EMBs and media organisations. Lastly, a comparative framework is used to further deepen the discussion on electoral integrity in Turkey. Pulling this together, the last chapter of Part One compares Turkey with other countries around the world and gives a more recent picture of the preceding two decades by drawing on a variety of datasets, such as the World Values Survey (WVS), the Perceptions of Electoral Integrity database (PEI) and the Varieties of Democracy database (V-Dem). This chapter also includes some introductory information regarding the EMB and the media in Turkey.

The volume's second part analyses attitudinal and behavioural factors related to electoral integrity problems and starts with an informational account of individual perceptions of damage to electoral integrity. Even though research on electoral integrity is on the rise among academics and practitioners, enquiries into popular perceptions of electoral integrity have received less attention. The purpose of this chapter is to describe the chief factors that appear to lead individuals to conclude that difficulties with the integrity of the vote have impaired the elections in their country. It finds that an individual's impressions of the political process are influenced by their level of education, their media consumption habits, the degree of confidence they place in various media sources and the level of economic well-being. The situation in Turkey demonstrates that adjusting for partisanship does not entirely eliminate the impact of where voters source their information and that partisanship has a role in moulding people's opinions of electoral integrity.

According to previous studies, one critical factor that helps establish electoral integrity is the existence of a free media. Chapter Four provides evidence to support this in the Turkish context and implies that a biased media environment favouring the government makes it more likely that people would regard elections as problematic. Similarly, existing research has proved that the fear of electoral violence reduces turnout on election day. This situation becomes even more problematic when we take into account the possibility that lacking a levelled media environment might also depress faith in elections. This chapter shows the gap between objective levels of electoral integrity and the popular views of it. Observation of this gap is crucial, to clarify the connection but also the clear distinction between these two, since several other considerations affect voter perceptions. Hence it becomes essential to analyse the influence of public and private media sources on people's understanding of the problems associated with elections, combined with the role of local and regional actors.

Chapter Five scrutinises the role of electoral management bodies as establishers of electoral integrity. It tries to explain what determines voter opinions about election officers and the bodies they work for concerning electoral integrity. In this regard, the chapter identifies the problems raised by the impact of EMBs on electoral integrity by first discussing the issue on a global comparative level and then relocating the discussion to the Turkish context, providing a historical outlook on the Turkish EMB, Yüksek Seçim Kurulu (the Supreme Electoral Council, YSK).

For electoral integrity studies changing the focus to look at EMBs appears crucial for several reasons. It is an under-researched area in the domain, which strangely contrasts with the significant function of these organisations in the electoral cycle. Evaluating the effect of the decisions made by these organisations, which are responsible for the conduct of elections, should help us develop a more holistic understanding of the issues surrounding the integrity of the electoral process. Although, in principle, EMBs all over the globe appear to adhere to international democratic norms, there is still a lack of information about how far they manage to do this and how choices made by EMBs are related to issues with election integrity. In this regard, our preliminary research on the subject analyses EMBs' organisational independence from governments, compares the degree of independence given to EMBs around the world as a benchmark for electoral integrity and finds a correlation between public trust in election management and voter opinions of the independence of electoral authorities.

In that sense, the YSK is no exception. The current structural and functional state of the YSK results from a series of historical developments in the institution, experienced parallel to the altering political climate of the country. In other words, changes in the structural and functional position of the Council stem from the specific demands of the dominant political perspective of the corresponding political era.

This chapter also provided empirical evidence about how voters' perceptions of electoral officers and EMBs impact on their perceptions of electoral integrity. If voters have confidence in the honesty and objectivity of responsible individuals and organisations, they are more likely to perceive that the election was conducted in an honest manner. This finding is expected since the EMBs are in charge of a range of electoral-process operations, such as voter registration, ballot design and handling complaints or objections. Hence, it would not be wrong to argue that the actions of EMBs can increase the overall level of honesty that the public associates with the election if they are seen as impartial, open and fair by voters. By the same token, the decisions made by the EMBs have potential to undermine public faith in the validity of elections. Accordingly, EMBs need to be open and accountable in making decisions, in order to maintain public faith in the legitimacy of the voting process. This can be accomplished by providing voters and other stakeholders with explanations of their actions and addressing any concerns. EMBs can help ensure that elections are regarded as being conducted with integrity, which increases the likelihood that the general public will accept the results of those elections.

At this point, I introduce additional factors that can shape the perceptions of EMBs. If citizens lose faith in the fairness and impartiality of elections, this can erode the legitimacy of the democratic process and lead to widespread mistrust in the political system. Thus, high levels of partisanship have the potential to operate as an additional negative variable within this framework since partisanship can affect opinions of the EMBs in a variety of ways, some of which can have a negative influence on the integrity of the election. It is possible, for instance, for political parties and candidates to hold divergent perspectives on the fairness and impartiality of EMBs and to make efforts to sway public opinion regarding these institutions. Such attempts can lead the public's opinions of the election process to divide along party lines, viewing the EMBs through a distorted lens. In addition, voters with strong allegiance to a particular political party or candidate are more likely to read EMBs through the prism of their political affiliation, further polarising perceptions of the voting process. This might give the impression that the election's credibility is based on whatever party or candidate is currently in power, rather than on the neutrality and fairness of the electoral process itself, which would be incorrect and unfortunate.

In general, EMBs should strive to be as impartial and objective as possible, to maintain the public's faith in the honesty of the electoral process. It is an arduous task to fulfil, especially in a highly politicised atmosphere, yet it is vital to ensure that the democratic process is taken seriously. EMBs should make every effort to make their decision-making processes public, accept responsibility for those procedures and be attentive to all stakeholders' interests, including those of political parties and candidates. They have the potential to help ensure that elections are perceived as administered honestly, which is essential for the well-being and consistency of any democracy.

Part Three of the volume shifts the focus to the consequences of damaged electoral integrity at the individual and institutional levels. Resting on the discussion in Chapter Five, it analyses the dynamics of the 2019 İstanbul repeat elections via the lenses of electoral integrity. Although the electoral integrity literature has touched upon many dimensions of the phenomenon, we still have limited knowledge of how citizens respond to these electoral problems when considering how to vote.

Political actors use manipulation primarily to win elections, resorting to a range of techniques such as ballot-box tampering, intimidation or buying votes. The current literature argues that, aside from winning elections, manipulation techniques may be used to build large vote margins, causing opponents to withdraw from the current election or discouraging them from putting up candidates in future ones, and making their supporters less inclined to vote. However, as noted in Chapters Two and Three, more recently political actors have not employed these tactics openly since genuine accomplishments are preferable to made-up ones for many reasons. Additionally, manipulating elections is expensive, countrywide electoral fraud has very high administrative expenses and, most significantly, recent research shows that voters generally disapprove of such practices: election tampering makes an election victory appear questionable. The same line of research also showed that fairness and integrity are normatively necessary for every election but, at the same time, voters' opinions about malpractice may alter depending on whether they favour the victors or losers. Accordingly, voters do not develop a uniform reaction to electoral problems. Instead, they first tend to assess whether any electoral problem has actually occurred, then consider its significance (for them), and finally decide whether or not to change their ideas. Partisans, as a result, tend to ignore their own party's election malpractices and become more sensitive to charges against other parties; and they do not change their vote. In parallel with motivated reasoning theories, such voters tend to ignore their own party's malpractice because they use different criteria for judging their own and other parties, and prefer to downplay their party's wrong-doings, to portray them as insignificant and mitigate the negative consequences.

However, voters may change their vote after considering misconduct claims. Although government supporters are more likely to feel elections are fair because they are more prone to trust regime propaganda, it is reasonable to argue that these voters might occasionally penalise incumbents when they learn of electoral integrity issues. Each incidence of election tampering has moral significance, and the available research shows that most voters think it is wrong. By providing empirical evidence for it, Chapter Six showed that perceptions of the legitimacy of elections play the most crucial role in voters' decisions under such circumstances. It showed that YSK's decision to order the 2019 mayoral election to be repeated damaged the election's credibility and created a legitimacy problem, leading large numbers of voters to alter their vote choice.

Chapter Seven analyses the relationship between the integrity of elections and trust in governments. Around the world, the credibility of elections appears to be under threat owing to concerns about fake news, widespread voter fraud, voter intimidation, cyber attacks and gerrymandering. The damaging impact of these events has spilt over and raised broader concerns, particularly about the cornerstones of democratic functioning, including trust in governments.

Elections must demonstrate integrity in order for the transition of governments to be orderly and peaceful, which is likely to boost the levels of trust in governments. In contrast, if individuals believe elections produce unfair results stemming from integrity issues, the effect will probably spread and trust in the political system as a whole will diminish. Among other factors, electoral integrity is a critical component, as most individuals see free and fair elections and the rule of law as cornerstones of democracy.

Despite its experience with many democratic breakdowns, Turkey has upheld the essential ideals of electoral democracy since the 1950s and, in this regard, the country offers a good context in which to examine the relationship between electoral integrity and trust in government. Existing research on the subject has deployed sociocultural, performance and party explanations to examine the drivers of trust in government, combined with differences in ethnicity and partisanship. The findings in this chapter demonstrate the explanatory strength of institutional and cultural approaches to political trust in the Turkish context, and show that voters' perceptions of electoral integrity can have far-reaching and long-lasting effects on public trust of governments. When voters lack confidence in the electoral process, they doubt the government's legitimacy and that of its supporting institutions, such as the court and the media. This lack of confidence can result in a decline in support for the government, making it more difficult for the government to carry out its programmes and accomplish its objectives. Doubts about the electoral process can also cause social unrest and political polarisation because voters who believe their views and votes are not being heard may resort to rallies, marches and other forms of action.

The eighth chapter of this volume elaborated on how perceptions of electoral integrity relate to electoral expectations. Conceptualising its argument with the umbrella term 'surprised voter', it examined underlying integrity and other individual-level factors that shape beliefs related to electoral outcomes. Integrity studies must address this gap for several reasons. For one, citizens' electoral expectations relate to their faith in government and contentment with democracy. We also know that supporters of political actors who lose elections hold more unfavourable views of democracy and government than those on the winning side, frequently blaming elections and arguing that they lack honesty, responsiveness and credibility. Based on these arguments and the well-established literature on media consumption and political behaviour, the chapter used explanatory variables for electoral integrity, preference for different sources of news consumption, trust in the media and partisanship to examine their impact on electoral expectations.

In parallel with four hypotheses tested in the chapter, the analysis of these variables revealed that strong perceptions of integrity are associated with accurate expectations of election results. Several factors may cause this outcome. First, an honest election builds voter trust. Voters' trust in election results is based on their assumption that their voices will be heard and that the political process will be fair and open. Second, election integrity promotes openness, giving voters accurate and trustworthy information about candidates, issues and voting. Complete and impartial information helps voters make informed decisions and set realistic election expectations. Third, strong electoral integrity assures every qualified voter that each ballot cast is given the same weight in the final total by making the voting process transparent and objectively verifiable. So, when the process is fair, and all opinions are heard, voters can form more accurate election expectations, even though these may be biased by their electoral preferences.

Chapter Eight also provides solid empirical evidence that choice of news sources and varied degrees of confidence in media impact on electoral expectations, in addition to views about the integrity of the process. Providing a base from existing literature, the chapter argues that repeatedly consuming material with which someone already agrees can strengthen expectations and lead to disappointment when these expectations are unmet. That is to say, uneven media exposure has the potential to perpetuate prejudiced political attitudes, exaggerate wishful expectations and foster misperceptions about political events, including election results. Similarly, it claims that seeking information from a range of sources, including the internet and social media along with TV or print news, increases the likelihood of being exposed to content with alternative and opposing viewpoints, which may lower the likelihood of being trapped in an echo chamber. Accordingly, the chapter hypothesised that diverse media consumption may establish a framework for more realistic and unbiased expectations and boost a voter's political knowledge, including election knowledge, reducing the likelihood of being surprised by the results. The chapter reasons that believing fake news and disinformation is related to a person's trust in particular media sources. Merely accepting what is read, listened to and/or seen with complete trust and without critical thinking can be connected with political misperception; skewed belief may alter political perceptions, and in turn election results.

Lastly, Chapter Eight also discussed the relationship of partisanship to electoral expectations based on motivated reasoning theories, with particular reference to partisanship in the Turkish context. Given that people's political opinions are impacted by their motives, efforts and knowledge of the political environment, affiliation with a political party can become a persistent and essential feature of a citizen's identity that shapes perceptions on a variety of topics: warfare, information exposure and the necessity for ideologically acceptable media material were touched on. The chapter also highlighted the regional dimension of the phenomenon, referring to the historical, political and social particularities of the eastern and south-eastern Anatolian region, where the Kurdish ethnic minority is highly concentrated. The related analysis provided empirical evidence for all of these arguments.

The COVID-19 pandemic began as this book was being written, prompting an unprecedented worldwide crisis that posed tremendous challenges for democratic institutions, including elections. Chapter Nine examines the impact of the pandemic on election timing in Turkey via a conjoint experiment embedded in a country-representative face-to-face poll.

Although political science has extensively studied elections, our understanding of postponed or delayed elections is limited. Around the world, elections may be postponed for several reasons, natural disasters, terrorist attacks and wars among them. The COVID-19 pandemic is no exception: at least seventy nations worldwide were forced to postpone forthcoming elections. These decisions were taken since conducting elections during a global pandemic clearly presented serious dangers, if for no other reason than the requirement that citizens travel to vote. Areas affected included voter and party control of electoral registers, door-to-door verification of these records, holding of rallies and canvassing during election campaigns. On election day, millions of people are on the move to vote; vote counts are typically made in crowded settings, such as halls or polling centres, where social distancing is difficult owing to the enormous number of people present.

It would not be wrong to argue that many other factors shape opinions about electoral postponement. Thus, even in extreme situations like pandemics, some firmly ingrained political concerns – for instance partisanship and polarisation – might continue to influence these perceptions. Our research about these factors in the Turkish context showed their relevance in the matter. Studies on partisanship have showed that party identification forms in the earliest stages of life; expectations of economic utility play a significant role in forming party identifications; and intense partisanship influences perceptions of political candidates and vote choices in Turkey. The works on polarisation in Turkey display a similar picture. Recent studies indicate Turkey is among the five nations ranked highest in affective and political polarisation indices, and especially the level of social distance – the desire of one group to be apart from another – is disturbingly high. So partisanship and emotional polarisation can politicise neutral circumstances, causing individuals to view these circumstances, and any proposals made to address them, through partisan lenses. This final chapter of the volume delivers two significant results. First, our findings indicate that expert policy advice is preferred to government or opposition policy proposals, but with limitations. A different picture emerges when policy preferences are examined after controlling for partisanship and polarisation. Those with high levels of partisanship and polarisation levels prefer policies developed by their parties instead of those of experts.

This volume is an effort to shed light on electoral integrity by combining the lenses of global comparative approaches and the contextual findings of a case study. Underlying the importance of contextual determinants, I believe this volume indicates the need for further research in the area, particularly in illiberal contexts, which will help us solve the democratic problems of our time.

EPILOGUE
GENERAL AND PRESIDENTIAL ELECTIONS
OF 2023 – AN INTEGRITY OUTLOOK

While I was writing this book, Turkish citizens went to the polls for the 2023 general and presidential elections. This is the second election that the country held after the constitutional amendments adopted in 2017, which came into force in 2018, transforming the system from a parliamentary to a presidential system. Since the 2023 election provided an opportunity to monitor the arguments in this monograph, this epilogue will highlight some of the essential developments that took place during this recent electoral cycle.

The Electoral Context

Turkey conducted the first round of presidential and legislative elections on 14 May 2023. Three alliances competed in the elections. The first was the People's Alliance, led by Erdoğan's Adalet ve Kalkınma Partisi (the Justice and Development Party, AKP) with the Miliyetçi Hareket Partisi (the Nationalist Action Party, MHP) and a few smaller parties. The second was the major opposition bloc, Nation Alliance, which includes the Cumhuriyet Halk Partisi (the Republican People's Party, CHP) and the İyi Parti (the Good Party, İyi) and four smaller parties, including two led by prominent former AKP figures. And third was the Labor and Freedom Alliance, the minor opposition bloc consisting of a few small left-wing parties alongside the Halkların Demokratik Partisi (People's Democratic Party, HDP). The HDP ran with the support of Yeşil Sol Parti (the Green Left Party, YSP) owing to the danger of a pending court case seeking to close the HDP. As discussed within the framework of integrity issues in detail below, the parliamentary election this year was governed by amendments to Turkey's election legislation implemented in 2022. As in the last election in 2018, each of the 600 parliamentary seats was allocated between Turkey's 87 electoral districts to party lists using the proportional d'Hont method. The 2022 amendment decreased the threshold for representation from 10 to 7 per cent. Under this new rule, parties can be represented in the parliament if they get at least 7 per cent of the national vote or are part of a bigger electoral coalition that manages to do so.

During the pre-election period, the vast majority of public opinion polls signalled a win for Altılı Masa – 'Table of Six'/Nation Alliance – by highlighting Turkey's economic and societal problems. Despite this, the opposition bloc faced severe problems both before and during the election cycle: it regularly displayed an impression of a lack of internal unity, while the government exerted its strong influence over court judgments, its financial strength and its effective control of the media. Additionally, there were doubts, including whether the country could manage to hold free and fair elections, whether Erdoğan would transfer power if he lost the election and the possible problems that would be presented by a close contest (Zanotti and Thomas 2023). The opposition was organised around a detailed plan that prioritises restoring Turkey to the legislative system that existed before the 2018 election and limiting presidential authority (CHP, 2022). This document also criticised the government's attitude to various international and domestic policy concerns, particularly challenges relating to democracy and the rule of law in Turkey, and pledged to make reforms, mainly prioritising economic issues.

However, early disagreements within the Nation Alliance over choosing a presidential candidate caused severe doubts about the alliance's performance right at the beginning of the campaign period. After long and tense discussions, the alliance decided to nominate CHP party leader Kemal Kılıçdaroğlu as the bloc's presidential candidate. This decision was not welcomed by Meral Akşener, the İyi leader, who left the bloc for a short period since he had campaigned for İstanbul mayor Ekrem İmamoğlu who had polled favourably against Kılıçdaroğlu. She eventually consented to support Kılıçdaroğlu's nomination with an agreement within the bloc that proposed İmamoğlu and

Mansur Yavaş – the nationalist-leaning mayor of Ankara – should be vice-presidents in the case of electoral victory.

The other problem that the Nation Alliance experienced related to external support the HDP and YSP offered to Kılıçdaroğlu. While Akşaner's nationalistic İyi party opposed a formal alliance between the Nation Alliance and the HDP, the HDP chose to back Kilicdaroglu in the presidential election rather than run its own candidate. Two other candidates also ran for the presidency. First was Muharrem İnce, who had run as the CHP's presidential candidate in the 2018 election. Early surveys predicted İnce would receive 5 per cent of the vote, but on 11 May he announced his resignation, which is discussed in the context of electoral integrity below. The fourth candidate was Sinan Oğan, an ultra-nationalist contender who had formerly served in the parliament for the MHP. After İnce withdrew, Oğan became the only independent candidate.

In the first round, Erdoğan received 49.5 per cent of the presidential votes, just a half-percentage point shy of the required 50 per cent. His main rival, Kılıçdaroğlu, received 44 per cent, while Oğan received an unexpected 5.2 per cent. Although Erdoğan and the AKP-led People's Alliance lost 21 seats, they managed to retain the majority at the TBMM with 323 seats.

These results make it necessary to conduct a presidential run-off election for the first time in the country's electoral history; the previous joint presidential/parliamentary elections, in 2014 and 2018, had ended in the first rounds. While Turkey's economic problems and the February earthquakes may have fuelled voter discontent with Erdoğan, the first-round electoral results apparently exceeded many analysts' predictions, and these results also appeared to signal victory for Erdoğan for the second round. The run-off will take place too late to be covered in this book.

It seems that the major themes discussed during the first round will continue to be debated in the second campaign period. As previously stated, Kılıçdaroğlu and the opposition bloc have based their campaign messages on Turkey's declining economic conditions, democratic backsliding and deteriorating human rights, all of which have worsened under Erdoğan's regime. On the other side, Erdoğan will continue to underline various successes at home and abroad over his twenty-year tenure, including Turkey's defence and energy industries, and he has blasted the opposition for siding with terrorists and LGBT+ rights. The ultra-nationalist Oğan's 5 per cent vote is seen as fertile terrain to exploit, especially for the Nation Alliance. Although the Alliance aims to collect these votes, by adopting an increased nationalist tone in the campaign, this strategy risks alienating the Kurdish electorate, which already proved lukewarm in their support for Kılıçdaroğlu in the first round. In the meantime, these developments have elevated Oğan to the position of 'king-maker', which is, simply put, an unwanted and undeserved outcome from the first round. Alongside the debate over nationalism, economic issues seem to dominate the electoral debate. These issues include a wide array of sub-fields such as high inflation levels, the balance of payments and populist measures. The third issue is relatively new: the possibility of electing a president whose party or alliance lacks a majority in the parliament. According to the regulations under the present Constitution, if the president's party coalition or alliance loses control of parliament after the elections, parliament might block the president in a variety of ways if the majority of members want to. Although the Constitution grants the president extensive authority to designate cabinet ministers and act in the absence of parliamentary initiative, decisions on several pivotal matters, such as budgeting, international treaty ratification and overseas military deployments, require parliamentary approval.

Last but not least, it is expected that issues related to electoral integrity will continue to dominate the pre- and post-run-off electoral debates. The following paragraphs will elaborate on these discussions in detail.

The Electoral Integrity Context

When analysed through the lenses of electoral integrity, several pre-election and post-election events seem worthwhile to mention. Despite some heated rhetoric on election night, with supporters of both Erdoğan and Kılıçdaroğlu accusing one other of releasing false information, all parties acknowledged the results in advance of the run-off. Considering the pre-election developments, the most important change proved to be the alterations made in Law No. 7393 in March 2022. These amendments incorporated significant revisions to several electoral and political party statutes, such as lowering the electoral threshold for parliamentary representation, revising the methods for determining parliamentary seat allocation and political party eligibility, updating campaign limits for public officials, and changing particular aspects of voter registration and procedures for appointing electoral boards. The alteration to the procedures for appointing electoral boards was heavily criticised because it changed the rule for selecting the members and the chairman of the provincial election board, who serve in the provincial centre, to require the first-degree judicial justice commission to draw lots among judges assigned to the first class instead of appointing the most experienced of these judges to the post. It was asserted that the new procedure would compromise the competence and independence of election administrators and the judicial security and stability of election legislation. Among other things, the decision to lower the national threshold for parties and coalitions to qualify for seat distribution from 10 to 7 per cent can be evaluated as a positive development. This amendment also allows minor parties that are members of alliances to be represented in the parliament since the regulation does not require each individual party in such an alliance to pass the 7 per threshold. Previously, seats were assigned in two steps: awarding seats within constituencies to pre-electoral coalitions, individual parties and independent candidates and then allocating the seats given to a pre-electoral coalition to its constituent parties. The law also foresees that, in order to participate in parliamentary elections, parties must have organisational structures in at least half of the provinces and one-third of the districts, and they must have held party congresses at least six months before election day. The amendments made in Law No. 7393 tightened these provisions and required the parties to have all held national, provincial and district congresses. Moreover the same regulation stipulated that parties that fail to hold (e.g. postpone or cancel) two consecutive congresses within the legally mandated time frame are not eligible to run for election.

As in previous elections, there continue to be integrity problems associated with the Yüksek Seçim Kurulu (the Supreme Election Board, YSK), the sole authority on electoral decisions. As mentioned in previous chapters, YSK's decisions are not subject to judicial scrutiny, whether they cover the final results of elections or disputes related to citizens' constitutionally protected rights. Especially in the pre-election period, in the absence of avenues for judicial review many parties formally asked that the YSK reconsider several of its decisions, and some of these petitions were from candidates barred from the elections. As experienced during previous elections, problems raised by YSK were not limited to these pre-election rulings. For example, the YSK has continued to operate outside its legally mandated framework by acting as a body of eleven members instead of seven, allowing all replacement members to attend meetings and vote, even though the law states decisions must be taken by a majority of the seven permanent members. Moreover, the council has not revealed to voters which judges have been appointed as substitutes and which as permanent members.

These problems once again bring up concerns about the YSK's legal position. The council's judicial procedures for election-related complaints lack openness and do not meet international standards; the YSK usually considers complaints in secret meetings and denies parties the opportunity to be heard. At this point, it is worth mentioning examples of the arbitrary use of judicial powers by the YSK. Just before the election day, the council shortened statutory deadlines for the filing and settlement of the majority of election-day disputes to a single day, without presenting a legal rationale, as required by statute. Although the Law on Basic Provisions gives the YSK the right to alter legal deadlines, it may only do so if absolutely required, and the rationale for the adjustment must be stated in the judgment. Needless to say, accelerating the limits for post-election complaints runs counter to international norms and may jeopardise the right to seek adequate legal recourse for election results. One last point to mention relates to merging and moving polling stations. At very short notice, the YSK moved or combined 861 polling locations throughout 28 provinces, predominantly in the south and south-east Anatolian regions, as late as one week before election day, citing security concerns, poor voting facilities or insufficient population, and at the request of governors. This regulation by the YSK jeopardised the right to vote of more than 50,000 voters in the region.

As far as the council's organisational and technical capacity for running the election is concerned, the YSK has provided satisfactory service despite the enormous problems caused by the earthquakes just three months before the elections. On 6 February 2023 Turkey experienced two earthquakes of magnitude 7.8 and 7.5, the most destructive national hazard to affect the region for a long time. More than 46,000 people died in Turkey alone, and over 130,000 were injured. An estimated 173,000 structures collapsed or received severe damage, displacing 2.2 million people. Based on evaluations made in the region, the council decided to hold the elections on the planned date. To help with the resulting problems, YSK also took measures such as providing mobile ballot boxes and made other preparations for the election to accommodate displaced individuals.

For all that, those evacuated from the earthquake zone faced several difficulties in adopting the new regulations. Voters who moved out of the earthquake zone and wanted to vote in a different district were allowed to declare an address and confirm their new location by 18 March 2023, to be registered to vote in their new district. In addition, the YSK allowed residents who had lost their major identity papers (passport, driver's licence, national ID card) to vote using a temporary ID document, valid for three months, that could be obtained through the e-government portal. The YSK also displayed an acceptable performance in voter registrations; the central voter registration was based on civil and address records. Voter lists were available for review at local government offices by 20 March, giving voters until 2 April to check their information and seek corrections. However, the main challenge was the voters living in cities in the earthquake zone. Approximately 2 million voters were moved because of the disasters, but the government made few steps to ease address changes and voting for those impacted. According to a report by the Organisation for Security and Co-operation (OSCE), around 500,000 citizens registered to vote in their new places of residence, which leaves nearly 30 per cent of voters in the earthquake-hit region unregistered (OSCE, 2023).

Like the flaws foundd for electoral administration above, the integrity problems related to the media seem to linger in the country. Although the Turkish Constitution protects freedom of speech and of the media, laws such as the Criminal Code, the Press Law and anti-terror laws limit this considerably in practice. Several administrative and judicial organisations have successfully demanded the banning of websites and individual webpages, including the YSK, and this practice continued during this electoral cycle. Moreover, the day before election day, Twitter and Facebook announced that they would limit access to some material in Turkey in response to blocking requests from the Turkish government.

The previously flawed structure of the conventional media continued during this election. For nearly two decades, the media market in Turkey has been organised in two camps. The first camp, which consists of media outlets supporting the government, is financially backed by state organisations. This situation was underlined in the European Union's Turkey Progress Report, which stated that the opposition-leaning channels Fox TV, Halk TV, Tele 1 and KRT did not receive any public advertising in 2022. Moreover, Radyo ve Televizyon Üst Kurulu (the Radio and Television Authority of Turkey, RTÜK) has regularly fined these opposition-leaning outlets, putting them into severe financial crises.

The bias of the state-owned media institutions towards the government was also visible when Türkiye Radyo Televizyon Kurumu's (Turkish Radio and Television Corporation, TRT) broadcasts during the election period are analysed. According to the OSCE report, TRT-1 and TRT Haber newscasts distinctly favoured the People's Alliance, who got 44 and 45 per cent of politically relevant coverage, respectively, most of it favourable in tone. What is even more concerning is that these sources did not distinguish between coverage of President Erdoğan as president and as candidate, often portraying campaign activities as coverage of the president. In comparison, the opposition alliances, namely the Nation and Labour and Freedom Alliances, earned a combined total of 35 per cent of broadcast coverage, all of which was primarily negative in tone (OSCE, 2023). Although the YSK used to have the authority to monitor and supervise the national broadcast media, a presidential order issued in 2017 eliminated the fines it could apply for any violations it found.

For this particular election, manipulation-related electoral integrity problems have been discussed within the domain of social media. According to a recent report, social media manipulation by bot movements has been a prominent feature of this election. Click farms, in which thousands of computers are lined up to produce false involvement, have been widely exploited, with accounts indefinitely creating fresh faces of individuals who do not exist or mimicking those who do (Özarslan and Wriedt, 2023). Twitter's decision to remove 'the blue tick', a reliable indicator of the user's authenticity, allows malicious actors to spread misleading or fake messages and have them read effectively. Moreover, these actors use artificial intelligence to create compelling content that is very difficult to distinguish from genuine tweets.

Against this background, Turkey has been called the country with the highest exposure to false news, and the current election scene has demonstrated this several times (Petersen, 2023). It has been reported that at least 20 per cent of hot topics on Turkish Twitter have been influenced by bot involvement, making them untrustworthy. During the campaign period, Muharrem İnce, a presidential contender, dropped out of the contest partly in response to a fake video clip. Even Erdoğan shared hoax movies purporting to link his major competitor Kılıçdaroğlu to PKK. What is unique in this election, however, is that suspicious bot movement, for instance thousands of Russian-, Hungarian- and Portuguese-speaking (Brazilian) Twitter accounts, has manufactured and circulated fake news, influencing Turkish Twitter trends. In line with these arguments, Kılıçdaroğlu alleged that Russians were at the root of all these digital manipulations. He also argued that specific profiles with more than 10,000 followers had been purchased, to influence the Turkish people through social media.

As in previous examples during the period since 2010, the first round of the election was primarily peaceful, with some minor disturbances. Election monitoring organisations like Vote and Beyond and Turkish Volunteers carried out parallel vote tabulation, either as accredited observers of political parties or as interested citizens without accreditation. The results showed that the country would require a run-off election for the first time in its history since no presidential candidates passed the necessary 50 per cent threshold.

The opposition parties have objected to the results declared in several locations and asked for recounts owing to irregular records. Indeed, in most cases there is hard evidence of miscounted tallies and erroneously recorded results. These anomalies have been made mainly by the opposition, frequently in social media, and echo electoral integrity problems that the country has previously experienced – for example, imprisoned former co-chair of the pro-Kurdish HDP, Selahattin Demirtaş, stated that elections have been rigged for years, citing concerns with signed counting reports, the composition of ballot-box committees and manipulation of counting reports. He also accused Interior Minister Süleyman Soylu of being involved in suspected election fraud. These allegations increased substantially as other opposition politicians and social media users conveyed evidence that several vote-box results have been erroneously registered in the YSK database. Being aware of this specific problem after experience of previous elections, the CHP has developed unique software to compare the signed ballot-box results with the records recorded at the YSK's registry system, to identify irregularities. Using this software, many citizens have spotted differences between the two sets of records.

The opposition bloc, the Nation and Labour and Freedom Alliances, have reported more than 1,000 erroneously entered ballot-box registries and filed official complaints to the YSK. Although the YSK has addressed most of them, the opposition bloc has still demanded openness and a truthful depiction of the election results, citing worries of persistent fraud. The opposition bloc has also underlined the problems related to disseminating early election results by two registered news agencies, blaming these agencies for picking ballot boxes in which the government bloc was leading and only reporting those to create a disappointing environment for the opposition.

In a nutshell, the 2023 elections have repeated what the country has experienced during the last two decades when electoral integrity matters have frequently come into question, both positively and negatively. It will not be wrong to argue that Turkish citizens had a genuine choice between political alternatives in the 14 May general elections, which were held in the aftermath of devastating earthquakes. Turnout rates were high, a distinct feature of Turkish democracy for years. However, as summarised above, the process has not been without difficulties. The media terrain was uneven, which created severe problems for the integrity of the elections. Although, to a certain extent, the limitations on association and speech have lingered for this election as well, the electoral campaign was competitive and reasonably free for most contenders. Technically, the electoral administration administered elections effectively, but at the same time, there was a lack of openness and communication, which calls into question the independence of the related state organisations. Instances of inadequate execution of some processes, notably during voting and counting, have been highlighted, but none of these irregularities has been major enough to change the evaluation of the election as, broadly, healthy. These developments show that the problematic areas mentioned in this monograph, particularly those relating to the electoral laws and regulations, seem to remain unresolved within the domains of electoral alliances, funding restrictions and the media.

References

CHP. 2022. *Memorandum of Understanding on Common Policies: Text of Agreement for a Strengthened Parliamentary System.* https://chp.org.tr/yayin/memorandum-of-understanding-on-common-policies/Open.

European Commission. 2022. *Commission Staff Working Document: Türkiye 2022 Report* https://neighbourhood-enlargement.ec.europa.eu/system/files/2022-10/T%C3%BCrkiye%20Report%202022.pdf.

OSCE. 2023. *Statement of Preliminary Findings and Conclusion: Türkiye, General Elections*. https://www.osce.org/odihr/elections/turkiye/543543.

Özarslan, O. and La. Wriedt. 2023. 'What's Fake and Not Fake in Turkey's Election'. https://inkstickmedia.com/whats-fake-and-not-fake-in-turkeys-election/.

Petersen, T. 2023. 'Mass scale Manipulation of Twitter Trends Discovered'. https://actu.epfl.ch/news/mass-scale-manipulation-of-twitter-trends-discov-2/.

Zanotti, J. and C. Thomas. 2023. *Turkey: Major Issues, May 2023 Elections, and US Relations*. https://sgp.fas.org/crs/mideast/R44000.pdf.

INDEX

EU representative:
Easy Access System Europe
Mustamäe tee 50, 10621 Tallinn, Estonia
Gpsr.requests@easproject.com

www.ingramcontent.com/pod-product-compliance
Lightning Source LLC
Chambersburg PA
CBHW050647270326
41927CB00012B/2912